How
to
Drink

Victoria Moore

How to Drink

Andrews McMeel
Publishing, LLC
Kansas City · Sydney · London

First published in 2009 by Granta Publications, 12 Addison Avenue, London W11 4 QR, United Kingdom

09 10 11 12 13 RR2 10 9 8 7 6 5 4 3 2 1

ISBN-13: 978-0-7407-8574-0
ISBN-10: 0-7407-8574-5

Library of Congress Control Number: 2009926282

www.andrewsmcmeel.com

ATTENTION: SCHOOLS AND BUSINESSES

For Mum and Dad

CONTENTS

ABOUT THIS BOOK

Appetite is not just about food, as Elizabeth David understood—it's there in the title of her seminal essay "An Omelette and a Glass of Wine"—yet somehow in the past few decades we've allowed the solid part of what we eat to take most of the attention. Drink is an integral part of any meal or snack, just like another ingredient on the plate. A sip should send you for another forkful of food, and vice versa. Yet drinks are often thought of separately or neglected altogether. I've lost count of the number of intricate, slaved-over dinners featuring organic rare breeds from the farmers' market to which I've sat down when the first thing to pass my lips has been a virtually flat gin and tonic with no ice or a glass of lukewarm white wine that no one has noticed is also corked. And as for trying to find a decent cup of coffee, or even tea, don't get me started.

It shouldn't be like this. It doesn't need to be either difficult or expensive to drink as well as you eat; it just requires a little care.

And there's another thing. It's often said that life's too short to drink bad wine, but I'd go further. Life's also too short to drink good wine, or anything else for that matter, if it's not what you feel like at the time. There's no point in popping the cork on a bottle of vintage champagne if really you hanker after a squat tumbler of rough red wine. Likewise a milky hot chocolate, served in a breakfast bowl as they do in France, can be delicious but really works only on dank, dark mornings in the middle of winter, when you've got time to wrap your hands round it and haven't eaten so much the night before you're still full from dinner.

A good drink—the right drink poured at just the right moment—becomes not just a thirst-quencher but part of our social fabric.

A passing moment can be burnished to become an event that fixes in your mind: the jug of homemade lemonade shared outside on a rare warm afternoon; the kir (far superior to kir royale) that was so good just before a coq au vin on that cold winter's night; or the glass of prosecco, too often thought of as a poor man's champagne when it is nothing of the sort, poured as a pick-me-up at the end of a grimy day in the office.

Sometimes it's worth memorizing a few easy recipes: one of the best drinks I've ever had was a negroni (Campari, gin, and red vermouth, in equal parts, poured over lots of ice) knocked up from the minibar of a hotel in the Middle East, which we savored on the terrace in the sticky heat as the sun dropped out of the sky.

More often it's the simple rituals of drinking that give the most pleasure: the rhythm of the morning cup of tea, whether a mug of strong English breakfast tea or a calming lemon-balm infusion, that helps you out of bed to start the day; the whirr of the blender pulverizing fruit that might otherwise have gone to waste but has been reinvented into a nutritious smoothie; or the pfft of relief as you pull open a can of tonic at 6:00 P.M. on a Sunday afternoon.

I've written this book partly as a response to the flow of queries I get from friends, acquaintances, and readers of my *Guardian* wine column, asking first what they could make to drink at such and such an occasion and second how to make a certain drink taste better. But also partly out of a sense that while we all have kitchens piled high with books telling us how and what to cook, few seem to offer advice on what to drink in the context of our everyday lives.

This book is a very personal collection of the things I like to drink at home. It is not intended to be encyclopedic—one that was would have been twelve times the size, taken the rest of my life to research, and done some serious damage to my liver in the process. So I apologize for the many, inevitable omissions, as well as for those drinks, some of which deserve an entire book to themselves, to which I have perhaps not given as much space as some might like. One of these is beer, a subject on which others are far better informed than I am. Cognac, whiskey, and Armagnac lovers may also feel slighted by the small amount of space given to those drinks. Part of the reason for these absences is that this book is mostly about the preparation of drinks, and how best you might enjoy them, rather than being a shopping guide.

What I drink depends not just on current whim but also on whom I'm with, what time of the year it is, and how cold it is outside, so the book is arranged by season and, to some extent, occasion. The idea is that this will make it easier for you to find a drink that will quench your thirst and suit your appetite, whether you have friends coming round, are throwing a big party, or just want to have a nice night in at home. Because what you drink cues up your taste buds, in some cases I have included a few food suggestions or recipes too, particularly for canapés. There are occasionally suggestions for what to have for dinner too—the whole package.

I'm no expert bartender, so there is nothing complicated or difficult in this book, but I think that's the point: every drink can be thrown together by anyone—provided the person is sober enough, of course.

BAS

STOCKING UP

The store cupboard

A drinks cupboard is just like the food section of your kitchen, in that with a good stock of basics and old favorites you should be able to add the simplest of fresh ingredients—a slice of lemon, perhaps, or an egg white, some milk or half a glass of freshly squeezed lime—and bring everything else alive. In the same way that you might keep two (or even three) olive oils—a cheap one for cooking and a superior extra virgin oil for dressing raw greens or drizzling on bruschetta—it's sometimes worth duplicating an ingredient on different quality levels, especially if you are a keen martini drinker or an addict of single malts. Here are some suggestions to give you the bones of a good liquid larder. Also, do remember that a drink can only ever be as good as the quality of its ingredients.

Vodka

Useful for vodka and tonics, martinis, and mixing with pureed or muddled fruit (and vegetables), from raspberries to cucumbers, in summer, or drinking icy cold in small tots with a spread of blinis and pickled herring in winter. I like to keep a couple of different kinds of vodka in the house. There may be something very cheap and fiery, the vodka equivalent of lighter fuel (see p. 259, "How rough do you like your vodka?"), generally a store's own brand, for mixing with tonic and fruit purees. A step up from this is required for cocktails. Smirnoff is a very decent standby and a good blank canvas for mixing with other ingredients. For sipping neat in shot glasses I like something with both smoothness and flavor, such as Russian Standard, a wheat vodka with its roots in St. Petersburg. It's a great all-arounder that works in tonic, martinis, or cocktails too.

Gin

Only gin-and-tonic or martini aficionados need to worry about keeping a wardrobe of different gins (see p. 300 for tasting notes on different gin brands). Tanqueray (the 47.3 percent Export Strength) is probably my favorite all-rounder, though throughout this book I've occasionally specified cases where one gin may work better than another.

Rum

In my household this gets heavy use in summer, when it is called on to make endless daiquiris, mojitos, and Cuba libres. I find a bottle of golden rum, ideally Havana Club—Anejo 3 Años answers most needs. See p. 145 for more information on rum.

Brandy

A bottle of cooking brandy is essential—go as cheap as you dare. And then a cognac is useful for sidecars and mixing with ginger beer to warm you up in winter. It ought to be good enough quality to sip on its own after dinner too. I have H by Hine.

Whiskey

It's useful to have just one bottle of this gravest of drinks around for serious conversations on late nights, medicinal purposes, and of course mixing with lemon juice and honey as a compensation for winter colds. But this is a spirit almost as personal as a perfume or aftershave, and I would not presume to suggest what you should buy, except that as it is most often sipped either neat or mixed only with water or ice, quality is important, whether your taste runs to the whiff of peat and smoke from an Islay single malt or the trenchant no-fuss of a blend.

Bourbon

The American whiskey is useful if you like to drink old-fashioneds, Manhattans, and mint juleps. See p. 305 for more details.

Vermouth

This fortified wine takes its name from the German *wermut*, wormwood, one of the herbs and roots with which it is flavored. It may be dry, medium, or sweet, and is used (sometimes in homoeopathically small quantities) in the likes of martinis, slings, and negronis, and older generations often like to mix it with a lemon-lime soda. The best-known brands are Noilly Prat (from southern France, the most complex of all the dry white vermouths and the one I prefer), Martini & Rossi (Italian, and comes in four styles—sweet and white, dry and white, sweet and pink, and sweet and red), and Cinzano (Italian again, and comes in the same range of styles as Martini). If you are going to buy only one bottle, go for a dry white; if you are a keen cocktail addict, you will also need sweet red (for negroni, and it's good mixed with tonic) as well as the sweeter white version.

Cointreau

This may not sound like a staple, but the colorless liqueur, invented in 1849 and flavored with the peel of bitter and sweet oranges, is used in a great number of classic cocktails, from margaritas to sidecars to white ladies. It's a vivid drink—the vigorous smell makes you think of freshly squeezed orange juice combined with candied orange peel—and you can also drink it neat on the rocks.

Bitters

Strictly speaking, the term covers all those alcoholic drinks flavored with herbs, roots, peels, and flowers, at least one of which lends bitterness and which were traditionally made by monks allegedly for their medicinal virtues. The bitter ingredient may be artichoke (as in the case of Cynar, an Italian aperitif), quinine, rhubarb root, or angelica. Famous bitters include Campari, Aperol, and Fernet-Branca. However, the term *bitters* is more often used as a shorthand for the highly concentrated angostura bitters and Peychaud's bitters, both of which are flavored with gentian. Just a few drops of either of these potent liquid seasonings will add kick and bite to a homemade lime soda, made with sparkling water and the juice of one lime. A dash of bitters gives pink gin its rosy hue and is an essential base-note in several other classic drinks, from a champagne cocktail to a Manhattan. A bottle is as crucial to a liquor cabinet as a supply of black peppercorns is to the larder. I also like to have a bottle of blood-orange bitters in stock—they give a warmer, fruitier note to any drink.

Wine

Whether through parsimony, habit, or perhaps lack of faith in our ability to choose the right thing, British people aren't very good at keeping a stock of wine in the house. I once read that over 90 percent of all bottles bought in England are intended to be drunk within twenty-four hours.

Ideally, however, you'd always have one bottle of red in the cupboard and one rosé and one white in the fridge. I'm not sure who first said that the three most depressing words in the English language are "Red or white?" Though I couldn't agree more, this isn't the place to be specific about what your red or white should be, save to say that the liquor-cabinet bottle of wine has to be something you almost always feel like drinking, rather than something you love when the mood and food are right. In other words, you need to have found that most elusive of bottles: one that suits your taste, is inexpensive and delicious too—that season's

VODKA

GIN

RUM

WHISKY

VERMOUTH

cointreau

BITTERS

wine

star bottle of wine. Last summer my white was a Saumur Blanc that cost £5.99 from the supermarket Waitrose, the rosé was a pale Provence thing picked up cheaply in Calais, and the red was an easygoing modern Rioja bought on sale.

Simple syrup

There are few obscure ingredients in this book (rose water and watermelon syrup spring to mind, but I think that's about all)—no ouzo, no crème de menthe, no Galliano, nor a battalion of odd liqueurs that taste disgusting on their own but are required for finicky cocktails and will do nothing more than gather dust and take up cupboard space. But the one thing I do use liberally, and which might seem specialist, is simple (sugar) syrup. You can make this yourself, by stirring equal volumes of sugar and water together and leaving until the sugar dissolves, which takes 5 to 10 minutes. But then you have the hassle of storing or throwing away the sticky syrup that's not used. That's why I prefer to buy it, ready-mixed. A friend of mine even packs a bottle of this (plus cocktail shaker) when she goes on holiday so as to be ready to make daiquiris at any moment.

Cordial

At least one good cordial is essential as a nonalcoholic drinking option. British supermarkets are full of old-fashioned British brands and you may be able to find some of these nonalcoholic mixes online. Bottlegreen makes some of the best, among which my favorites are aromatic lime and elderflower.

Tonic water

Buy cans of Schweppes and keep them in the fridge. See p. 293 for more information on tonic.

Sparkling water

There's no need to pay for club soda or seltzer, which is more expensive, if mixing drinks such as Campari and soda or mojitos that call for it. The cheapest fizzy bottled water will do just as well—only take care to find a neutral one with larger bubbles. Badoit, for example, with its fine mousse and distinctive taste of bicarbonates would be an odd choice as a general mixer, though Badoit and cognac makes a delicious long drink— the teeny bubbles suit the finesse of the cognac, and the underlying minerality dovetails with the richness of the spirit.

Tea and coffee

Try not to buy coffee too far in advance: even when kept under a vacuum seal it will still go stale. Once opened, a pack of ready-ground coffee begins to lose its freshness in a matter of days and should not be kept for more than two weeks. Keep opened coffee in an airtight container in the fridge to prolong its life span, or in the freezer, where it will last up to around two months after opening. Tea keeps for about a year, provided you have it somewhere dry and cool. See p. 45 for more information on tea and coffee.

Cooking alcohol

Marsala, sherry, brandy, and Calvados are all useful in the kitchen. See Chapter 5, Autumn, for more details.

Fresh basics

Lemons and limes

A house is not a home without a constant supply of fresh lemons and limes, both of which should feel heavy and yield to pressure for the greatest amount of juice.

Mint

Everyone seems to drink mint tisane these days, and as it's a healthy alternative to (yet) another glass of wine at the end of dinner, I try always to have a bunch of fresh mint, or a windowsill mint plant, available.

More specialist stuff

Campari

Campari is actually a staple for me. During spring and summer I eat even more of it than I drink. I make a sorbet (see p. 97) so delicious friends invite themselves around just for a fix. But Campari is the alcoholic equivalent of marmite in England—people seem to hate or love it, so it won't be on everyone's list.

Sipping spirits

I count among these all the more expensive, finessed versions of whiskey, rum, and brandy: the single malts, the rare American bourbons, the ancient Armagnacs, fine cognacs, premium vodkas, and dark aged rums—all the spirits you might like to savor and for the most part would consider too good to mix with anything else. So, for example, I usually have a bottle of Belvedere, a silkily soft Polish vodka, in my freezer that I use for the occasional vodka martini; Gosling Black Seal, a treacly dark rum from Bermuda; and a selection of Islay whiskey, among them Ardbeg Ten Years Old.

Tequila

Distilled from blue agave in Mexico, this is an essential if you are a margarita addict. See p. 137.

Glasses

You could go crazy buying the perfect glasses—one for this, one for that—and end up with cupboards bursting with different shapes and never having enough of the same one to go around when friends come over. So I have tried to consolidate.

Wineglasses

Once you have seen how different wine can taste out of different glasses (see p. 33 for more on this), a kind of madness sets in and it is hard ever to be satisfied—you are constantly wondering whether it might not be better to drink a wine out of this or that. Would a bigger glass elicit more perfume? Would a taller one reduce the sensation of oak? But budgets and common sense suggest it may be wise to impose some limits. Choose one set of glasses that curve in, even if almost imperceptibly, toward the rim and use them for everything. If you want to splash out, then buy a set of smaller ones for whites, larger for reds. Supplement the basic wineglass wardrobe with a few specialties according to what type of wine you drink most.

Glasses for sparkling wine and champagne

There are two traditional models, the coupe and the flute. The coupe has three drawbacks: its large surface area means that bubbles disappear fast, the center of gravity is unnervingly high for anyone on a second top-up (or is that just me?), and someone is always guaranteed to mention that the shape resembles a woman's breast.

I prefer small flutes because the wine doesn't get tepid and clammy before you are halfway down the first glass, and you get a lot of pours out of one bottle—it's always better to be in a position to issue top-ups than to have to reduce portions partway through a round.

However, I use flutes only for cocktails or cheap sparkling wine, such as cava or prosecco. Good champagne I now drink out of ordinary wineglasses, after the Bollinger incident (see p. 34).

Tumblers and highballs

As a G&T addict, I can't help buying glasses that strike me as being perfect for the drink—a set of tumblers tinted palest blue and so thick they seem to have been hewn out of a glass mountain was my last extravagance. In theory some cocktails call for a short, squat tumbler and others for a tall, narrow Collins glass; breakfast orange juice seems to demand small beakers, water and milkshakes large. In practice two shapes and sizes will easily see you through.

First, a set of small, heavy-bottomed tumblers for the serious stuff—spirits served neat or on the rocks. Second, a hybrid that is neither tall and thin nor short and squat. I use the Aino Aalto tumbler made by the Scandinavian design company Iittala. It's attractively ridged and capacious enough to take a lot of ice.

Though in the recipes that follow I have sometimes specified that the ideal glass might be a long, tall Collins, say, in case that's what you have in your cupboard, you can be sure that whether drinking water, mint juleps, or smoothies I am using my Aino Aaltos instead.

Martinis and other short cocktails

Instead of the traditional martini glass shaped like an inverted cone, which is angular and annoying to hold, I have a set of cocktail glasses that are halfway between that and a champagne coupe. I also use them to serve sorbet. They are made by Alessi, are exceptionally fine, and objects of beauty in themselves.

What else?

Inevitably there are other things kicking around in my cupboard—some cognac bulbs I never use, a set of shot glasses that have spent most of their lives serving me boiled eggs, and so on. The only thing I feel I lack is a small Campari-and-soda glass. But I know that as soon as I have found the perfect one, there will be something else.

Other equipment

As someone who lives in a tiny flat with virtually no cupboard space, I have worked on the basis that you should be able to make these drinks with pretty basic kitchen hardware. Of course, for good tea you need a **teapot**, ideally made of china rather than metal, as well as a **tea strainer** for loose-leaf tea, and a **cafetière** or a **moka** for coffee (see p. 56 for a discussion of different coffee-making methods).

For cocktails you will need a **cocktail shaker**. The most common version is the three-piece stainless-steel sort that comprises a cup, a lid with a built-in strainer, and a cap that fits over the strainer and often doubles as a measure. I also like the glamour of Boston shakers, which consist of two tall cups, one made of glass and one of stainless steel. The idea is that you put the ingredients in the glass cup, so you can see what you are doing, put the two things together to shake (be warned: they are more unwieldy than a standard shaker), then pour the cocktail out of the stainless-steel cup so that it arrives as a surprise in the glass of whomever you are making a drink for. As there is no built-in strainer with a Boston shaker, you need to buy this separately. You could make do with a tea strainer or small sieve, but the thing to get is a Hawthorn strainer, a flat metal plate with holes that sits over the mouth of the cup and has a spring around the edge to help you hold it in place. As the holes in both a **Hawthorn strainer** and a shaker are quite large, you may sometimes need to double-strain a cocktail—that is, use a small sieve as a secondary strainer balanced on the top of the glass. This is particularly useful if you are trying to remove small debris, say raspberry pips, from the drink, or if you like it to be completely smooth with none of the tiny shards of ice that sometimes form as the cubes smash against each other when they are shaken.

What else? A **hand blender** often comes in, well, handy when pureeing fruit and is easier to store than a bulky countertop model. Aside from that, it's almost always possible to do without specialist tools. For example, professional bartenders use a **muddler**—a sort of miniature wooden baseball bat—to squish fruit gently in drinks such as caipirinhas and strawberry daiquiris. As long as you are careful, you can use a pestle, or even the back of a spoon instead, though of course if you are planning on making a *lot* of cocktails, it might be nice to own a muddler. You don't need one for anything in this book, but if you become really obsessed you might also invest in an ice crusher, which is useful for frozen margaritas and daiquiris as well as mint juleps. But crushed or not, the one thing that is really important in any cold drink is the ice.

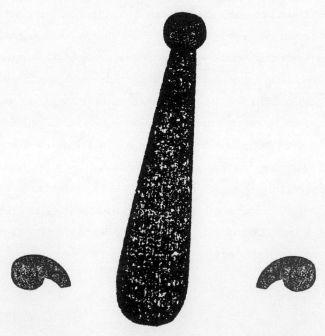

ICE AND OTHER TECHNIQUES

Ice freakery: is an ice pick essential to cocktail making?
Until I met a bartender called Kevin Armstrong, it had never occurred
to me that anyone living outside the Arctic Circle—and certainly not
someone in the metropolis of London—might feel a piece of climbing
gear was a necessary part of their drink-making kit. I still find I can get
by without one, but Kevin was adamant that if you are entertaining,
"You *need* an ice pick."

His explanation made a degree of sense. "Look," he said, "making
a cocktail requires a phenomenal quantity of ice. People don't always
realize that. Sometimes I watch people's faces when I'm making them a
drink in the bar. The first thing I do is to fill their glass up with ice, and
I can see they think I'm trying to short-change them on the spirits. I'm
not. They get just the same measure, but the drink is better if it has a lot
of ice in it as well. If you're having a party, you're going to get through a
lot of ice. You're not going to have enough ice-cube trays, so the easiest
way to make it is to freeze water in big roasting trays, then crack it with a
baby ice pick. That's what I do at home."

It would certainly be interesting to see if this explanation washed if
you were apprehended by the police on a dark street with an ice pick
tucked inside your jacket: "I am merely on my way to a party where I
intend to make gin and tonic for several good friends, officer."

I didn't actually meet Kevin, who is the head bartender of Match
bars and also oversees Milk & Honey and the Player in London, to talk
about ice. I asked to see him so we could chat about cocktail fashions.
The ice conversation started when I confessed that I really can't drink a
caipirinha unless I've done my best to fit the ice cubes closely together
in the glass when making it. Before long, we had discovered we were
united in our loathing of those bags of ice you can buy at supermarkets
and liquor stores.

"The cubes have holes in them," spat Kevin. "Holes. So they have a huge surface area, melt really quickly, and if you use them in a shaker, they smash to bits and dilute the drink horribly."

Needless to say, there was more. Kevin prefers ice made with mineral water: "It gives you an amazing purity and clarity." And if ice-cube trays are to be used, he favors spherical molds, "because that gives you the smallest possible surface area so the melt-speed is lower." It's because it deters the ice from melting that it's best to cram plenty into the glass. More ice cools the drink to a lower temperature, so although there are more cubes, each one melts more slowly, the drink stays both cold and relatively undiluted, and you don't find yourself in that half-panicky, half-miserable state of trying to slurp a cocktail down faster than you really want to in order to enjoy it before it gets tepid and loses its edge.

Kevin was also very specific about the temperature, -18°F, at which he freezes his ice. Ice stored at a lower temperature will keep your drink colder for longer, because as well as absorbing latent heat in the process of transforming from solid to liquid, ice also requires energy—specific heat—to raise its temperature to the melting point. In other words, the colder the ice, the colder it will make your drink before even beginning to melt.

The temperature at which ice is frozen also has an aesthetic impact. Peter Barham, a professor of physics at Bristol University, freezes his in the laboratory, using liquid nitrogen, at -321°F. An ice cube made in a domestic freezer would probably have four or five ice crystals in it. "What happens at much lower temperatures is that you get very, very small crystals and lots of them," says Barham. "The effect of this is to make the ice opaque. It's a bit like having a transparent pane of glass and then grinding it down into a dust that will appear white, even though each individual speck if viewed in isolation would be transparent."

-18°F

Ice cubes can appear cloudy for other reasons too. If the freezer door or the freezer compartment in an old-fashioned fridge-freezer is opened a lot, water vapor will condense on top of the ice-cube tray to form a fine frost. And if the water is oxygenated (as it will be if run into the trays from a spraying tap), it will also form ice that looks milky rather than as clear as Britain's ice-cube-shaped Fox's glacier mints.

How to make ice cubes in a hurry: why hot water freezes faster than cold

You are desperate for a vodka martini but have just discovered there is an ice-cube crisis. Should you fill the empty ice-cube tray from (a) the just-boiled kettle or (b) the cold tap, which you have just run to get the water as chilly as possible?

This is clearly a trick question: the answer is (a) because, in most cases, hot water freezes faster than cold. This is wonderfully counterintuitive, but, according to Peter Barham, "It is a well-established and accepted scientific fact." In his book *The Science of Cooking* he explains how the mind-twisting phenomenon was first revealed to twentieth-century scientists by an African schoolboy called Erasto B. Mpemba. Erasto had conducted experiments using identically sized containers filled with precisely the same amount of hot and cold liquid, but every time he nagged his physics teacher to explain why the hot water kept freezing more quickly than the cold, he was told flat out he must have made a mistake and got it wrong.

You can hardly blame Erasto's teacher, because the basic thermal laws of physics suggest that the cold water will most definitely freeze first. It seems logical that the hot water ought to take a certain amount of time to reach the temperature of the cold water when it was first put into the freezer and after that require the same amount of time as the cold to freeze. In other words, it should always be playing catch-up. This is why Erasto's findings were taken seriously only when a British physicist,

Professor Osborne, visited the school and Erasto once again put his question to him. Professor Osborne's initial response was the same as that of the African physics teacher: impossible. But once back home he repeated the experiment and was astonished to find that Erasto was right.

The conundrum was discussed for years in the reader Q&A section of the *New Scientist*, and scores of physicists have since tried to explain why hot water freezes faster than cold. Says Peter Barham: "Every year I get my undergraduates to chip and hammer away at the problem, and every year we uncover another small detail. One of them recently found that the phenomenon was first observed in ancient Greece—Aristotle wrote about it." He breaks off and adds glumly, "At the moment I've got half the physics department working on it."

Barham explains that one key part of the solution to the puzzle seems to be connected to "supercooling"—the process by which liquids can be reduced to a temperature below their normal freezing point without changing state. "One thing we do now know is that when you put cold water in a freezer it will normally supercool more than hot water— that's to say, it will actually reach a lower temperature before it starts to freeze—and that's how the hot water manages to win the race, by freezing at a higher temperature. It has also been proposed that boiling water might precipitate impurities that act as nucleating sites for ice crystals. But while lots of different bits of the problem have been solved, we still haven't got all of it."

It seems incredible that in the twenty-first century we can't crack a problem as elementary as this. Meanwhile, if you have two identical ice-cube trays, you can conduct the hot/cold water experiment for yourself.

How to shake (when making cocktails)

There are many wonderful drink moments in the 1934 film version of Dashiell Hammett's *The Thin Man*, in which William Powell and Myrna Loy play a couple, Nick and Nora Charles, who hardly have time for sleuthing in between hoisting cocktail glasses, issuing rapid-fire one-liners, and flouncing around dressed for the boudoir (and sometimes all three at once).

At one point Nora, impeccably glamorous but lying flat-out on the bed, removes an eye mask to ask, "What hit me?" "The last martini," retorts her husband.

But my favorite is when Nick decides to teach the bartender how to shake a cocktail. "The important thing is the rhythm," he says with a mannered flourish. "Always have rhythm in your shaking. A Manhattan you shake to fox trot. A Bronx, to two-step time; a dry martini you always shake to waltz."

Certainly it's a nice idea. But as with so many apparently delicate pastimes, such as baking a cake, what is actually important is the amount of brute force put in. Cocktails need to be shaken with vigor. The point is to make the drink as cold as possible, and to get a little dilution, which will help release some of the flavors in the spirits. So, put your back into it and don't stop until the metal is so well chilled your skin feels raw and almost as if it might peel off when you put the shaker down.

A note on quantities

Where possible in this book I have written recipes in terms of "parts," giving the proportions you need for a drink but not necessarily the quantities required per person. This way you can use whatever you like, from a bottle cap to a shot glass or a wineglass, as your measure. As a rough guide, when making cocktails consider that a standard measure of spirits is 1 ounce and that a cocktail for one person will usually contain up to three measures. All recipes serve one unless otherwise stated.

For accuracy, I've often listed ingredients such as lemon or lime juice in terms of parts too. When shopping it might help to know that an average lime yields about 2 tablespoons or 1 ounce of juice, a lemon closer to $1\frac{1}{2}$ ounces, but some limes and lemons are much bigger and juicier than others.

An aide-mémoire

Some people are so determined to drink exactly what they want that they will go to extreme lengths. Out with a friend one night, and failing to make our request for a sidecar understood, I was amazed to see her primly produce a piece of paper from her wallet, explaining that the recipe had been written out for her by the head barman at the Ritz in Paris and that she carried it with her everywhere she went, rather like a driving license or organ donor card, in case of emergency. "I'm thinking of having it laminated," she said, and I don't think she was joking.

WINE BASICS

One of the most pleasing sounds is the pop of a cork being plucked slowly from a bottleneck, followed by the unsteady gurgle as it is poured into a glass. But what wine to drink? And when? Wine is a vast, chameleon subject, the very nature of which—vintage changes, small production, availability—means it is impossible to make particular recommendations here. In each of the seasonal chapters I suggest generic wine and food combinations that are particularly worth trying as well as suiting the time of year. And there are a few important things to say about how to choose wine generally and how best to enjoy it.

Drinking with confidence: recognizing wine faults

When opening a bottle of wine, you should always taste before going on to pour a drink or before mixing it with other ingredients. The most common fault to find is that the wine is "corked." This doesn't mean that the wine has little bits of cork floating around in it; it means that it has been tainted by a chemical called 2, 4, 6-trichloroanisole (TCA). The effect may be very mild, damping down the flavor, making the wine taste "less" of everything than it usually would. This is almost the worst possible scenario, because you might not notice that anything is wrong unless you have just opened a bottle of something you know well, but you probably won't enjoy the wine very much. Severely corked wine is much easier to spot. First of all, when you are sniffing it, look for a muted quality and an absence of attractive smells. A lack of fruit and a general flatness is the first giveaway. If you then notice that it smells of soggy cardboard, walking through a damp old cellar, or the sort of mustiness you find in a bag of slimy old mushrooms, you can be certain. If unsure, leave the wine in the glass for ten minutes and then retaste—by now any musty odors will have flourished and be much easier to discern.

If drinking at a friend's house, I hate to see the host opening a bottle of good wine and then immediately making his way around, generously filling up the glasses of a dozen or more people. If the wine is corked, he may as well be giving them a cabbage-water top-up. Not only is everyone then stuck with a glassful of alcohol they're not going to enjoy, but the perfectly nice wine already in the glasses is now polluted too. I can never quite bring myself to say anything, and because it seems pointless to gulp a glass of wine I will actively dislike, and then find myself drunk (my alcohol tolerance levels are hopelessly low), I end up looking for ways to make a sneaky deposit down a sink. Absentmindedly taking your glass with you on a bathroom trip is the most discreet way.

If you think you've never had a corked bottle of wine, consider that 4 to 10 percent of bottles sealed under cork are thought to be affected. The strange paradox is that people are much better tasters than they think. I've watched countless friends knock back countless bottles of corked wine without complaint, but if quizzed they usually admit to not enjoying it very much and say they had assumed the wine wasn't a very good one that they won't buy again.

There is no shame in a bit of uncertainty—it happens even among wine tasters, particularly with wines that are not badly corked and which no one has tried before.

As for sending bottles back in restaurants, this can be traumatic even when you have the backing of professional expertise. A colleague tells how she once summoned the waiter in a pizza restaurant and, not wishing to be rude or intimidating, gently asked him to replace the wine because she thought it might be corked. Unfortunately the waiter also felt on top of his game. He tasted the wine himself and reassured her that it was perfectly fine. My colleague demurred. The waiter refused to capitulate. In the increasingly heated debate that followed my colleague, now abandoning charm and goodwill, found herself yelling that she was the head buyer of a national wine chain, she knew a corked wine when she tasted one, and even if they had to pay for the damn bottle could he please take it away and bring them a new one because neither she nor her guests were prepared to drink it.

"Well," said the waiter triumphantly, "I've done a wine course too."

So forget the hovering waiter, the clueless bartender, the bullying maître d', or the sommelier who has just ceremoniously pronounced the wine fit to drink (even he sometimes makes mistakes). The best person to listen to is yourself: trust your instincts and your subconscious. Sometimes I notice a wine is corked only when I realize that I keep picking up the glass and putting it down again without taking a sip or I keep taking sips in the hope of finding something that's not there— pleasure. If you are not enjoying a wine, do not drink it.

Do not assume, either, that a wine under screw cap is going to be trouble-free. It may suffer from a phenomenon known as "reduction," the word that, confusingly, tasters use to describe a wine in which undesirable sulfur compounds have developed in the absence of oxygen. This is a complex problem on which it is hard to find consensus, but telltale signs include the smell of a just-struck match or burnt rubber.

Sometimes the wine will sort itself out if poured into a decanter (never be afraid to decant white wines and don't worry if you don't have a decanter either—I usually use a flower vase) or given a bit of air in the glass—you could always try the old sommelier trick of pouring the wine from one glass to another. You could also try throwing a handful of loose change (perhaps wash it first) into the glass. This might sound bonkers, but the result is that tarnished coins begin to shine, and the wine stops smelling and tasting dirty and springs into expressive focus.

Wines can also be dulled or even ruined by poor storage. And just occasionally you will find a wine that's oxidized—it smells of sherry when it shouldn't and will taste dead and be darker in color.

Most important of all, don't be in awe of the wine: you're the one who's paid for it, and you're the one who's going to be drinking it. Trust your responses.

How to choose wine to go with your food

So much fuss is made about the art of choosing a wine to go with your food that it has acquired at best a mystique, at worst a reputation as a prissy pastime on a par with making matchstick sculptures or hunting rabbits with beagles. There is nothing strange or particularly specialized about taking what you drink into consideration when planning a dinner. Deciding on the wine is no different from working out what other ingredients will be on the plate. And just as there may be certain foods you would not usually put together—cauliflower with cheese with pasta amatriciana, ratatouille with boeuf bourguignonne, avocado with roast lamb, or bread sauce with lobster, all of which would be cases of two delicious things spoiled—some wines and foods don't sit comfortably alongside each other.

The biggest problem for most people is that they don't have enough experience with enough wines to be able to imagine what one will taste like before it has been poured from the bottle. There is a way around this, and that's to choose a wine from the same area as the food you are eating. So, for example, a pale, dry rosé from Provence is one of the best things you can drink with the pungent aïoli and salty olive tapenade eaten along France's Mediterranean coast. The protein in a Florentine-style T-bone steak cooked with olive oil and salt will soften the perception of tannins in a Chianti and make a delicious savory pairing. Pesto alla genovese is good with the herbaceous white wine made from vermentino in Liguria. Gewürztraminer from Alsace goes with the local smelly Münster cheese. If eating the rich magret de canard or cassoulet of Gascony, you could go with one of the two contrasting local wines: Marcillac, an acidic, light red grown in iron-rich soil that seems to quiver with the metallic taste of blood and offers relief from the thick food, or Cahors, a red as sturdy and unyielding (particularly in its youth) as a Cathar fortress, which acts as a kind of stoic balance to the weighty meat and goose fat.

I could go on.

The theory behind why this works is that in places where the gastronomic culture has had time to simmer slowly, the wines and food have developed in tandem to please the same palates at the same tables. This certainly explains why a humble wine like dry Frascati is consumed with such relish in Lazio, where it is made—with what else would you want to wash down a rich, eggy pasta carbonara? It's a process equivalent to the daily accommodations made between married couples who by the time they reach retirement have a partnership that operates like a complex and subtle dance.

You can see this dance taking shape in places like New Zealand and Australia, where the eating and drinking cultures are in rapid motion (people are always surprised to learn that the first sauvignon blanc grapes were planted in Marlborough only in the 1970s). Already, for example, antipodean whites—from New Zealand sauvignons with their characteristic pungency to aromatic pinot gris with a touch of off-dryness that complements spice—are proving good mates for the vibrant, exotic flavors of the fusion food of the region.

Sometimes it can also be useful to think laterally. The other day, stuck for something to eat with a handful of clarets (red Bordeaux) I needed to taste, and cooking for someone who didn't want to eat red meat, I thought back to the sort of food popular during Britain's claret-drinking era, roasted a loin of veal, and served it with egg and anchovy cream sauce, and it worked perfectly.

This rule of thumb is intended only as a guide; I don't wish to suggest that you should restrict yourself to drinking wine from the same country as the food you are eating. So what can you do if you're not cooking a classical dish? Or want to branch out?

Broadly speaking, there are two directions you can take. You can choose a wine that melds with the food. So, for instance, if you were eating roast pork with sweet, mellow roasted root vegetables, you might pick a mellow, aged Rioja with autumn-leaf flavors and a kind of strawberry-softness to echo the caramelized woodiness of cooked parsnips and carrots. Or, to take a more unusual example, you might try smoked eel with an off-dry pinot gris. It might sound odd, but there's a textural correspondence between the fleshiness of the wine and the oiliness of the fish, and both have a smoky quality.

Alternatively you can pick a wine that acts as a contrast, cutting across the food, like fruity chutney with cold meat or a squeeze of lemon over fish. A good example of this is drinking Beaujolais, with its bright, cheery fruitiness, with Christmas dinner; in a similar vein, Beaujolais is also lovely with duck rillettes.

Watch out for herbs and spices, because they have a huge impact on the taste of a dish. Acidity is another thing that can wreck a well-planned glass of wine. If you're going to be eating a lot of vinegar (in vinaigrette, say), tomatoes, or lemons, try to find a wine with enough acidity to stand up to it; otherwise the acidity in the food will make the wine taste dull and empty. Roast chicken with buttery gravy will be delicious with a rich, buttery oaked white Burgundy or South African chardonnay. Marinate chicken breasts in lemon juice and lemongrass and grill them fast, and the crisp vim of a sauvignon blanc or lemony-tasting Gavi from northern Italy will be better.

It's mainly instinctive, but weight and intensity should also be taken into consideration.

The most critical food and wine matching exercise of my life occurred when a newspaper for which I was working as a features writer asked me to go and have dinner with a man who lived off roadkill. On the phone with Mr. Boyt, it became clear that we were not talking about the odd pheasant or grouse.

"There are some dead foxes on the verges at the moment," he said, rather too cheerily. "They're a bit old and stinky, and fox is the only thing I don't really like eating because it tastes of petrol, but if you like we could take a steak off one anyway. And don't worry. Just in case we don't find anything, I'll get a badger stew out of the freezer and have it bubbling on the stove, ready for when you arrive."

Lovely. I gave a lot of thought to what wine I would take to drink with that badger stew. Would it be South African pinotage, for the reek of rubber and smoke, the better to go with the tire marks? Or maybe industrial vodka, for the anesthetic effect? In the end I settled on the biggest, burliest Australian shiraz I could find, in the hope that it would obliterate the taste of anything else I put in my mouth.

Unless you are trying to drown out the taste of badger with a roar of shiraz, or cut through a heavy meal with an acidic wine, it's a good idea to look for a reasonable parity of intensity. This is why bold, oaked, high-alcohol reds from Argentina, Chile, South Africa, and Australia are so often teamed with barbecue food: they have a volume similar to that of pungent marinades and charred red meat.

Two other things play havoc with wine: chile and bitterness. The best way to counteract chile is to put it with a wine that has some sweetness. Try drinking a bone-dry wine with a hot marinade and the wine will seem stripped of all flavor, like water. With an off-dry rosé, or pinot gris, however, you might just succeed in being able to taste both wine and food. As for bitterness, which you find in chicory and artichokes, this is something wine drinkers learn to dread, and it is not easily resolved, though a glass of fino sherry is one answer.

Finally, there is the do-as-you-please school of wine and food matching for those who prefer to eat what they like best and drink what they like best without making any link between the two. This reminds me of the uncle who used to put tomato ketchup on his breakfast cornflakes on the grounds that they were his two favorite things and that he could. Not everyone shared his taste, but it made him very happy.

How to store wine

Few of us have the luxury of a cellar, but we can follow a few basic rules. Wine should be stored in the dark, ideally at a temperature of 50°F. Keeping the temperature steady is more important than getting it exactly right, so don't put the wine rack near any radiators or outside walls, where the heat fluctuates.

What to do with leftover wine

Rather than throwing wine away, or allowing it to linger for a third day, freeze it for culinary use. I freeze small quantities of wine in ice-cube trays, to be popped into gravy, and larger amounts in plastic cups to make stews and casseroles.

The shape of a wineglass and its effect on taste
My face must have inadvertently scrunched up as I took a sip of the expensive champagne. "What's the matter?" asked the friend whose new job we were supposed to be celebrating. "Corked?" It wasn't corked. It was just . . . horribly unsatisfying.

This was a wine I had drunk in France only three months earlier, on a December afternoon so cold our hands had turned first blue and then as deathly white as the frost on the Bollinger vineyards we had toured before being rewarded with a glass of their 1999 vintage. I had loved it then, so what was the matter now? Did the wine refuse to express itself away from its homeland? Did it taste that good only if you almost caught pneumonia before trying it? For five more minutes I sipped from my flute, tasting only disappointment, drinking too quickly because I was hoping to find in the next mouthful what I had missed in the one before. This wasn't something for which I'd willingly fork out £60 again. More like half that.

Then it came to me. In the kitchen I tipped the champagne out of the flutes and into two large white-wine glasses. This time, given space to breathe and a stage to occupy, the wine was as gorgeous as I'd remembered it, like "tasting stars," to quote the monk Dom Perignon on one of his own brews.

I think we all intuitively realize that the type and shape of glass we drink out of affects our drinking experience to some extent. After all, doesn't everything, from what you've just had in your mouth, to your mood, the temperature, its age . . . the list of variables is almost endless. So what we should be asking is how much? And in what way?

To take two extremes, I suspect only the very perverse would argue that it's more pleasurable to drink wine out of a polystyrene cup than fine lead crystal. But what about all the things that fall in between?

The word *glass* derives from an Old Teutonic form of the word meaning "to shine." Pliny tells us that in his time it was preferred over gold as a drinking vessel, and there is a lot to be said for the way a clean glass sparkles on the table and how your eyes enjoy running over its curves. But change the taste of the wine in a way an ordinary person might actually notice? For a long time I thought the idea was nonsense, but a lot of tasting and a lot of drinking have changed my mind. Now

I realize glasses can make such a difference that they are as big a part of the equation as deciding how much money you're going to spend on a bottle. And tipping vintage champagne out of a narrow flute to give it a bit more space is only the beginning.

My education began when I was invited to a fancy dinner hosted by Georg Riedel, the head of the Austrian glass company that bears his family name. Riedel is like the Armani of wineglasses. Its drinking vessels come in dozens of different shapes. But they are not just designed to look and feel good when you pick them up; each one is made with a specific wine style, say Chablis or zinfandel, in mind, and is supposed, by some mysterious process, to hone its best points, like a fun house mirror that makes you appear taller and emphasizes your waist.

In the event we didn't really put the Riedel range through its paces that night. We tried wines in pairs of glasses—the one designed specifically for it and a second glass that splayed out toward the top, more martini than tulip. Each time the wine smelled significantly less intense in the glass that splayed out. The effect was a bit like shouting into a gale that's howling past your ears—you have to make more effort to make yourself heard, and even when you do, words and inflections simply disappear. Lesson one learned: a glass that doesn't curve in, at least slightly, around the wine lets it down in the same way, and included in this category are many of the thick-stemmed, goblet-shaped glasses you are sometimes given in restaurants and that I have found waiters change only with irritation.

The other, very basic thing that makes a big difference is space. Pour wine one-third of the way up a decent-sized glass (this will often mean that the meniscus is at the widest point of the bowl, giving the greatest surface area contact with the air), give it a swirl, and it's going to smell much better than if you poured a student-sized portion right up to the rim, giving the nose no room at all for maneuver. For red wines, a glass is effectively a personal decanter, and the bowl should generally be larger than it is for a white.

Then something even more disconcerting happened. I invited my friend Joe over for dinner. Joe Wadsack is a food and drink nut. He had just finished helping to design a range for Dartington Crystal and, rather than turning up with wine or flowers, he offered to bring a few of them, eager to show them off. Buying a set of good tasting glasses, which revealed wines in brighter, sharper detail—in much the same way that the hazy green mass of a tree suddenly resolves itself into individual leaves the first time you put on a pair of contact lenses—had already persuaded me that good glasses could make a difference, but I was still skeptical about all this different-shapes-for-different-wines business.

Joe called ahead with instructions that made him sound like a stage magician and almost made me wish I hadn't agreed to the whole performance. "You'll need a pinot noir," he said. "Any pinot noir—it doesn't matter which; you can choose. And a sauvignon blanc, any sauvignon blanc." Yes, all right, I said, I get the idea.

According to Joe, when designing glasses intended to flatter certain types of wine, you have to look first not at the wine but at what people expect of it—what they want it to taste like—and work backward from there. "For example," he said, "from sauvignon blanc people expect lively, grassy scents, citrus, vigor. It's a wine you'd have sitting outside, watching cricket. Wallop. And it should be refreshing."

When Joe starts talking, it's sometimes hard to get him to stop. I tuned out, stuck my nose in several glasses, and began sniffing like a hound of the Baskervilles. I had to admit that something seemed to be going right. In the Burgundy glass the sauvignon smelled weak and diffuse. In my cheapie Habitat number, and in our control "taster" glass, it was doing OK. In Joe's wine glass for unoaked white something was happening: on the nose it felt more sculpted, pointy, and firm, much more like sticking your head out of a car window and catching a gasp of crisp mountain air, which is exactly what I want from a sauvignon blanc.

"Exactly," said Joe. "Now taste. You're going to have to do this as if you're drinking rather than spitting, and tell me which one seems more thirst-quenching."

Again, Joe's unoaked—white wine glass outperformed the Burgundy one. He explained why: "The bigger brim of the Burgundy glass directs the wine under your tongue. The others send it straight on to the sides of the tongue where your mouth waters when you drink something acidic, so it seems leaner. Also, when a glass is narrower at the top, you can't get your nose into it, so you have to tip your head farther back to take a sip. The wine then hits your mouth with a higher velocity—whoosh—which creates a different sensation and alters the flow across your taste buds."

There were more revelations. A bottle of young Meursault, an oaked white from Burgundy, tasted creamier, richer, and more opulent in a glass with a short, shallow bowl.

"That's because most of the volatile components from the oak hover just above the wine," explained Joe. "Because this glass is wide, you stick your nose right in—and you catch them."

This wasn't always a good thing, I discovered after experimenting with a few more whites. I preferred some of the more flagrantly oaked, sumptuous New World whites from the control taster glass—but that's because I liked them better if those qualities were restrained and they were "Frenched up," as Joe put it. "Again, it's about looking at what you want from the wine, as well as at the wine itself."

Perhaps most interesting, from the point of view of anyone who drops this sort of money on a wine but doesn't invest in glassware, were the changes wrought on the more expensive reds. In the right glass (a wide bulb) an expensive pinot noir fanned out like a peacock spreading its tail, so much more expressive than in our control that I was forced to conclude you'd be wasting your money spending so much on a bottle of wine unless you had something halfway decent out of which to drink it.

It would be like buying a state-of-the-art sound system and fitting it to cheap speakers—or a Ferrari and sitting in it in traffic.

It's hard to buy, unless you've seen it in action, that anyone whose nostrils weren't trained to the nth degree might be able to pick up such a change. But not only have I experienced it enough times now to believe there really is something in it; I've even sat down at my kitchen table with my mum, who knows nothing about wine except that she likes to drink it, and got her to sniff and slurp the same wine from different glasses. Every single time she told me that she preferred the wine from the one designed specifically for it—and she didn't know which the "right" answer was.

There is one small scrap of good news, though: a one-size-fits-all wineglass, such as my Habitat specials (perhaps a smaller one for whites and a bigger one for reds), can do a pretty good job with most wines, provided it tapers slightly at the top.

Nonetheless I reserve great respect for sticklers like the head waiter at the Taj Mahal hotel in Mumbai, who refused to let standards slip during the terrorist siege in November 2008. As one guest-hostage who had been holed up in the restaurant while explosions shook the building later reported, "Come 5 A.M. we were fairly confident the police were going to get us out, so I marched over to the bar and found a bottle of vintage Cristal, opened it, and began pouring. Then the head waiter came rushing across and said, "No, no, you can't do that!" And I said, "Well, we're going to!" and he said, "No, sir, those are the wrong type of glasses."' Quite so.

BREAKFAST & BRUNCH

From the moment we get up, promising ourselves a mug of tea, splash of juice, or jolt of coffee as a reward for braving the temporary awfulness of shaking ourselves out of sleep, until bedtime, drink and its rituals are among the rhythms that give shape to our day. We all have our own routines. They might begin with the rushing glug of coffee streaming through an Italian stovetop coffee maker, move on to a series of gossip pit-stops en route to the office water cooler, include a nicely brewed pot of tea and a cookie to punctuate the afternoon, swing into the relief of a glass of wine, and finish with a late-night whiskey or chamomile tea. Whatever, the business of preparing a drink—slicing up oranges to juice, warming the teapot, setting out cups on a tray, grinding coffee, heating milk—feels like a civilizing process. It needs to have a bit of joy to it, though, and a bit of care, otherwise we would end up measuring out our lives with coffee spoons, like T. S. Eliot's J. Alfred Prufrock.

WEEKDAY MORNINGS

Tea: a call for rebellion

A cup of tea is so much more than a drink. George Orwell once called it "one of the mainstays of civilization in this country," and I don't think he was exaggerating. It is a unit of time ("stopping for a cup of tea" is as much about the break as about the drink), a highly effective security blanket (in the most devastating crises the British can seldom think of a better course of action than to brew up), a social glue, and a kind of magical fuel that in the morning helps bridge the gap between sleep-in-your-eyes muddle-headedness and wide-awake getting-on, then throughout the day provides restorative solace. Perhaps it is because many of us will manage with a polystyrene cup of something that only vaguely resembles tea rather than forgo the reassurance altogether that so much of the tea we consume is made to such poor standards. There is another reason too.

"Have you ever sent a cup of tea back?" I once asked one of Twinings's master blenders. He looked momentarily startled, then abashed, before he confessed he had not. Neither have I. But oh, how I wish I had.

The closest I ever came was on the morning of my honeymoon, in 60 Thompson, an expensive New York hotel, when we ordered room-service tea that turned out to be just about as bad as tea can ever be. The water had either not been boiled at all, or been left to cool before the tea was added, so the flavor would not take, and just to slight us further, when we tried to pour it from the teapots, a good half of the liquid spilled all over the tray and dribbled down our arms. My husband and I looked at each other. We had already changed rooms because we wanted that other peculiar English thing, a bath. I thought he might be upset if I intimated he had chosen a hotel where they could not even serve a decent cup of tea. I said nothing. He did the same. We settled down to silent fury but later agreed that if it hadn't been our honeymoon, we would have complained. We then did so, vigorously, to a receptionist who clearly thought we were slightly insane and refused to remove the drink from our bill because it was no longer there to examine for flaws. We paid something like $7 apiece for that hopeless cup of tea.

It was neither the first nor the last time I have overpaid for shoddy tea. From the cafés of Paris to the hotels of Sydney, to the 10:06 train from Paddington to Penzance, the global standard of tea making is frankly appalling. In an age when every little railway station kiosk can froth milk to make cappuccino, and every other sandwich shop serves sushi without poisoning its customers, why can't pay-through-the-nose hotels with apple martinis on their bar menus get a simple thing like making tea right? I have come to believe it is our fault. In Britain, we drink 165 million cups of tea a day—only the Irish have a higher per-capita consumption—but thanks to that British habit of Not Wanting to Make a Fuss, we are utter wimps when it comes to putting people straight about the lamentable quality of their tea. "Oh, well," we think to ourselves, "no one abroad ever understands about how to make tea; it was good of them to let me have a cup in the first place." Or "Never mind; it's not that poor chap's fault. He's probably not allowed to use boiling water for some health and safety reason. We'll have a proper one when we get home."

I would like to propose a tea revolution, an international rout of lousy cups of tea. All we tea drinkers should begin to make a fuss. We should complain when we are given hot instead of boiling water, we should take up arms against horrible little plastic cartons of shelf-stable milk, and most of all we should riot against caterers on airplanes and trains who pour tea from giant thermos jugs that have previously been used for coffee.

How to make a proper cup of tea

Of course, I am talking about ordinary black tea here. Water is the first thing. It must be freshly drawn. Do not reboil half a kettle of water left over from the last cup. As Twinings's Jeremy Sturges explains, "When you boil water, you boil the oxygen out of it. It affects the quality hugely and means you end up with dull, flat tea. It doesn't happen with modern electric kettles because they switch off as soon as the water boils, but if you are camping or perhaps have a stovetop kettle, you should make sure it doesn't sit there boiling away for a long time. In our tasting rooms, if we see the water has been overboiling we throw it away and start again."

The water you use will also make a difference: the harder the water, the less expressive the tea. This is why Taylors of Harrogate supply some areas of the country with a special "hard water" version of their Yorkshire Tea. If you live in a hard water area, filtering will improve the tea, but take care not to leave the water standing around or you will lose the dissolved oxygen that gives it freshness.

Next, the tea. Tea bags have their place, but they must be good quality. See below for a discussion of tea types.

The best tea is almost always made in teapots. This is because if you do the mug dunk, the mug will rarely be the right size for the amount of tea in the bag, so in order not to make the cup too strong, you end up underextracting the tea and missing out on a few layers of flavor.

In winter you will need to warm the pot by swirling hot tap water around it while the kettle boils. On a warm summer's day this isn't essential. Empty the warming water from the pot and put in the tea. For loose-leaf tea, the old measure of one heaped teaspoonful per person is a rough guide, but it will depend on what type of tea you are using, so you need to experiment.

NICE

Have the pot ready and waiting. Immediately after the water comes to a boil, pour it over the tea. The use of freshly boiling water is the single most important point in this whole performance and the one most often ignored outside the home.

Now leave the tea to brew. Some teas require only two to three minutes; others six to seven. The color and flavor do not come out of the leaves at the same rate—the tea usually gains color before it is quite ready to drink. The mistake made by mug dunkers is to judge when the tea is ready by its color and take the bag out too early, thinking that if they leave it in longer, the tea will be too strong. Well, it might be. But it will not just taste stronger; it will taste different, because over time different elements of flavor are extracted from the tea, and to get the depth and bite that make a cup of tea worth drinking, you need to give it time. Part of the problem here is that most tea bags contain too much tea to make a single cup. If your tea tastes too strong when a bag has been left in for two to three minutes, this is easily dealt with—use a bigger cup or a teapot.

Once the tea is ready to pour, you have to make a decision about milk. Americans usually drink their tea black, but in Britain 98 percent of people drink it white. In my view only 2 percent milk makes a good cup. Skim is too light and you need to use too much of it; whole milk is too creamy. In the past there has been a lot of snobbery attached to whether you pour milk into the cup first or second. In the eighteenth century it is thought that aristocrats would pour the milk first, perhaps so as not to stain or crack their fine china. By the early twentieth century this social habit had reversed: putting your milk in first had come to be seen as an irredeemably middle-class affliction. In *Noblesse Oblige*, published in 1956, Nancy Mitford refers scathingly to "MIFs' (Milk in Firsts), whom she defines as being "non-U" (non-upper-class). There's even a moment in the film *Gosford Park*, set on an English country estate in the 1930s, that points up this notion: when a lowly policeman, Inspector Thompson (played by Stephen Fry), prepares a cup of tea for Lady Sylvia (Kristin Scott Thomas), she interrupts him at once in terribly pained, cut-glass tones: "Would you mind putting the milk in afterwards?" Poor Thompson is so embarrassed by his social gaffe that he is thrown into a fluster: "Of course, of course. I don't know what came over me there. I usually put the milk in afterwards but on that occasion . . . Mrs. Inspector Thompson always prefers the milk in first, so I get used to pouring it for her—I don't know, some nonsense about bacteria. You know what women, well, you know what wives are like."'

I usually put my milk in first because I am lazy and don't like the paraphernalia of teaspoons.

A guide to tea leaves: from oolong to what goes in a tea bag

Tea is made from the glossy green leaves of *Camellia sinensis* var. *sinensis* and *Camellia sinensis* var. *assamica*, members of the same genus as *Camellia japonica*, whose flowers, so improbably bright they look as if they have been painted by the queen in *Alice in Wonderland*, are loved by gardeners. The tips (hence the suggestive name of the brand PG Tips) are the most highly prized part of the plant, and for good-quality tea only the top two leaves on the bud will be picked. Lower-quality teas use perhaps the first four or five leaves and, because more stalk is included and the lower, older leaves are more veined, there is more fibrous material and the tea is less refined and less tasty.

The difference between black and green tea

Black and green tea are from the same plant. The difference lies in the processing. To make black tea, the cell structure of the leaves is broken down by rolling, and they are then exposed to the air so that they oxidize and darken. Leaves destined for green tea, on the other hand, are given a direct application of heat, by being warmed in a wok or pan or by being steam-treated. This process destroys the enzymes that react with oxygen in the air, and the tea retains its color.

What's in a tea bag?

The tea inside a bag is usually, but not always, different from loose leaf. While loose leaf generally resembles long, tightly twisted slivers that swell into something resembling a leaf when they come into contact with hot water, tea bag tea may be tiny, granular specks, like very small grape nuts, or even dust. This is because loose-leaf tea is usually processed using what's called the *orthodox method*—rolled between two surfaces so that the leaf twists—while tea-bag tea is classically made using a process known as *CTC*, or *cut, tear, curl*—the leaves are passed through a series of serrated-edged rollers, getting finer and finer. Once it has been rolled and dried, the tea is shaken over different sizes of mesh so it can be graded by size. The lowest quality is the stuff, little more than dust, left at the end, which is called *broken mixed fannings*, or *BMF*. The cheapest tea you can find will be tea bags filled with BMF made from tips that have been plucked five leaves down the stem. However, better-quality tea bags may be made using tea processed by the orthodox method and a larger grade of leaf. Tea sold in bags is usually a blend and may come from as many as forty different tea gardens.

Darjeeling

Grown in India, in the foothills of the Himalayas, this is sometimes known as the champagne of teas and sometimes, rather less romantically, said to taste of sawdust. It is true that lower-quality Darjeeling can seem thin-bodied and astringent, but the good stuff has vitality and finesse. I thought I didn't like Darjeeling until I tried loose leaf, and it was pointed out to me that it is a major component in some of my favorite bagged blends; Darjeeling is often used in afternoon tea because its briskness, delicacy, and bite make a more refreshing pick-me-up drink.

Assam

This has a broader, maltier taste and because of its rich, robust flavor is a mainstay of English breakfast blends. It is grown in the lush landscape of Assam, to the east of Bangladesh in the far northeastern corner of India.

Ceylon

Like Darjeeling, Ceylon tea is said to do well in hard water. It comes from Sri Lanka and is lively, light-liquoring (produces light-colored tea), and less rounded than Assam.

Lapsang Souchong

It is no quirk of imagination to say that Lapsang Souchong tastes smoky. It is smoky. It comes from southeast China, where it is laid out in bamboo baskets and allowed to dry over fires. The fires are stoked with pine logs from the nearby forests, so the smoky character also has a medicinal, resinous quality from the pinewood.

Earl Grey

This is named after the second Earl Grey, who was the British prime minister from 1830 to 1834. Apparently he was given a diplomatic gift of black tea, scented with oil from the rind of the bergamot orange, a citrus fruit that grows in Calabria in Italy, and enjoyed it so much he asked British tea shippers to re-create the blend.

Oolong

This is like the rosé wine of tea. The leaves are allowed to oxidize—or "ferment" to use proper tea terminology—only partially so they look reddish black and bruised along their edges and make tea with a slight rosy-green hue. They traditionally come from Taiwan and Fujan province in southeastern China and, as they are delicate and fragrant, are usually drunk without milk.

White tea

To make white tea, brand-new buds and leaves are not subjected to the usual withering, rolling, and oxidizing process that black tea undergoes, nor are they steamed like green tea. Instead they are simply dried, sometimes in the sun.

Loose-leaf tea: the beginning of the affair

I will always love tea bags. They are convenient, quick, make no mess, and make it possible for tea to be brewed in office lunch rooms or in a grumpy hurry early on a Tuesday morning. Tea-bag tea is reliable, sturdy, fortifying, and thickly calming. But once you upgrade to loose leaf, a new realm of tea unfolds. The flavors may be subtle, but they are also brighter: alert, refined, and yet strangely intense.

You can buy loose-leaf tea in the supermarkets, but for specialty teas I buy from a number of people. Whittard shops in Britain are uninspiring places, but they have a highly knowledgeable and enthusiastic buyer and their better teas are available online. I sometimes buy Margaret's Hope Darjeeling through them: either the first flush, which is picked earlier and is green and spinachy, almost metallic in its astringency, or the sweeter, richer, more grape-nutty second flush. In London, East Teas in Borough Market (or online, at www.eastteas.com) also sells fine tea. As does Jing Tea (www.jingtea.com), from which I recently had a bag of Ali Shan Oolong that made a creamy, cleansing pick-me-up after an exhausting run and would also be an ideal post-yoga tea, if there is such a thing. And Twinings has a treasure chest of a shop on the Strand.

Tea-bag manufacturers use a blend of teas to achieve a consistent flavor for their brand. Sometimes I will put a bag of English Breakfast and one of Earl Grey in the pot together, because I like to have just a tinge of bergamot scent. If you are using tea leaves, you obviously have free range to create your own blend, tweaking and refining, adding more Assam, perhaps, for richness and Darjeeling for edge, until it is as perfect as Goldilocks's third bowl of porridge.

There are, however, teas so fine it would be sacrilegious to mix them with anything else. My own loose-tea appreciation is in its infancy compared to that of a colleague, Chris, who became very restive when Twinings failed to stock his favorite Russian Caravan for a whole year (because, apparently, there was a global shortage), while Jasper Morris, a Master of Wine and a buyer for the wine merchant Berry Brothers & Rudd, is as keen on tea as he is on Bordeaux and Burgundy. He keeps his wine in a damp cellar, but his tea is safely stashed in his wardrobe behind the winter sweaters, where it remains warm and dry. He particularly likes Pu Erh, which is sold in dried-out cakes; a good vintage can, much like wine, be aged for over a decade, becoming increasingly complex in flavor the longer it is kept. Such fine tea does not come cheap. Jasper once spent HK$3,800 on a small amount of Pu Erh. How much, I asked him, would that be in sterling? "About the same price as a case of Chasse-Spleen," he explained breezily, leaving me not very much the wiser. "There are twelve bottles in a case, and I have about enough tea to make twelve pots, so that seemed about right."

This is probably not the sort of thing you would guzzle with fried eggs and bacon at breakfast; Jasper drinks his fine tea with his wife in the afternoon, when they want to reward themselves and have time to appreciate it. I'm partial to a spot of afternoon tea myself—especially if it comes with a slice of Christmas cake, buttered crumpet, or toasted currant tea-cake, eaten on the floor beside a real fire—and often eat a smaller lunch on purpose to accommodate it.

But a sparklingly fresh cup of your own personal tea-leaf blend? That is a good start to the day.

Coffee: how to make it

We live in an age of baristas and world coffee-making championships, and in Britain we boast around 3,000 branded coffee outlets in which we spend millions every year, yet it's unusual to buy a cup of coffee that meets even fairly low expectations. Skinny lattes are too milky or too bitter; espressos lack the proper *crema* (the creamy-textured top that shows the espresso is both fresh and properly made); there's not enough balance or not enough punch, or there's an earthy edge that reminds you of dishwater. At home, even though we control every variable, it is often just as bad.

Most of us drink coffee, but I have still to find more than a dozen people who make it well and do so without hesitation or apology. With a filter machine or French press no one is ever sure how much coffee to use—there is always a great deal of conferring, and then, "Well, I'll put four spoonfuls in and a bit extra," followed by some uncertain fumbling as a few more grounds are shaken in, just in case. With a French press there is also the plunging dilemma: How long ought one wait? Will it be done yet? Should I give it a quick stir? And so on.

The smell of freshly ground, fresh-roasted coffee beans is one of the most stirring and intoxicating I know, yet the gulf between that and the dead taste of murky brown liquid when it hits your mouth can sometimes feel as wide as the Grand Canyon.

My own coffee making improved immeasurably when I realized I only ever enjoyed the first cup I made from any packet and it dawned on me, in a cartoon-like revelation, that I was letting the coffee go stale. Once opened, a vacuum pack of ground coffee will keep only about two weeks before it loses its brightness and edge, and that's if you look after it by storing it in an airtight jar and then put the jar in the fridge. The other major mistake most of us make is that we don't use enough coffee. To get freshness and punch without mud and flatness, you need quite a lot of it. But using coffee that's still fresh enough to taste of anything and putting enough in is only the beginning.

The domestic espresso machine

A friend once texted me, in a temper, from the kitchen of Gordon Ramsay's family house to say someone was trying to make her drink instant coffee because Gordon had no idea how to work his shiny new espresso contraption. These hulking, gurgling machines have become de rigueur in middle-class homes over the past few years, but they owe more to engine appreciation than they do to a desire for gourmandism. Few people actually seem to drink espresso, preferring to use the machine to produce an espresso base for coffee that is then diluted with milk. It's a style familiar and therefore reassuring to our taste buds because it's what we all now buy when we go out. But though it feels consoling, coffee made in this way doesn't do much to showcase the bean itself.

An espresso machine works by putting the coffee under pressure. Flavor, tannin, bitterness, and acidity are all extracted hard and at speed from the grounds to give a strong, short drink with a creamy head, the *crema*. But the feeling among coffee experts is that while an espresso is a delicious drink, the coffee-making method has more impact on the flavor than the beans. That is, an espresso reveals the nuances of an espresso more than it allows your finest Java, Colombian, or Kenyan coffee to express itself.

A. J. Kinnell, one of the three buyers for the Monmouth Coffee Company, goes further. A rigorous New Zealander, she has been hooked since she began visiting coffee shops at the age of fourteen, ordering espressos and asking questions, intent on finding that holy grail, "a coffee that might taste as good as it smelled." She says, "I tell everyone not to buy an espresso machine, because unless you can afford to buy one made to commercial standards, which would probably cost you

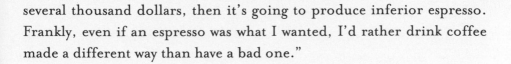

several thousand dollars, then it's going to produce inferior espresso. Frankly, even if an espresso was what I wanted, I'd rather drink coffee made a different way than have a bad one."

Filters

The electric filter machine is the antichrist of coffee making. It is almost painful to watch the liquid dripping lethargically through as the already-made coffee sits on the scalding metal plate, stewing to dullness, or, even worse, to see the jug languishing on the heat in restaurants, waiting for someone to order a cup, while the coffee rapidly loses whatever vestige of decent flavor it may once have had. A child equipped only with a bag of chicory, hot water, and a sieve could not make a worse drink. Indeed, this is virtually what we fell back on during a vacation in France when the gleaming kitchen of our rented house contained no coffee-making equipment but for an electric filter machine. Despite repeated attempts with three different types of coffee, we could not coax it into making anything we wanted to drink, so we ended up putting grounds and hot water into a jug, waiting briefly for the solids to settle, and pouring the coffee off the top. It tasted better.

This does not mean that filters are no good. The problem with the electric machine is two-fold. The hot metal plate and the hanging-around time destroy the freshness. And because water is passed for several minutes through the same grounds, muddier flavors are extracted. Both these issues are avoided if you make coffee directly into the mug using individual filters. This method had not occurred to me until I visited the Monmouth Coffee Company, which imports individual ceramic filters from Japan (which you can also buy in its shops if you happen to be in London), and makes all the non-espresso-based coffee it sells in this way.

You simply rest the ceramic filter, with a filter paper inside, on top of a mug, put about 2 tablespoons of coffee in the paper (this is an awful lot, but the method works, although I defy anyone to drink more than one cupful without getting twitchy), dampen the coffee with near-boiling water so that it blooms up slightly, then fill the filter to the top with hot water so that it gushes through. The coffee made in this manner tastes very similar to that made in a French press, but a little cleaner, because the filtration process removes some of the solids in suspension in the water. It's also much easier to clear up—all you have to do is chuck the filter paper and its grounds in the bin.

French press

There is a school of coffee hoity-toitiness that sneers at the French press. I do not subscribe to this. Along with individual cup-filters, this is to my mind one of the two coffee-making methods that shows the beans off fully. It just requires a little care. First, as with a teapot, you need to warm the beaker up, which is easily done by filling it with hot water from the kettle and leaving it to sit while the kettle reboils. Mike Riley, a buyer for Taylors of Harrogate, introduced me to another tweak. "If there are any small grains of old coffee caught in the press's mesh, they will dull the taste," he said fastidiously. "So when I'm warming the press I clean it at the same time, by giving it a few vigorous plunges before I throw the warming water away."

Most people don't use enough coffee in a French press. Unlike tea, coffee tastes sharper and brighter if it doesn't have much steeping time. This means you need to put enough coffee in the pot to give instant flavor. It's no good relying on leaving it to sit in the water to make it stronger. Doing so will only extract all the earthy, dull flavors you don't want. There should be at least a couple of fingers of coffee in the bottom

of your press when the water—just off the boil or boiling; it makes no difference—goes in. Now either leave the coffee for thirty seconds before plunging or give it a stir with a spoon and then begin to plunge, slowly, immediately.

Moka

This is the Italian stovetop device that comes in three metal parts. You put cold water in the bottom and the grindings in a perforated metal cup above it; steam from the water as it boils passes through the coffee, gathering flavor, before condensing and gurgling through into a jug screwed on the top. A bad moka—and when you get one of these there is nothing for it but to throw it away—makes coffee that tastes tinny and uninspired, as if the bag has been open for several weeks. A good one makes glossy, strong black coffee that always tastes a little baked—it acquires a charcoal or toasted edge sometimes reminiscent of cocoa nibs and has less fruitiness than the same coffee when brewed in a French press or individual filter system. You can prevent it from burning too much by turning off the heat the moment the coffee has all spurted through so that it doesn't boil in the jug at the top or by dropping an ice cube into the liquid as it begins to come through, so that it never gets hot enough to boil and retains a creamier texture. Thanks to the slight burnt taste it gives, a moka will never do justice to an expensive bean. But I happen to like it, not to mention the preparation ritual and the satisfying gurgle that alerts you to the fact that the coffee is ready, and I tend to alternate among a French press, filter, and moka according to my mood. I particularly like to drink Italian blends of coffee in a moka if having pain au chocolat for breakfast, as the toasted, more savory edge it gives to the coffee is a good foil for the sweet chocolate, while the same coffee made in a French press would make for too rich a combination.

A word on water

There is one other thing. Yes, really, the water. "Such a big considera-tion," according to one person. "Dangerous territory," said another. The fact is that real coffee freaks would not dream of using tap water without first filtering it. Just as it is with tea, hard water is unforgiving on coffee, destroying the nuances and damping down the style. In some cases, it makes coffee taste harsh. But coffee is less sensitive than tea when it comes to the temperature of the water with which it is made. My father always taught me to make coffee with water just before it came to a boil, but even the most persnickety coffee experts tell me that their experiments show that whether you use water just before it boils, just on the boil, or slightly cooled makes no discernible difference to the taste.

Know your beans

The roasted beans of two species of coffee plant, *Coffea arabica* and *Coffea robusta*, are widely used to make drinks. Of these, arabica is considered superior—smoother, more finessed and elegant—while robusta tends to have a flatter, earthier, more rustic profile. It is robusta that is found in many instant coffees, but it's not confined to them. I have a sneaky attraction for the gutsy smell of robusta in the morning, which in coffee circles is akin, I am told, to declaring a passion for Black Tower. Oh, well. The robusta I drink is actually mixed with arabica and is the blend Lavazza sells under its red label, Qualità Rossa. It is a little too plain-spoken for drinking later in the day, but first thing seems to me just right.

Many espresso blends, and by association some of those coffees labeled "Italian blend," are based on Brazilian coffee. Partly this is because there's a lot of it about. It's also because it works well in an espresso. According to Taylors of Harrogate, which sells coffee under its own name as well as producing some private-label blends, "Acidity comes out much higher when you put beans through an espresso machine. So you might really love Kenyan coffee, which tends to have high acidity, made in a cafetière [French press], but find it too much in an espresso. Brazilian coffee, on the other hand, has lower acidity and is much more chocolaty. You give it a dark roast to bring up that flavor and it makes a fantastic espresso."

Darker roasting emphasizes the toasty, cocoa, and caramel notes already present in a coffee. It may also be used as an intensifier: French blends are traditionally roasted even darker than Italian because, according to Taylors's Mike Riley, "Their beans historically came from the colonies in West Africa. There would usually have been a lot of robusta in there. It needed a dark roast to give it flavor, and also to punch through the creaminess of a café au lait."

Though coffee-growing countries will all produce different styles and qualities of coffee, there are broad characteristics associated with each one. Java tends to be heavy, rich, and chocolaty. Kenyan typically has a zesty, citrusy acidity and a broad fruitiness. Brazilian is quite neutral. Ethiopia, the country where the coffee plant, with its white flowers that smell unexpectedly of jasmine, is first thought to have been persuaded to give up some of its "coffee cherries" for roasting and turning into a drink, is said to have "the most coffee-tasting coffee."

Buying coffee

Freshness is key. In an ideal world, you would buy from a place that roasted the beans themselves, because while the green beans will keep relatively well for up to a year, once roasted they rapidly begin to fade. If you can grind them yourself at home, so much the better. Equip yourself with a grinder with a variable setting so you can churn out grounds the size of coarse bread crumbs for French presses, fine bread crumbs for filters, and something between confectioners' and superfine sugar for espresso machines. If you don't have a grinder, for reasons of space (in a kitchen too small for a toaster, this is something I really can't manage) or time spent messing about, then try either to buy vacuum-packed with as long as possible on the sell-by date or coffee that is well stored and ground to order. Staleness is your enemy.

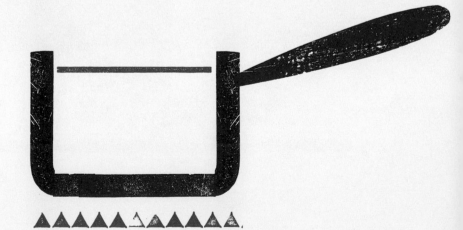

A word on milk

Because I like my coffee made very strong, then heavily diluted with milk, I always need to use warm milk. It is very important not to overheat it. Boil it and the coffee is lost to the taste of cooked milk, not to mention floating skin debris. Take great care, testing the temperature with your finger as it warms as you would if feeding a baby, and use it as cool as you can get away with.

And a trick for frothing

You can buy small frothing devices, but if you have a French press this can also be used to make the milk foamy. Just put the hot milk in the press. Don't fill it to more than halfway up. Then pump the plunger vigorously up and down and the milk will become aerated.

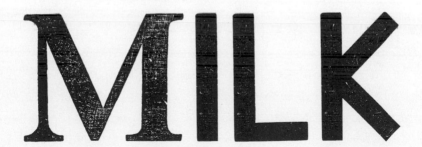

The right cup

Getting out of bed on the wrong side is nothing compared to the irritant of having your first, or indeed any, drink of the day out of the wrong sort of cup. My cousin and I are both very particular on this matter. She once confessed she felt she had been deliberately undermined by a flatmate who repeatedly poured my cousin's tea into the only cup in the kitchen she actively disliked.

For some time I concealed our strange habit from others, presuming it was an odd family thing and that people would laugh. Then I noticed my boss always flinched slightly when given a certain mug for his afternoon tea. There were three of us in that office, and only two bone-china mugs, so someone always had to be the odd one out. One day my boss made the status of the third mug, which was actually quite attractive, explicit. "When we have new people," he said, lowering his voice confidentially, "they cannot have the nice mugs for a long time." After that when he made tea he began to ask, "Who would like the thick mug?" Sometimes when we made the tea we presented him with that mug as a silent rebuke and he would know he was in the doghouse; on a good day one of us would volunteer, martyr-like, to take it.

It now seems strange I should ever have thought my cousin and I were peculiar in the matter of cup preferences. The quickest way for anyone to fall out with new colleagues is to march into the communal kitchen and jauntily help him- or herself to any of the cups on the shelf. This will often prove as provocative and unwise a move as marching into a country pub, settling into a plum seat at the bar, and then spending the night feeling the eyes of a wronged local boring into the back of your neck, wondering when you will dare to brave the dark rush back to the car. Careful observation is imperative before approaching the office mug tree.

milk

two
sugars

Nor is it always easy to predict who will want to drink out of what. I have been surprised at the number of republican households in which I've been offered tea out of a Silver Jubilee mug (or perhaps that's part of the joke). I once interviewed a writer whose crumbling house was piled so high with books and papers I doubted he could locate anything so mundane as a piece of crockery, yet he served me tea in a very pretty, old-fashioned floral set of teacups and saucers. And I remember reading a report sent back from Afghanistan by a noted war correspondent who, amid the fear of the alien territory and perpetual threat to his life, reserved his most somber indignation for the fact that he was reduced to drinking tea out of a cup that was chipped.

This is not just about having a favorite mug. Cup preference is also determined by mood, time of day, and what you are drinking (Lapsang Souchong, in my view, is ruined if drunk out of a thick mug). It is also intensely personal. Unlike wineglasses, which can alter the way the liquid tastes, what seems more important for tea, coffee, and hot chocolate, is the sensory pleasure. You might drink slowly, and want a cup that keeps the tea warm, or require the comfort of earthenware in the morning and the delicacy of china in the afternoon. Or you may not care, in which case please try to be understanding of others' cup madnesses.

Hot water: an oddly reassuring start to the day

Hot water is something we should probably all drink more. It may sound unexciting, but first thing a mug of it can provide much of the reassurance of tea, not least because it warms your hands in just the same way. It also hydrates without being as boring as plain old cold H_2O. And it leaves you feeling fresher and livelier than any caffeinated drink.

BRUNCH

Brunch may be nothing more than a drink: a homemade smoothie swigged on your own after a sweaty workout at the gym, say, or a bowl of hot chocolate consumed for energy before setting out on a long walk. It may equally well be a sociable event over which you linger with a jugful of Bloody Marys and too much food. What it does require is a bit of time.

Juices and smoothies

Even plain orange juice, made from concentrate and not refrigerated until it was opened, was considered a luxury in our household when I was growing up. Now there seems to be no limit to the fruits that can be pulped, squeezed, pressed, or flung around until they give up their essence, nor to their price—the juice of pomegranates, which for obvious reasons (all those pips) are hard to process, can cost as much as a decent bottle of wine. No matter. The tang of fresh fruit pulp is so popular that sales of smoothies have risen by 500 percent in the past five years and are set to triple in the next three. But what differentiates a smoothie from something we might otherwise call a juice? Consistency seems to come into it somewhere, but how far? Must a smoothie contain some form of thickening dairy product? (And if so, what does it take for a smoothie to become a milkshake?) Most books on the subject seem to bandy the term around according to whim, and contradict each other. The *Oxford English Dictionary* says that, aside from being "a slick but shallow or insinuating fellow," a smoothie is "a smooth, thick drink consisting of fresh fruit, especially banana, pureed with milk, yogurt or ice cream." I suspect the *OED* is already out of date: some of the most fervent smoothie drinkers I know would certainly not expect to find yogurt among the ingredients in their favorite fruit pulp. So I'll settle for saying a smoothie should contain either yogurt or ice cream, or bananas, which, when liquidized, give a gloopy texture.

Now on to the equipment. I did once borrow a collection of juicers to test, and though I enjoyed the experiment, I found that, given the small proportions of my flat and consequent need for any piece of kitchen machinery to justify its space, there was no great incentive to buy one. I would like to be able to juice apples (see p. 200 for more information on juicing apples), but I can live without juiced spinach, broccoli, or beets, all of which I think are better eaten than drunk. Most of the fruits I really enjoy drinking are best dealt with in other ways. Grapefruit, limes, lemons, and oranges require a citrus squeezer. Nectarines, peaches, strawberries, melons, blueberries, raspberries, kiwis, pineapples, bananas, mangoes, and papayas can all be blended. I use a hand blender in a small jug, because it seems to create less waste, but you could just as easily use a larger machine. I haven't included all the ingredients above in the concoctions that follow, but juicing has few rules: you can always make up your own combinations.

The original: orange juice

Most supermarkets now sell bags of "juicing oranges," which for a long time I avoided, presuming suspiciously that they were inferior oranges not fit for eating rather than oranges particularly suited to juicing. It's certainly true that some seem hard to peel, and have tough segment membranes, but all the ones I have tried have tasted very good.

Juicing fruit, according to the citrus buyer for the supermarket Waitrose, tend to be Valencia (which includes Midnight, Delta Valencia, and other Valencia types) and midseason oranges (for example, salustiana, and some of the blood oranges like sanguinelli). Not only do juicing oranges produce a lot of tasty juice, but the juice usually keeps better in the fridge than that of navel oranges, which can pick up off or bitter flavors. Freshly squeezed orange juice is so sharply delicious that people are surprised to find what good value it can be. In my local supermarket you can often pick up 4 or 5 pounds of fruit, which will give up to a quart of juice, for much less than the cost of buying the same amount of juice marketed as "freshly squeezed." And though you have to put in some elbow grease to convert the fruit to something drinkable, I think the added freshness shows.

Orange and cranberry juice sharpener

A handful of fresh cranberries adds pep to a glass of orange juice and a welcome tinge of astringency if the juice is very sweet. You can buy fresh cranberries at the holidays and frozen ones year-round. If using them straight from the freezer, leave them to soak and begin to defrost in a small amount of juice for a few minutes before blitzing; otherwise you risk having shards of frozen cranberry flying all over your kitchen.

3 oranges

12 cranberries

Squeeze the oranges in an ordinary citrus juicer. Put the juice of I orange into a small jug if you are using a hand blender or into the jar of a blender. Add the cranberries and blitz until smooth, pour in the rest of the juice, mix, and drink.

Citrus bite

Orange and grapefruit juice is a popular combination in Britain, but I like the sweet-sour finesse that a squeeze of lime adds. This has a real vibrancy and alertness to it: you feel as if you really ought to go out for a run after drinking it, or better, perhaps, as if you have just come back from one.

1 white grapefruit

2 oranges

1 lime

Squeeze in a citrus juicer, combine, and drink.

Green winter livener

The choice of fresh fruit available to put in a glass dwindles in winter, and this recipe makes a pleasing change of pace from all the citrus fruit. The kiwi's distinctive markings, which make it look like an exotic green and black butterfly, once helped to make it fashionable and now seem to count against it. But though neglected after a long period gracing 1970s Pavlovas, it still tastes good—sparky and simultaneously sweet and tart. If you have a juicer, you could use homemade apple juice here. I cheat with fresh-bottled from the store. The lime adds a touch of perfume but isn't necessary. Makes two small helpings.

2 ripe kiwis
⅔ cup apple juice
squeeze of lime
(optional)

Peel the kiwi fruit, chop into large chunks, and puree in a blender. Stir in the apple juice and lime and serve.

Nectarine and mint pulp

White-fleshed nectarines have a lovely cool, aromatic quality. This is something I make as a treat on summer weekend mornings, but it's also very good if you need to use up fruit from a basket of nectarines that all seem to have moved from rock hard straight to the almost-rotten stage. If you score the nectarines from pole to pole with the point of a knife, the peel should just slip off in your fingers. This makes enough for two small helpings.

Remove the stones from the nectarines, chop the flesh coarsely, and blitz to a puree with a hand blender. Stir in the freshly squeezed orange juice and pour into glasses. Use a rolling pin or knife handle gently to bruise the leaves of the mint—just give them a very light roll; there's no need to go in hard—then drag the sprigs through the thick juice in the glasses to give it a suggestion of flavor. Leave the mint in the glass and serve immediately, because the mixture separates out quite rapidly.

2 nectarines, peeled

2 oranges, squeezed

1 sprig mint for each glass

Pineapple and raspberry juice

My mother used to make fruit salad containing nothing but pineapple and raspberries. It's a blissful combination, both invigorating and luxurious, that I convert into a juice. This makes two generous portions.

    Peel and core the pineapple and chop into pieces, removing all the gnarly bits. Blitz the fruit together using a blender. Serve.

½ pineapple
one 6-ounce box
  raspberries

Strawberry and orange juice

Do not make the mistake of thinking the orange is here merely as a cheap carrier for the expensive strawberries. I first came across the coupling in a Josceline Dimbleby recipe for strawberry tart with an orange cookie pastry; as she wrote, "The combination of strawberries and orange is one of those marriages which is an inexplicable success."

    Pinch the green tops off the strawberries, halve them, and puree. Halve the oranges and squeeze in a juicer, then blend the two juices together, adding the orange juice to the strawberry, which will create less waste than doing it the other way around. Serve.

10 medium strawberries
2 oranges

Strawberry, orange, and banana smoothie

This doesn't sound as if it will be much different from the preceding recipe, but while the juice is clean-tasting and runny, flickering between the sweetness of the strawberries and the lively citrus, the addition of banana gives the smoothie a glutinous texture and a creamier taste. Serves two.

Pinch off the green tops, halve the strawberries, and blend with the banana until smooth. Add the squeezed orange, blitz again to combine, and serve.

14 medium strawberries
⅔ banana, peeled
2 oranges, halved and
  squeezed

Mango lassi

This is a take on the yogurt drink that in India is usually diluted with water, may be drunk sweet or salted, and is often flavored with lime or rose water or with roasted spices. Mango is so sweet I don't think you need to add sugar or honey. Instead I prefer to add salt and drag a couple of cardamom pods through for an aromatic flavor. This makes a good Sunday brunch, drunk on the move, when you've had a big dinner the night before and don't quite want to sit down to anything as filling as croissants or bacon and eggs. Makes two to three helpings.

Blitz the mango to a smooth puree using a hand blender. There should be about ⅔ cup of it. Stir in the milk and yogurt. If using cardamom, gently squash a pod or two and stir

½ mango
¾ cup skim milk
¾ cup nonfat natural
  yogurt
1 or 2 cardamom pods
  (optional)
salt to taste

them through the thick liquid. Salt to taste, stir, then pour over ice into glasses and drink with a straw.

Frozen berry smoothie

You can use any single variety of berries or mixed berries, available frozen in various combinations. You could of course use any berries—either a surplus from a fruit-picking expedition or the bits and pieces left in the fridge after a dinner party. That way nothing goes to waste. It does help if the berries are frozen, because the cold crunchiness of the thick, slushy liquid is one of the nicest things about it, but it's a movable feast.

3 heaped tablespoons low-fat natural yogurt
3 heaped tablespoons frozen berries
juice of ½ to 1 orange
honey to taste

Put the yogurt and berries in a jug; stir and blitz with a hand blender until they form a smooth puree. I usually find this is too thick to drink on its own, though that will depend on the berries you have used, so add the juice of up to one orange, stirring it in a bit at a time and tasting to check the flavor. I don't have much of a sweet tooth, so I don't sweeten this, but black currants and red currants can be quite sour, so if they are part of your mixture, you may want to stir in some honey.

Bloody Mary

Glugging a slug of vodka into any other fresh fruit juice or smoothie before noon would be considered the act of an alcoholic. With tomato, things are different. Not that Bloody Marys are simple. Has any drink been more hotly debated? Not even, I think, the martini causes such controversies and fallings-out about how it ought to be made. No one can even agree on the decade in which the Bloody Mary was created. However, it was probably first made a few years after cans of tomato juice began arriving in Paris at the end of the First World War. In fact the tomato juice is the most important ingredient: find a good-quality one and your Bloody Mary is guaranteed to come up to scratch. Vodka is also an essential. Over the years, dozens of other variations have been mooted, with ingredients that range from fierce chile sauces to Clamato to beef consommé, wasabi (for a very clean, Asian-style take on the drink), horseradish, or celery salt. This may be the ultimate brunch drink—especially if you make it up in a jug to feed to disoriented house guests on a Sunday morning after a big Saturday dinner. The original Bloody Mary was strong stuff—equal parts of vodka and tomato juice. I prefer mine a little weaker, but I don't believe in giving a firm recipe for this sort of thing. You have to make it yourself, taste, taste, and taste again. Following are the ingredients I use—I leave it to you to find your own level of seasoning. For me, it's the sherry that really makes it, bridging the gulf between the hot but clean spirit and the fruity tomatoes. See p. 315 for a recipe for Virgin Mary that uses fresh tomatoes.

Mix all the ingredients in a jug or shaker, tasting, tasting, tasting until it is right. If making in small quantities, you should then shake with ice and strain into glasses. Otherwise, just add ice to the jug and serve.

2 parts vodka
5 parts tomato juice
¼ to ½ part freshly
  squeezed lemon juice
dash or 3 fino or,
  better still,
  amontillado sherry
few drops Lea & Perrins
  Worcestershire sauce
few drops Tabasco sauce
salt
black pepper

The occasional bowl of hot chocolate

If there is a remedy for a dank, grey morning when the wind and drizzle seem to creep through the window frames and into your skin, then it is this: hot chocolate. It isn't something you'd drink often, but at the right moment the sugar boost and the act of warming your hands around the bowl can be very welcome. The more ungodly the hour, the more comfortingly milky I like to make it. In the pitchy cold of winter, a mild French drinking chocolate, drunk from the bowl, seems most appropriate. If wider awake, then you may have more of a stomach for the thick bite of sweetened cocoa. At brunch, by which time you ought to be less sleepy, you might feel like something richer, and there is certainly time to make it by melting solid chocolate in milk. I always use dark chocolate for this, usually Lindt 85 percent, to which I sometimes add half a teaspoon of sugar, but obviously you should just use a chocolate you like. This recipe makes quite a rich drink, so if you are not keen on the bitterness of dark chocolate or prefer a gentler taste, either use a brand with a lower percentage of cocoa solids or put a bit less in.

Snap the chocolate into small pieces. Warm the milk in a jug in the microwave or in a small saucepan on the stove. Once it is warm, but before it approaches the simmering point, add the broken-up chocolate. Stir with a wooden spoon and keep heating gently until the chocolate is dissolved but without letting the milk boil. Pour into a mug, add the cream, sweeten to taste, and drink.

¾ cup low-fat or whole milk

1 ounce dark chocolate

a good glug heavy cream (optional)

½ teaspoon sugar (optional)

Grown-up hot chocolate, with chile

The Mayans drank hot chocolate, which they frothed by pouring it into a drinking vessel from a great height. They also added extra flavorings, which included vanilla and chile. The combination of dark chocolate with chile is a good one: the chile expresses itself as a tingly heat that counterbalances the bitterness of the chocolate, and its ripe warmth adds breadth to the drink too. Until relatively recently, chile and chocolate was considered an odd combination, but the modern fashion for flavoring chocolate with herbs and spices, from lavender to cardamom, has made it fashionable again. You can even buy bars of Lindt flavored with chile in the supermarket, which would be an even simpler way of doing things, though not quite as good. To make chile hot chocolate, seed half a fresh red chile (the more robust flavor works better than that of a grassy green one) and let it infuse for ten minutes in a mugful of lukewarm milk. Remove, then use this milk to make hot chocolate in the normal way.

spring

As the days grow longer, and trees show the first green signs of unfurling leaves, we begin to leave behind the protective comforts of winter food and drink and start looking for brighter, lighter, zestier flavors. With the windows open, and the smell of new life in the air, a glass of grassy sauvignon blanc acts as a reminder that the asparagus season is on its way. The first warm weekend is always an excuse to crack into the Pimm's. And the first white peaches always have me rushing to make a Bellini.

SAP RISING

The first Pimm's day of the year

The first day when you can smell spring and the sun shines unexpectedly hot, despite the still-watery light, usually falls somewhere between the spring equinox and the May bank holiday. It happens when the gorse is burning yellow and the lawnmower has come out of the garage for its first few runs, but the heads of peonies haven't yet burst and the first bluebells aren't quite beginning.

This is the first Pimm's day of the year, and on it nothing will seem more intoxicating than the fruity, sweet, just very slightly woody, orange-peel scent of Pimm's No. 1 poured into a tall glass, mixed with cheap lemon-lime soda (or tonic if, like me, you find lemonade too cloying), and topped with a sprig of mint and slice of cucumber. Standing outside, feeling the sun warm on your skin, with a sparkling glass of brownish amber liquid in your hand says one thing: summer is on its way.

From now until the weather turns, Pimm's will be poured by the river, on the patio, after a game of golf or the church raffle on weekend afternoons with the tennis spooling on the telly. . . . We have been drinking it since 1840, when one James Pimm, owner of an oyster bar in the City of London, put this cup—essentially a gin sling with some extras thrown in—on the menu and served it in silver tankards, diligently explaining that it would aid digestion.

The recipe was secret then, and still is now, by virtue of a somewhat irritating marketing quirk, but Pimm's No. 1 is based on gin and flavored with various fruit extracts and herbs. At selected points in its history there have been other numbered Pimm's: No. 1 has always been gin-based, No. 2 was whiskey, No. 3 brandy, No. 4 rum, No. 5 rye, and No. 6 vodka. The others have gradually died out, and today you will find only No. 1 and No. 3—repackaged as "Winter Pimm's"—and No. 6 on the shelves.

A bottle of No. 1 feels a bit like a prop on the film set of the warmer months, always promising to deliver a slice of quintessentially English relaxation. Before the Great War Pimm's was advertised by a gentleman in a pith helmet remarking, "By my gaff and ghillie—I could do with a Pimm's No. 1." In the 1930s its slogan depicted it as the savior of aristocrats, whose fortunes were ebbing and stately homes being sold off: "We had to let the west wing go, but thank heavens we can still afford our Pimm's." This century it's a little more egalitarian, but the play on traditional Englishness is still there in "Anyone for Pimm's?" and, "I make that Pimm's o'clock."

But here is the bad news. Unless you are a committed Pimm's fan, and probably even if you are, the first time you drink Pimm's each year is also the only day on which it will meet expectations. After that, it's all downhill. Pimm's for me is much more about the moment than the taste, which is perhaps why pleasure decreases exponentially until what began as a glowing glass full of promise becomes a sickly confection lacking definition and no more irresistible than an old piece of bubble gum. I only ever drink it once a year. But on that first Pimm's day, I love it—so enjoy it while you can.

Pimm's dos and don'ts

Do use ordinary lemon-lime soda; the fancy cloudy stuff doesn't work as well. Don't make a fruit salad: cucumber peel, mint or borage, and a slice of orange if you want to be extravagant are all that's required. Don't put the fruit and herb bits in a jug; they'll get waterlogged, so put them in individual glasses as you pour.

Grown-up Pimm's alternatives

Sometimes, even at the beginning of the year, Pimm's seems too cloying. Instead I often drink red vermouth with tonic—you can still put all the bits in it—which has the virtue of being more bitter, and also one of the few mixed drinks pubs are unlikely to wreck. To get a bit closer to the real thing, you can mix one part gin, one part red vermouth, and half a part of Cointreau, then dilute with either lemon-lime soda or tonic in the same way that you would for Pimm's No. 1. If you have lots of friends coming over, you could mix up the spirit element in advance, keep it chilled in the fridge, then put out jugs of it on a table alongside glasses, lemon-lime soda, tonic water, a bowl of ice, orange slices, mint sprigs, and cucumber parings. Let people make their own drinks from the buffet as they prefer—lemon-lime soda for those with a sweeter tooth, tonic for those who like it bitter, and dressed as they please.

Campari, and why it gets more bitter the more you dilute it

The sense of bitterness is thought to be one of the ways our ancestors identified—and knew to avoid eating—food that was likely to be toxic. This might explain why it is an acquired taste and why those who relish the oral pinch of, say, endives, dark chocolate, radicchio, tonic water, or lemon pith very often seem to be contrary, if not bloody-minded, individuals. As for Campari, it does not just taste bitter, courtesy of the quinine and wormwood it contains; it is one of a set of drinks that are actually classified as "bitters."

To my mind this is partly why, despite the beautiful carmine glow of the liquid in its distinctive bottle and the effortless cachet you would expect of a drink from the country that gave us Armani, Ferrari, and La Scala opera house, Campari has always stubbornly refused to catch on quite as well as it ought to outside Italy (with the exception of Brazil, when they also love it).

If I had a pound for every person who has sighed wistfully and told me how much they wished they liked it, well, I'd probably have a tenner. I've watched countless friends take a sip for the first time and seen their mouths pucker as if you're trying to poison them. Of course, the idea that it's a connoisseur's drink is one of the draws for those of us who do like it. At university I used to buy Campari all the time simply because, even toward the end of term, when severe financial drought threatened, no one else would touch it.

Yet when it comes to explaining why a drink that has everything in its favor, from looks to an Italian heritage, is not more popular, Campari discount the idea that bitterness might have any impact. "Taste is not a barrier to anything, to my mind," a Campari top dog once told me. A sinister concept, though when you consider some of the stuff that does sell by the truckload—I'm thinking about the likes of Red Bull and some branded wines—it does seem to hold true. So what is the problem? There's no doubt that the infamous 1970s ad starring Lorraine Chase, a bloke in a dodgy flared white suit, and the devastatingly tacky catchphrase, "Nah, Lu'on Airpor" hasn't helped over the decades. That aside, I'm completely foxed as to why we don't drink it more. In both Italy and Brazil, two countries with beautiful people and ultra-hip bar cultures, Campari is ubiquitous. Lombardian in origin, it was put together by a drink maker called Gaspare Campari in Novara in 1860. Its particular flavor comes from infusing a secret list of sixty-eight herbs, roots, peels, spices, and barks in alcohol and water and then coloring it a glossy shade of red. The Italians drink it as an aperitivo—the bitter herbs are said to stimulate digestion—which is certainly the best way to enjoy it. Don't, as they apparently do in St. Lucia, even think of mixing it with milk! The classiest way to drink it is to mix it with soda (or look for the premixed volcano-shaped bottles so cute that my cousin buys them because they cheer her up when she opens the fridge door).

If the bitterness makes you wince, there is a surprising way to reduce its impact. The mistake most people make when they're being tentative about Campari is to overdilute it, thinking that this will give it a gentler taste. It doesn't. Our perception of bitterness is very acute and is barely affected by increasing the dilution. What does change, though, is our perception of the sugar concentration, which you will notice decreasing with more dilution; and without the sugar to balance the bitterness, it will make you flinch even more. In other words, the less you like the bitterness, the shorter you should drink it.

Campari and soda

I like this with ice and a slice of orange in a small glass, mixed roughly 50:50, which makes it about 12.5 percent abv (alcohol by volume), about the same strength as a table wine.

Campari and orange

One of the most popular ways to drink Campari is with orange juice, ideally freshly squeezed. Put an inch or so of Campari into the glass, pour the orange on top, and let the colors mingle like a good sunset. Add plenty of ice. Black olives or tapenade is killer with this drink; failing that a bowl of green olives will do.

Campari and grapefruit

Even better than Campari and orange, because the briskness of the grapefruit is a good match for the bitter Campari. Try it with pink grapefruit too.

Campari in the kitchen: blood-orange sorbet

The combination of blood orange and Campari is almost unbeatable. A scoop or two of this is a great way to start an evening or a sophisticated way to finish off a dinner. You do need an ice-cream maker to get this to work. And beware, because alcohol has a lower freezing point than water, it is Svalbard-cold in the mouth. Makes six helpings.

1 tablespoon plus
* 2 teaspoons sugar*
1 tablespoon plus
* 2 teaspoons water*
5 ounces Campari
1 cup blood-orange juice
juice of ½ lemon
1 egg white, hand-
* whisked until white*
* and frothy*

Make a simple syrup by mixing the water and sugar together; stir and leave for 5 minutes until the sugar is all dissolved. Combine the syrup with the Campari, orange juice, and lemon juice, and then fold in the egg white using a metal spoon. Pour the mixture into an ice-cream maker and churn until set. Thanks to the alcohol content of the sorbet, this needs to get very cold before it will solidify, so you may need to transfer the bowl to the freezer for the last 20 minutes of freezing. Serve immediately.

Campari addicts should also see "My favorite drink" on p. 108.

The Venetian way to drink bitters

There are two classic Venetian bar experiences. One is the smart Bellini at Harry's; the other is "lo spritz" in a shabby bar with a couple of rickety plastic tables, a dirty floor, a telly high on the wall in the back room, and lots of old men shuffling in and out. The men all drink spritzes: small tumblers of murky liquid, which turns out to be a bitter of choice—sometimes Campari, more often the artichoke-based Cynar, sometimes Aperol—topped with white wine and a dash of soda, dressed, if you're lucky, with a hunk of lemon. This seems to taste better in situ than it does at home (though best mind the canal, which often moves toward the door as you head out), but it's good outdoors, at lunchtime, in only-just-warm-enough weather, with a bowl of green olives.

Gin sling

Slings were popular in the eighteenth century, and the best known is, of course, the Singapore sling, made famous by the Raffles hotel, which is flavored with cherry brandy. This version, which adds bitters to the standard combination of spirit, lemon juice, sugar syrup, and soda, has a distinctly urban feel. We drank it on a friend's roof terrace, just behind King's Cross, one surprisingly warm afternoon in April as we made the first barbecue of the year. You can find blood-orange bitters at many liquor stores and online—they give the drink a warmer feel than ordinary angostura.

2 parts gin
1 part freshly squeezed lemon juice
1 part simple syrup
couple dashes blood-orange bitters
sparkling water

Mix the first four ingredients together in a jug, then pour into tall, ice-filled Collins glasses until they are half full, top with sparkling water, and stir with a straw.

SOMETHING A LITTLE HARDER

Philip Marlowe's gin gimlet

It's been so long since I drank my first gimlet that I'm no longer sure whether I was introduced to them by Raymond Chandler or whether gin gimlets introduced me to Raymond Chandler. In any case, I think it is safe to say that just as everyone knows that James Bond liked his martinis "shaken and not stirred," so any gimlet aficionado can tell you that Chandler's private eye Philip Marlowe drank his with no bitters, a cigarette in his hand, and a wry observation about blondes in his back pocket. In *The Long Goodbye*, one of Marlowe's clients, Terry Lennox, an Englishman, even supplies us with a recipe.

"What they call a gimlet is just some lime or lemon juice and gin with a dash of sugar and bitters," he complains. "A real gimlet is half gin and half Rose's lime juice and nothing else. It beats martinis hollow."

I know: it doesn't sound very appetizing, but it is strangely delicious, simultaneously sweet and sharp, provided you pour the whole lot over plenty—and I really do mean plenty—of ice.

Lennox is right on another count too: this is perhaps the only drink I know that cannot be improved on by replacing the liquor-cabinet mixer with the more chi-chi option of freshly squeezed juice. Actually, it would be unbearable with fresh lime, because it's the bittersweet contrast of syrupy mixer with citric acid and the harsh rawness of the gin that gives it such a mean kick.

You'll notice that Lennox specifies the use of Rose's, which, until the recent trend in Britain for upmarket nonalcoholic fruit cordials, was easily the best around. Now if I'm buying lime cordial, it's always Bottlegreen's Sweet Aromatic Lime (which includes a dash of bitters), but I wouldn't dream of using it for gimlets—that would be like putting homemade tomato relish on your burger when what you actually want is Heinz tomato ketchup.

This is too moody and too down-at-heel a drink to be terribly sociable. You're not going to put on your dazzling host smile and hand it around at a cocktail party. You should sip it, as Marlowe does, alone or with one other at a bar, or, provided only you order it, in company after a bad day. The beauty of it is that it is almost impossible to ruin, which makes it the perfect thing for non–beer drinkers to order in a pub (though never ask for it by name; just give the barman Terry Lennox's immaculate instructions, and don't forget the ice). And it even tastes good from a plastic glass, shivering outside on a field or in a park at the beginning of the summer.

A note on Rose's Lime Cordial

The reason Americans often refer to the British as "limeys" is that during the nineteenth century British ships carried supplies of citrus juice—usually lime, because it contained less sugar than lemon and so was less liable to ferment—to prevent their sailors from succumbing to scurvy. The common practice became compulsory with the passing of the Merchant Shipping Act of 1867, which suited a certain Scot called Lachlan Rose very well. His family were shipbuilders, but he chose instead to deal in grain and flour; by 1865, in the port of Leith, he had established L. Rose & Company, as a "Lime and Lemon Merchant." All the lime juice then taken to sea contained a healthy dose of rum as a preservative. Rose saw an opportunity here: he developed a way of preserving fresh lime juice using sulphur dioxide, patented it, then sat back and watched his Lime Juice Cordial, "entirely free from alcohol," take off.

Mint julep

Every year on the first Saturday in May, the crowds gather at the Churchill Downs racecourse in Louisville for the Kentucky Derby. The horses' hooves thunder, the bookies gesticulate, and everyone downs mint julep after mint julep after mint julep. The cocktail has been the official drink of the event for almost a century, and 120,000 of these refreshing yet potent cocktails, incorporating 1,000 pounds of mint and 60,000 pounds of ice, are drunk there each year. No one can agree on when the drink first came into being, but it belongs to the Old South. The word *julep* comes from the Arabic *julab* and Persian *gulab*, "rose water," and means a sweet drink, one that is sometimes used as a vehicle for medicine, which is certainly how some see their favorite spirit.

How to make it is a subject of so much discussion that to stand up in a Kentucky bar and offer an opinion would virtually qualify as a breach of the peace. There are some things most would agree on, though, notably that this is an idyllic spring afternoon drink and a blissful sundowner. As for the four ingredients of ice, bourbon, sugar, and mint, mint is the most contentious. The debate rests not only on how much of it you use but also on what exactly you do to the mint to ensure the drink is infused with its flavor. I find that minimal intervention (no bruising) but a little time (patience is never a bad thing) are the important points to note. There's a lot of alcohol in here—at 3 ounces the measure is almost a double double—so you should be drinking it slowly and don't want to feel, when you hit the halfway point, that it's stewed so badly you're downing alcoholic mint tea. As for the bourbon, I use Buffalo Trace because I like the savory rye character that feels almost like sucking on pumpernickel bread. I know many people who are attached to Woodford Reserve, but to me it's too fruity and boisterous for the mint. You need a lot of ice—I'd say about ten large cubes per drink. At the Kentucky Derby they make this in bulk with precrushed ice, and they certainly don't fool around like I do with the mint. This drink is traditionally served in pewter cups that have been frosted in the freezer.

3 ounces bourbon
½ teaspoon sugar
1 sprig mint
over ½ tray of ice cubes
or lots of precrushed ice

You also need a tea towel and a rolling pin or a dowel. And to drink it from, a large tumbler that comfortably holds about 10 ounces of liquid.

First, deal with the mint. We're not going to bruise the leaves. Pick off the bottom 2 leaves and, using a small knife, cut through the stem on the diagonal just beneath the point where they were attached. Make another diagonal cut just beneath the next pair of leaves. Now you should have 1 small sprig of mint, 2 separate leaves, and 2 bits of stalk. Put them all to one side for 5 minutes to allow the sap to begin leaking at the cut ends. While that's happening, sort out the ice. Shake the ice cubes out of the tray into a tea towel, wrap them up, take them outside, and beat the living daylights out of them with a rolling pin or dowel. When the ice is coarsely crushed, transfer it to a jug or bowl. In a glass, put half the bourbon, the sugar, the mint, and a handful of crushed ice and stir a couple of times to dissolve the sugar. Add the rest of the bourbon, fill the glass up with crushed ice, and use a teaspoon to drag the mint through the ice a couple of times, trailing its flavor through the drink. Sit outside in the sunshine and sip.

FRIENDS OVER

The following drinks are particularly suitable for serving to groups. They are easily made, and the first three are not too strong, which means people can sip, chatter, and lose track of how much they've had without suffering too much, while the others involve opening bottles of fizz (two people going on to have dinner may not finish a whole bottle). Prosecco and antipasti are also better for groups because they allow you to have a greater variety of food with no waste.

White-wine spritzer

These are three words that many people find hard to say in public. Secretly, they would like to. Or perhaps they don't know deep down that they would like to, but if they did they might be surprised to find that actually it was something they rather enjoyed. Deep breath now . . . white-wine spritzer. Or, to put it another way, thirst-quenching, effervescent, delicate, which sounds much better but describes the same thing.

Under pressure from the wine snobs at the top and suburban-girl jokes at the bottom, this ladies-who-lunch former staple has largely died out. For me it was an accidental rediscovery. My conversion was made in a pub when I asked for a second, empty, wineglass so as to share a single, queasily large, 8-ounce measure of Chilean sauvignon blanc with a friend. I almost had second thoughts about asking for soda water on the side. "They'll think we're going to make white-wine spritzers," I hissed. "Are you going to make up your own white-wine spritzers?" asked the barmaid. "No," I denied, a little too emphatically and a little too loudly. So then, of course, we had to, and blow me if they weren't delicious and just the thing when you want to drink but not get drunk.

There are a few rules, though. Don't use oaked wine or chardonnay of any sort. Pinot grigio will do in extremis but is not ideal—unless you have happened upon a rare good one, it doesn't really taste of anything, so let down with water it will be so bland as to be almost undrinkable. Sauvignon blanc, particularly from the New World, is good because the vibrant gooseberry, melon, and papaya flavors work in this context, and it has enough intensity to punch through the dilution. I tend to favor Chilean, on the grounds that New Zealand sauvignon probably does cost too much and is a little too elegant to be treated like a mixer. Even cheaper are the colombard-ugni-blanc blends from the south of France, which produce a prettily floral spritzer. A keen, green verdejo from Rueda in Spain also does the trick.

chitter
chatter

Don't premix the white-wine spritzers if you have people coming over. A large jug of well-iced, sparkling water and a bottle with beads of condensation placed on the table so people can adjust to their own preferred strength feels better. I like this at lunchtime, when eating a bowlful of salad such as bacon and avocado with grated Emmenthal, soaked with hot mustardy dressing, or crab and papaya with spinach leaves. It muddles the head less, barely feels like "lunchtime drinking," and if people snigger, well, you can console yourself with the idea that you know better. There really is nothing of which to be ashamed.

chitter

Strawberry grog

This adds up to far more than the sum of its parts. I came up with it when looking for a drink that, like Pimm's, would suit sociable situations but taste more delicious. I've simply taken the gin base and lemon-lime soda mixer (cloudy this time), but added ginger beer and fruit in the form of fresh strawberries, which apart from providing natural sweetness make it feel as if it might almost be good for you. The ginger beer might sound odd but actually gives an essential kick and base note. It's important to use the old-style Jamaican ginger beer that tastes of spicy gingerbread, which comes in cans, rather than one of the neo-old-fashioned (and more expensive) brands, which tend to be too fiery for this and lack the growl that grounds it so nicely. The result is harder to put down than I can say, and the nonalcoholic version, easily

scant 1 pound strawberries

⅔ cup ginger beer, chilled

1¾ cups old-fashioned, cloudy lemon-lime soda, chilled

5 ounces gin

chatter

made by leaving out the gin, is good for anyone who is driving or can't drink. Also, strawberry puree freezes very well, so if necessary you can make a batch when there is a glut and defrost it as you need it. The gin I use is Tanqueray Ten because its aromatic quality shines through, but bear in mind that at 47.3 percent abv, Tanqueray Ten is one of the stronger gins, so you may want to beef up with an extra splash if you use something else. This recipe makes just over a quart of strawberry grog, enough for about five glassfuls. Oh, and one last thing, the name. *Grog* to sailors is rum, but to Arthur Ransome's *Swallows and Amazons* it's ginger beer, and the idea of messing about on a lake in a boat, as in these classic British children's books, seemed to fit in with the uplifting taste of this drink.

First, pinch the stems out of the strawberries. I don't bother with hulling, but I do cut out any rotten or unripe bits. Use a hand blender to puree the fruit in a measuring pitcher. You should have about 1⅓ cups of puree. If you have to throw away too many rotten or green berries or you've accidentally eaten so many that there's less, then you may need to adjust the quantities of the other ingredients. The important thing when doing this is that there should be 3 parts of soda to every 1 part of ginger beer to get the right concentration of spice, so sometimes I mix the ginger beer and lemon-lime soda separately in those proportions, then add it to the strawberry mixture until I'm happy with the strength. Combine all the ingredients in a jug, then pour into glasses over ice.

Devon lemonade

This recipe comes courtesy of Plymouth Gin; hence the name. You could use other brands, but I do prefer this one—it sits crisp and calm as the white of a distant sail on a flat sea against the aromatic elderflower, and mixing it with soda ensures that you will still be lucid after drinking a couple.

1 part Plymouth gin
½ part elderflower
* cordial*
3 parts sparkling water
1 small sprig mint for
* each drink (optional)*

Combine the ingredients in a jug, stir, and serve in tumblers over ice. Add a sprig of mint to each glass.

My favorite drink, with spring crostini

This doesn't have a name—in my family we call it "the Campari and blood-orange thing"—but it's one of those discoveries that make you wonder why you ever bother with anything else. We get through more jugfuls of it than I can say: we had it when Grandma came to stay one April to visit her first great-grandchild; I often make it before dinner when people come over; and when a friend tried it as a possible offering for her son's christening party, she declared it "the perfect spring afternoon drink." Besides the general deliciousness, the beauty of it is that, unlike most things you make up in a jug and slosh around, it tastes more, not less, alcoholic than it actually is, thanks to the tenacious bitterness of the Campari. It's essential to use blood-orange juice (often available at specialty groceries and health food stores, but if you make this early in the year, you should be able to get hold of fresh blood oranges and squeeze your own), not only for the color but also for the warm flavor-boost. For the sparkling wine, don't go too expensive—champagne would be overkill in this case. Prosecco is fine. I tend to use a big brand of New World sparkling wine, such as Lindauer from New Zealand or Jacob's Creek from Australia, which I perhaps wouldn't buy to drink on their own but are ultra-reliable and more than good enough for this job (and relatively inexpensive). On holiday I've also made this with ludicrously cheap bottles of Gaillac Perlé, a sparkling white wine from the Tarn district in southwest France. As the other ingredients have quite a lot of flavor, you could put more or less anything in, apart from sparkling Riesling, as long as it was more or less dry. Get the ingredients very cold—twenty minutes in the freezer if necessary—before you mix them, because the drink is already quite diluted and the fizziness can't afford to be stretched any further. This makes a good eight glassfuls.

Pour the ingredients into a jug. Serve in small champagne flutes or wineglasses.

I usually make mozzarella and arugula crostini and salmon and fennel toasts to go with this. The savory Italian ingredients go well with the Campari, and the salmon recipe makes an expensive ingredient go a long way. Don't buy the small mozzarella bocconcini, as the dry skins don't stick as well to the toast.

1 bottle sparkling white wine
2 cups blood-orange juice
5 to 6 ounces Campari

Buffalo mozzarella and arugula toasts

Break up the mozzarella with your fingers and combine with the arugula and lemon juice. Press onto the toasts, put on a plate, and season with the pepper.

1 buffalo mozzarella
1 handful arugula leaves, chopped
freshly squeezed lemon juice to taste
8 small slices sourdough bread, cut in half; toasted, and drizzled with olive oil
black pepper

Salmon and fennel toasts

Poach the salmon fillet by putting it with a little milk on a plate above a pan of boiling water and covering with a dish until cooked through. Leave to cool. Break up the fish and mix with the fennel, crème fraîche, lemon juice, and half of the dill. Spread the salmon mixture on the toast, sprinkle with the remaining dill, and season with the pepper.

about 4 ounces wild salmon fillet
½ large fennel bulb, finely chopped
3 heaped tablespoons low-fat crème fraîche or yogurt
juice of ½ lemon
2 tablespoons chopped dill
8 small slices sourdough bread, cut in half and toasted
black pepper

Prosecco with antipasti

A tinge of pear skin and the feathery lightness of a snowflake just about to melt: this is how a glass of prosecco ought to taste. It might sparkle, and it might be wine, but it has nothing to do with the ritzy, sit-up-straight expectation of champagne. It has been damned for years as poor man's fizz, and I can see exactly why, because if you take a mouthful anticipating blowsy warmth and brioche, and fall flat into prosecco's lagoon coolness, it will inevitably disappoint. Yet as a pick-me-up (especially if you choose one with a hint of off-dryness—a little sugar can be very restorative; few people realize how much a tired person craves it), or as an effortlessly glamorous way to fall into the evening, it is impeccable.

Prosecco is the name of both the grape and the wine. Unlike champagne, it will not improve with age and should be drunk in its first flush of youth while its light florality and easy step are still engaging. The good stuff—which accounts for about 40 percent of the prosecco in Italy—is made in the DOC region of Prosecco di Conegliano-Valdobbiadene in the Veneto, in northeast Italy, which is why you see people swigging it in just about every bar and restaurant in Venice.

I can precisely remember the first glass that really gave me a sense of prosecco magic. It was made by Bisol, still one of my favorite producers, whose style is so airy it whispers through your mouth, and I drank it perched at a bar beside the Spanish Steps in Rome, with a plate of cured meats and bite-sized pieces of Italian cheese and a few slices of pear: perfection.

Antipasti are the thing to eat alongside prosecco. Usefully, if you are pressed for time, this requires no preparation, only shopping. Ideally you would have a few slices of proper prosciutto (not from a supermarket package), which I usually ask the delicatessen to cut more thickly than is typical to give it some chew, and lay these out on a small wooden chopping board, perhaps with a salami as well. Put a hunk of grainy

Parmesan on a plate and let people cut off their own slices, and a bowl of olives won't be amiss either. With a bit more time, you might slice some zucchini very thinly, lengthwise, and grill the strips on both sides so they are striped black, then dress with freshly squeezed lemon juice and olive oil.

My Italian reading group is keen on prosecco, and sometimes we drink it with an insalata caprese (or even a tricolore, which has avocado slices in it too)—just tear up a buffalo mozzarella, halve some cherry tomatoes or cut larger ones into wedges, arrange the lot on a plate, throw over some torn-up basil leaves, and drizzle with olive oil. We know each other well enough to mill around a kitchen with salad plates and forks or even just to eat messily with our fingers; in less casual company this is really more appropriate if you want to let the prosecco drinking bleed into dinner and sit down to eat the insalata as a starter. In that case, I'd probably follow up with a sturdy bowl of pasta, maybe penne with ragù or pasta all'arrabbiata with freshly grated pecorino, and a bottle of Tuscan red wine.

Bellini and Harry's Bar in Venice

The birthplace of the Bellini is well known: it was first created in 1948 by Giuseppe Cipriani at Harry's Bar, Venice, still one of the greatest bars in the world. What fewer people realize is that it was named after a Venetian Renaissance painter, Giovanni Bellini, whose work was exhibited in the city that year, as a tribute to the tender shades of skin found in his paintings (one of which, *Agony in the Garden*, is in the National Gallery in London if you want to examine it for yourself).

The drink is nothing less than sublime: a mixture of one-third white peach puree (made by peeling, stoning, coarsely chopping, then hand-blending fresh peaches) and two-thirds prosecco. Together these two ingredients are heaven itself, but, as with so many marriages that work, no substitutions may be accepted. Or at least almost no substitutions.

Harry's Bar uses white peaches—for this reason the drink used to be available only from June to September. Yellow peaches are fine, though more fruity and less intoxicatingly perfumed. If you are even considering using canned, then go throw yourself in a canal. Sometimes when you ask for a Bellini in a bar, it is made using peach nectar, or even peach liqueur. I hardly need say this will not be worth drinking and should not be repeated at home; when ordering a Bellini, you should always ask how it will be made before committing. Peach puree freezes well, so you can make a stock and keep it so as to enjoy Bellinis outside the prime peach season.

Put the drink together by pouring a little prosecco into the flutes (this helps the peach not stick to the glass); carefully spoon the puree in, and then top with prosecco, which you will need to pour very slowly down the side as it froths up when it hits the peach. Stir to combine, and then drink.

1 bottle prosecco

3 small or 2 large peaches

FOOD AND WINE

White wine in shot glasses with crab: an easy way to impress
Apart from using them as egg cups, it has always been hard to know what
to do with the shot glasses I was given as a birthday present after leaving
the university. It's not that we didn't drink neat vodka back then—just
that a shot glass was never big enough. And when I got older I graduated
to martinis instead, which was the same thing as an extra-large vodka
shot, but in a more expensive glass. So the shot glasses stayed at the
back of the cupboard, moving house a couple of times without being
used, until I went on a wine-tasting trip to Chile. In a relaxed little
restaurant in the port of Valparaiso, where brightly painted houses cling
and cluster on the vertiginous sea front, we were given the most perfect
of amuse-bouches—a plate of crushed ice and on it a single oyster, half a
lime, and a shot glass full of shivery sauvignon blanc, whose acidity and
citric shock was a brilliant knock-back for the oysters. It didn't just taste
good; it looked sensational too.

Now I borrow the template all the time, not least because it demands
virtually no effort. It's also a good way of getting around the question of
white wine with a starter for those who really drink red—you know, the
way it seems like such a good idea to have a glass of white to begin, which
you then down practically in one so you can move on to red, and realize
too late that you've overdone it.

I don't eat oysters at home, but I like to serve crab with the shot glasses
of sauvignon blanc—or another white grape with elbows, never anything
oaked or expensive; see below for some suggestions. Just add a teaspoon
or two of mayonnaise to a 4-ounce pot of crabmeat, squeeze in some
lemon, chop in two spring onions, and serve in a small hillock with
toast and the shot glass on the same plate. This works best with small
portions; otherwise everyone wonders why you're being stingy and not
giving them a larger glass.

Crisp white wines: Sancerre and alternatives

Sancerre—the very name glitters with promise—is so much more than just a wine. The most famous of the Loire sauvignons blancs, it comes with an aura attached, like champagne or Chablis. Ask for a glass of sibilant Sancerre and you don't just get the liquid, alive with the smell of newly mown grass and tense with brain-rinsing acidity; you buy into the idea that you are sipping spring itself and rewarding yourself in the process. Sancerre has a flinty keenness and finesse that, it is true, is hard to find elsewhere, but perhaps a little trust in wines that have similar characteristics, as well as a willingness to experiment, is all that's required to broaden your vinous horizons. There are many wines that, in theory at least, should please the Sancerre lover.

The most obvious, and safest, place to begin is with some of the other Loire alternatives made from the same grape: Pouilly-Fumé, Menetou

Salon, Quincy, Reuilly, or even a cheaper Sauvignon de Touraine. New Zealand's Marlborough is another source of excellent sauvignons blancs, though I never find their glowing pungency quite as satisfying. For value, South Africa is a good bet: here you find sauvignon blanc made in a style that is a halfway house between the rocky minerality of the Loire and the exuberance of New Zealand. As for Chile, for a long time I disliked the ripe, sweetly alcoholic style of sauvignon blanc so often made there, but you can now find some superb wines being made in cool-climate areas such as Leyda.

But it's not enough, or it shouldn't be enough, to be satisfied just with sauvignon blanc, when there are other grapes that have the same bracing appeal while offering something slightly different.

To begin at home, there is bacchus, a grape created in Germany in the 1930s that has taken hold in the vineyards of southern England. A good bacchus tastes of nettles, smells of hawthorn, tastes of crabapple and quince, is almost uncomfortably bony, and is nervy with acidity. If you were drinking bacchus, you would want to eat food from the same damp climate, with the same subtle, rain-on-fields undertones—a poached brook trout, for example, with homemade mayonnaise and a watercress salad.

Moving on to the European mainland, there's a grape in Burgundy that is similarly austere. Aligote is a clean, sharp, virtually invisible-tasting thing that reminds me of needles and streaks down your throat so fast it barely touches the sides. I once drank aligote with the writer Polly Devlin when I went to Somerset to interview her about her wildflower meadow. We sat in her conservatory on Midsummer's Eve, eating tomato, mozzarella and basil salad. "Isn't this just the perfect wine for this sort of evening?" said Polly with obvious pleasure. It was.

If in Spain, the best place to look for Sancerre alternatives is Rueda, an area on the Duero River to the northwest of Madrid where they make crisp, green-tasting white wines from verdejo as well as sauvignon blanc, which are delicious with garlicky shrimp.

Cross over to the Mediterranean Sea and Liguria, the curl of Italian coast that corners from the French border into the bootleg, and you find another grape to try. Vermentino (known as "rolle" in the south of France) makes a lively, herbaceous, slightly bitter-edged white that is perfect with spaghetti and homemade pesto, a local specialty. Add a few pieces of boiled potato and some cooked green beans to the mixture for a more filling and authentic dinner.

Traveling east again, you reach the blue Aegean. Here, in the scorching heat of Santorini, in the volcanic soil around the island's crater, they grow a grape called *assyrtiko*, which makes white wine that is heavily minerallic and so charged it almost feels as if it might explode in your mouth. It's as clean and sharp as an axe-blade too; drink it with barbecued swordfish and a squeeze of lemon.

Just one more to try: grüner veltliner (pronounced "grooner felt-leaner") from Austria. This is a relatively delicate wine, but it has a diamantine structure: precise, pure and clear, with a grapefruit undertone. The more expensive versions acquire a softer, spicier flavor too; young, cheap ones are usually leaner; both taste good with mild Thai food.

THIRST-QUENCHERS

Ginger infusion

Ginger has long been prized for its medicinal properties, among them its efficiency at reducing nausea caused by seasickness, morning sickness, and chemotherapy. Poorly or not, a single paring of ginger root, sliced to the thickness of a penny (you don't even need to peel it, provided you're not using the end of the root), dropped in a cup, covered with boiling water, and left to stand until just cool enough to drink, is a great pep-up afternoon drink. I also like to add a squeeze of fresh lemon juice for acidity.

Citron pressé

Citron pressé is proof that ritual vastly increases the amount of pleasure a drink gives. There are three ingredients here, and, if the fun is not to be spoiled, they must all be served separately. First, the juice of one lemon (two if they aren't very juicy) must arrive at the table in a long, tall glass. Second, there must be a jug of cold water so the lemon can be diluted to the required strength. Third, there must be a bowl of sugar and a long metal spoon, or a carafe of homemade sugar syrup for sweetening. For some reason the separate arrival of these things, and the mixing and jangling as everyone measures out their drinks, make it taste so much better than if the same thing had been done in the kitchen. This is a drink with café connotations: it makes you think of sitting under the awnings of a French brasserie, and dawdling, and being on holiday, and these associations also increase the pleasure. Here is one odd thing, though: a friend's pen pal claims that real French people rarely drink citron pressé. But then she also asked if it was true that British people always ate gelatin that had been set in rabbit molds and turned out on to a sheet of green gelatin grass. I was on the brink of protesting until I remembered that we had not one but two rabbit-shaped jelly molds at home. And that we always used them, which made me wonder if the French only think they don't drink citron pressé. It's a good thing to make when friends come over and no one quite feels like coffee or alcohol.

How to make your own elderflower cordial

If you only read Richard Mabey's entry for *Sambucus nigra* in his *Flora Britannica*, you might have second thoughts about drinking anything to do with it. "It is hard to understand," he writes, "how this mangy, short-lived, opportunistic and foul-smelling shrub was once regarded as the most powerful of plants. . . . [it] is now widely regarded as little more than a jumped-up weed, a ragamuffin haunter of dung-heaps and drains." Come, come, Richard, don't equivocate.

It is true the elder can be pretty pungent; that is why its crushed leaves have traditionally been used as insecticides, to ward off grubs from precious plants, and as insect repellents, to perform the same task for humans. There is also an old association with the devil—traditionally elder wood was never thrown on the fire because burning it was said to conjure up Beelzebub himself. But its curative properties have been admired for centuries (it's said to be good against a cold and even rheumatism); elder water is used as a skin cleanser; and the cordial made from its delicate, creamy flowers that grow in flat-topped heads sometimes as big as frying pans is utterly delicious.

The nonalcoholic drink, its taste reminiscent of drowsy hawthorn-hedgerows, seems to capture the very essence of idealized country life, filled with bluebell woods, church bells, and ducks swimming on the village pond. It can simply be diluted with water (still or sparkling), mixed with white wine or gin to make an alcoholic drink suitable for the backyard on a summer afternoon, or even put to work in the kitchen.

Elderflower cordial is now so popular in Britain—sales have more than tripled in the past decade or so—that it seems hard to believe it was not made on a commercial scale until the early 1980s. The availability of ready-made versions hasn't stopped people from making their own. On the contrary, it has only inspired more springtime expeditions to gather the blossom that, depending on the year's weather, and where you are, begins to appear in early May and is usually gone by mid-June.

The clusters of flowers are easy to spot: they grow in snowy drifts on bushes that can be up to 30 feet tall. If you are making cordial, it is necessary to be a little choosy because Mabey has a point when he calls the bush foul-smelling. "Some elderflowers can be really smelly," says Richard Kelly, who was the first grower for Bottlegreen. "Particularly the ones that are cultivated for their berries. But some can smell lemony and really sweet. The variation from one plant to another, especially in the wild, is tremendous."

The finished cordial will obviously bear the traits of the flowers you pick, so "Use your nose to select a bush," advises Kelly. "And when you've done that, use your nose again. You don't want to pick too early, when the flower is not quite open, or too late, when it's begun to turn brown. The flower should look and smell creamy, and when you sniff it you should get some pollen on your nose. We always used to say that good pickers will have their face covered in pollen by the end of the day."

It's wise to pick from several bushes so as to build up layers of complexity from their different characteristics in the finished cordial. You should avoid harvesting on a wet day or immediately after heavy dew, when some of the flavor-carrying essential oils will have been washed away. And unless partial to the taste of traffic pollution, you should also steer away from elders growing by busy roads. I usually take a couple of trays with me rather than bags, the better to carry the flowers, undisturbed, back home.

The cordial is no more than an infusion of flowers, sweetened with sugar and given a bit of zip. Some use powdered citric acid for the zip.

I prefer to get my zip from fresh lemons. If the elderflowers are small, then use more of them.

Trim the stems of the elderflowers back as far as you can—they will only make the drink taste stalky—and remove any obvious, large insects. Put the flowers in a large pan or jug with the lemon parings. Put the sugar and water in a large pan and heat gently until the sugar is dissolved. Bring to a boil and pour the syrup over the elderflowers. Allow to cool, add the lemon juice, steep for 6 hours, and then strain through a piece of cheesecloth into sterilized bottles or jars. Keep in the fridge. Depending on how well you sterilize the bottles, this will keep for around 4 weeks, or you can freeze it for later use.

20 heads of elderflower
juice and pared rind of
2 lemons
3 cups sugar
4 ¼ cups water

Elderflower and tonic

Homemade elderflower cordial, which usually tastes more musky and more of hedgerows than the store-bought versions, is particularly suited to the bitterness of quinine. Use more cordial than you would if diluting with water, and serve over plenty of ice with a slice of lemon and sprig of borage from the garden. The astringency and wildness make it more of a sipper than a glugger.

HERBS FROM THE GARDEN: CALMING DRINKS

Melissa tea

When I first moved to London and lived with my cousin in a tiny attic flat in Willesden Green, we once had our grandmother and my mother to stay simultaneously. We couldn't persuade Grandma that she wasn't allowed to smoke anywhere on the tube (on outside platforms she would whip her mobile ashtray out of her handbag and before either of us could say "Silk Cut," there would be a loudspeaker announcement asking her to stop), nor could we dissuade them from making pan-banging forays to the kitchen to make cups of tea at 4 A.M. I often used to find Mum in the kitchen drinking nighttime tea if I couldn't sleep as a child. Sometimes it would be the ordinary stuff, but she also liked to pick lemon balm from the garden, bruise the wrinkled leaves in a mortar and pestle, then make a fresh tisane with boiling water. Lemon balm, or *Melissa officinalis*, is supposed to have soothing properties—it was used in the Middle Ages to reduce insomnia—and is also thought to ease digestion, so it makes sense to drink it at night. It's also relaxing to have on a sunny afternoon and makes a refreshing alternative to mint.

Mint tea

Until recently, if mint tea was mentioned, it was Moroccan mint tea that sprang to mind—a viscous, tooth-dissolvingly sweet infusion of tea or green tea with mint, traditionally served in a silver pot with a curved spout and poured into tea glasses from a height. This is the stuff that has oiled countless carpet transactions in the souks of Moroccan medinas where, in the stinking heat, a shot of sugar is no bad thing. Over here, mint tea has come to mean something much simpler: nothing more than a few sprigs of mint put in a clean teapot with scalding water poured over and left for a couple of minutes before being poured into white china mugs. It's what I order now when I go out for dinner and think I fancy another—inevitably fatal—glass of wine, because the truth is that by that stage in the evening I actually prefer the freshness of the mint tea to more alcohol, and it performs the same role of prolonging the night. It's become so popular in Britain that waiters now seem to offer it with a knowing smile, almost as if they know how pleased you will be by the idea. At home I often drink it before going to bed or in the afternoon on a warm day as a means of getting more water down in a less boring manner. Some like to add a couple of teaspoons of honey to the pot, but I prefer it plain.

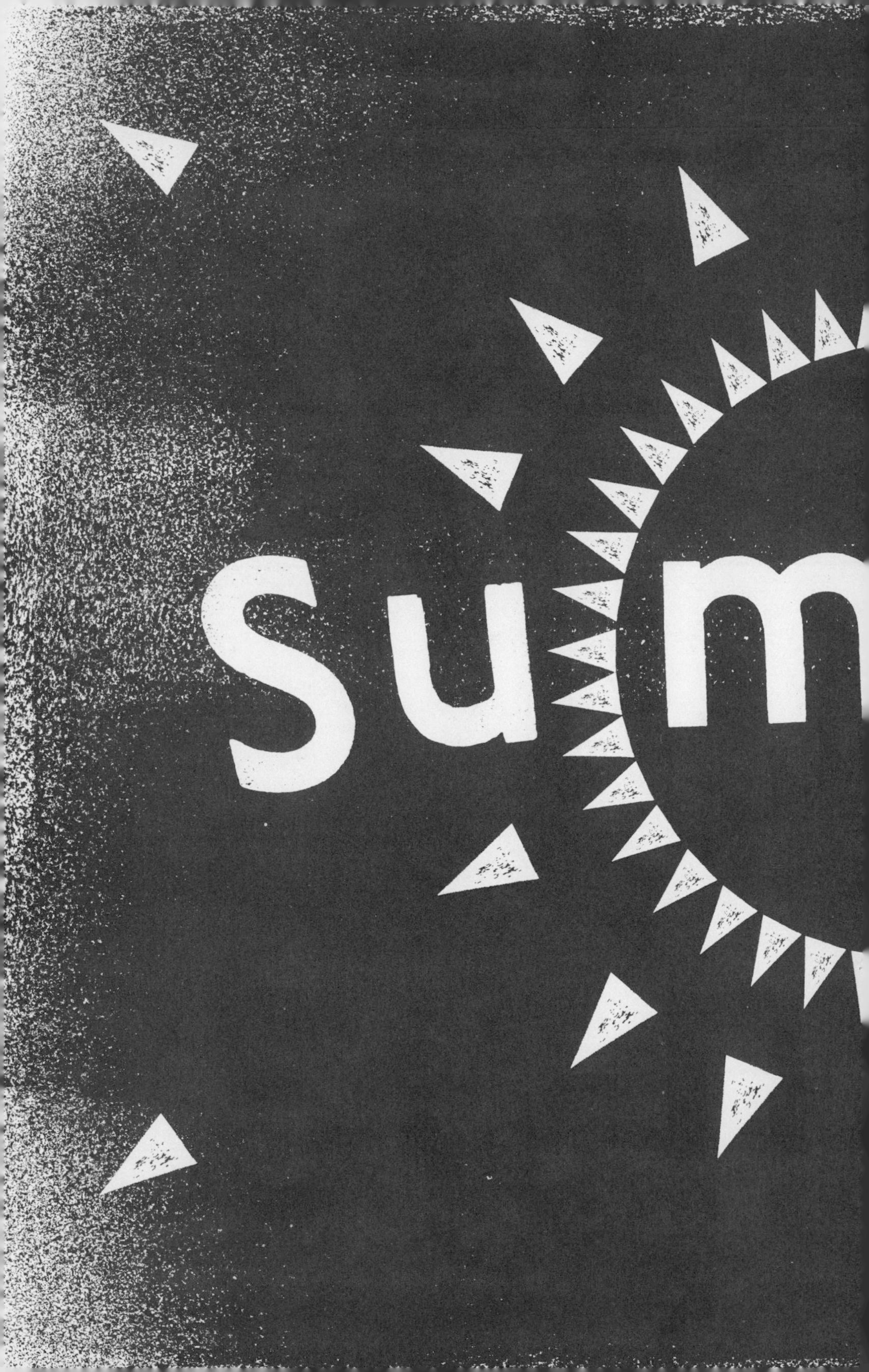
Sum

This is the season in which cocktails really come into their own. An abundance of summer fruits can be mixed with spirits to make drinks that taste like being on holiday. We plan to eat outdoors on terraces, at beaches, and in gardens, hoping it will be hot enough to long for ice to cool us down, citrus to pep us up, and sugary ingredients to replenish lost electrolytes; even if it isn't, drinking those things can at least, in a Pavlovian way, help convince us that summer is here at last.

IN THE GARDEN

The following are evocative of being in the garden in the cool twilight of a summer evening. Beautifully fragranced and delicate yet potent, they are sipping drinks.

Cucumber martini

Cucumbers have a bare, green taste that in a martini shows through with subtle detachment. You could insinuate the cucumber into the vodka by making a fresh puree, but the result is uniform and simplistic; you get a more haunting, edgier flavor if you muddle chunks of it with the vodka instead. The result is an elegant and calm drink.

To make one, take a 2-inch piece of cucumber, wash it, and pat it dry. Halve and seed it, but keep the peel on—there's a lot of flavor in the skin. Cut into slices about ⅓ inch thick, then cut each slice into cubes. Put the cucumber in the bottom of a cocktail shaker, pour over 2 ounces of vodka from the freezer (Zubrówka, the Polish vodka made from rye and flavored with bison grass, is particularly good because the grassy herbaceousness makes a good marriage with the cucumber), and use a pestle gently to bash the cucumber. The idea is not to make a pulp, just to bruise the skin and split some of the chunks slightly. Add several cubes of ice and shake hard before straining into a cocktail glass. I like to serve smoked salmon on plain brown bread with a squeeze of lemon with this. It's a take on the classic 5 o'clock tea with cucumber and salmon sandwiches. The bright pink of the salmon also looks stunning beside the pale green drink.

Hendrick's and tonic

Hendrick's may officially be a gin, but I think of it as its own beast, and as it is flavored with both cucumber and rose, it is perfect on an early summer evening. Don't add lemon or lime; instead float a dark green slice of cucumber peel with the ice.

Raspberry hound

The name doesn't quite do it justice, but this is a version of a forgotten classic called the *bloodhound*. It looks like water that has run off deepest pink peonies, somehow taking the color with it, and thanks to the fresh berries, it smells intensely of summer and of walking between rows of ripe raspberry canes. Bloodhounds are usually made using strawberries, but to my mind raspberries make a more piquant marriage with gin. Don't be tempted to skip the sweet vermouth or to replace it with dry; the ingredients mingle perfectly as they are—this really is one of those drinks that is more than the sum of its parts— and you need the sweetness to play against the raspberries. Drink after a game of tennis. Or just drink.

1 ounce sweet vermouth
1 ounce dry vermouth
3 ounces gin (I use
  Plymouth)
6 ripe raspberries

This recipe makes two drinks. I've included the quantities of gin and vermouth so you can see how they correspond to the amount of fruit required. The proportions—3 parts gin to 1 part sweet and 1 part dry vermouth—are what's important, and you can adjust quantities to the size of the glasses used, remembering that melt-water from the ice will mean you get more liquid out of the shaker than you put in.

Combine the vermouths and the gin in a cocktail shaker. Add the raspberries and, using the back of a spoon or a pestle, press them against the sides of the shaker to squash them. Now add ice and shake very hard and very well. Pour into two martini glasses, double-straining the drink through the top of the shaker and a tea strainer to get rid of the pips and other raspberry bits and pieces.

Rose water fizz

The intoxicating scent of roses ought to be evocative of an English cottage garden, but in the kitchen it becomes exotic, reminiscent of the food it is used to flavor, from Persian rose water ice cream to the sticky, deep-fried, sweet gulab jamun you eat in India.

1½ ounces gin
juice of ½ lemon
1 teaspoon superfine
  sugar
½ to 2 teaspoons
  rose water, to taste
sparkling water

It also makes me think of a dinner I once ate in a Marrakesh palace restaurant, deep in the twisty streets of the medina. Inside was a fountain with rose petals everywhere; the food was studded with raisins, pine nuts, and cinnamon—and all the perfumes of the roses and the spices mingled sweetly. I mention this to show how the flavors meld with the food I want to put this drink with. The nonalcoholic version of rose water fizz is good outside on a hot day, toward the end of the afternoon, with sticky pistachio baklava—a restorative shot of sucrose to match the prettiness of the drink. The ginny one is a good precursor to, say, a slow-cooked shoulder of lamb with dates, spices, and couscous or cinnamon-scented meat. The drink is perfumed, and girly, so not to everyone's taste, but when it works, it works well.

Mix the gin, lemon juice, sugar, and rose water in a tall glass (some rose water is highly concentrated, and you will need only the tiniest bit, so taste after adding ½ teaspoon to see how you feel about it). Stir until the sugar is dissolved, add ice, and top with sparkling water.

LAZY WEEKENDS

White port, tonic, and salted almonds

Not all port is red, or even a shade of purple or russet. White port is made in the Douro valley in Portugal from white grapes, among them malvasia fina and the wonderfully named rabigato, which means "cat's tail," a reference to the long, narrow shape of the bunches of grapes. It may be sweet, medium, or dry (and anything in between) and is often disappointingly vapid, though if you chance on a good bottle, you'll find an unusual, subtle, nutty drink. At its best drunk in the late afternoon (it's good at 5 or 6 o'clock, in place of tea) over a lot of ice and a slab of lemon peel or made into a long drink with tonic. It's good with roasted, salted almonds or cashews and always reminds me of sitting by the quay in Oporto, looking upriver to the Ponte de Dom Luis I, whose ironwork straddles the Douro like an Eiffel Tower lying on its side.

How to drink melons: watermelon "martinis" and other treats

Considering the abandon with which melons ooze a scent of sunny sweetness (and make the butter taste odd if you leave a cut melon in the fridge), you'd think you could do anything with them in cocktails. Not so, as I learned after begging a barman in a basement bar on the Portobello Road to make a drink from some golden rum and the orange-fleshed Charentais I had in my handbag (it's quite a capacious handbag and quite messy). The idea was that the vanilla warmth of the rum would play off the ripeness of the melon. Instead it drowned it.

As to so many other questions, vodka is the answer. (There is also a professional trick for boosting flavor, but we'll come to that in a moment.)

The simplest way to drink melons—any kind you like the taste of will do—is just to peel and seed them, puree the flesh using a hand blender to make a thick soft drink (which children will enjoy), then add as much vodka as you like. I particularly like honeydew, a discovery I made after getting stuck in the office too late to cook for the friends who were coming over for dinner. When I eventually turned up, wired and jumpy, I was relieved to find they'd taken the evening in hand by ordering in a Lebanese takeout. Besides the expected feast of falafel, hummus, lamb kebabs, spicy sausages, and tabbouleh, they'd also asked for a couple of rounds of fresh fruit purees—mango and honeydew melon—to which we added a good slug of vodka from the freezer, a handful of ice cubes, and a straw. The mango-vodka was nice; the honeydew-vodka was like nectar—an instant stress dissolver. Apart from tasting good with the food, it also proved dangerously intoxicating, making us think of bikinis and flip-flops and kissing boys on the beach aged sixteen—for which I blame the melon-scented Body Shop suntan lotion we all slathered on as teenagers.

These are easy, instant, casual drinks, though. The party piece is the watermelon martini (like so many of the other concoctions you find on snazzy cocktail lists, I admit it's not really a martini, but there's no need to get picky). For a while, it was the cocktail de rigueur among the Notting Hill pilates, wind-turbines, and cashmere set. Fashions move on, but the drink, as poised as a pink flamingo, served in a precarious martini glass, never fails to provoke coos and sighs of pleasure. It has catwalk glamour and also recalls those scorching days in high summer when you hack off gaudy pink mouths of watermelon to quench your thirst rather than sate any hunger. There is, however, a snag: making a drink with such a high water content or, to be more precise, low flavor concentration is a problem.

Bartenders often solve it by fortifying with a tot of watermelon liqueur and another of simple syrup (sweetness always pulls out the flavor in fruit—think what a sprinkling of sugar does to a bowl of strawberries).

An alternative is to use a watermelon syrup, thus bolstering flavor and adding sweetness in one go. I use one made by the French company Monin (their range of over ninety syrups, from almond to violet, will be familiar from gourmet coffee shops as well as the shelves of some supermarkets, or you can find more information at www.monin.com). Failing that, find the least insipid watermelons you can and add a splash of either store-bought or homemade sugar syrup (see p. 10 for details on how to make this) to enhance the natural flavor.

Cut a seeded and, preferably, chilled watermelon into chunks about 1½ inches square and ¾ inch thick. For each drink, put four pieces in the bottom of a cocktail shaker and use a pestle to pound them to a pulp. Add 1½ ounces of vodka—if you don't keep this in the freezer, you should—and a dash of either simple syrup or watermelon syrup. Shake with ice, strain into a martini glass, and serve—ideally by a swimming pool (mine, sadly, is imaginary).

You could pick at crumbly little cubes of feta with this and perhaps black olives (not marinated—the cocktail is sweet, and garlic doesn't taste nice with it) and mint leaves, for a modern take on a Greek breakfast, although you might not necessarily want to start on the vodka quite so early.

Taking the cactus out of tequila

One tequila, two tequila, three tequila . . . floor, as the old joke goes. But let's dispel a couple of myths. Drinking tequila is not the cause of the jackhammer-inside-your-head the morning after. Drinking a lot of tequila is one reason for it; the other is drinking slammers. A horse would ask to borrow the waiter's sombrero and start singing along to the mariachi band if it were drinking slammers—of anything. Nor does tequila contain a worm (that's mescal, and it's not actually a worm; it's a larva). Nor is it made from cacti, though the idea of such a totemic, spiny desert plant being transformed into a thunderously potent spirit has a certain William Burroughs—style self-destructive glamour.

The raw material for tequila is the blue agave, which, like aloe vera, is a succulent member of the lily family. It grows at high altitudes on the scorched volcanic plains of Mexico and has long, bladelike spikes the silvery blue-green of lavender or eucalyptus, which jut out of the ground, giving it a martial appearance. The Apache used to use thorns from those tough leaves as sewing needles and pins. But it is the huge, starchy heart of the plant, known as the *piña*, which is hacked out of its leafy cage with a machete and can weigh up to 175 pounds, as much as a grown man, that interests tequila-makers.

Once it has been crushed and cooked, the heart of the blue agave makes a syrup that smells something like a cross between honey and golden syrup; fermented, it tastes . . . well, that depends on the quality of the tequila. Even those who work in the industry have been known to admit that just unstoppering a bottle can make them gag (probably because a mere whiff takes them back to a nasty slammers experience, but this explanation hardly helps).

One niche tequila brand described to me a disastrous tasting the company held at Gatwick Airport with the aim of introducing people to its version of the spirit. "We kept asking, 'Would you like to try a new tequila?' and no one wanted to know. Once we started asking, 'Would you like to try Patrón? We'll tell you what it is once you've tasted it,' we had a much more positive response."

In truth the problem with the taste of tequila is not just psychological. Many of those cheap tequilas to which we are first introduced with a lick of salt and a squirt of lime are "mixtos" made with a minimum of 51 percent blue agave and up to 49 percent of neutral cane spirit. They can have a taste that rears up like a wave of nausea, then falls off into a harsh, acrid finish. Even at its best, tequila has a dirty kind of smell. It's freshly sweated salt; the roiling, delves-down-your-nose-right-into-your-stomach, raw complexity of pot-distilled alcohol; an almost sickly edge of sweetness—and then a gulp of alcoholic heat. Perhaps that's not a great sell. But this is a feral spirit, and that's what's so good about it. The new-wave tequilas have elements of brutality but, being made from 100 percent blue agave—which they will boast about somewhere on the label—are more finessed, softer, and polished than the mixtos you may once have known. To put it bluntly, you don't need to take your taste buds out with salt and sour to get them down; it's possible to sip and relish.

Some brands, like Patrón, which likes to boast that it's been name-checked in the lyrics of over fifty rap songs, and comes in a tactile recycled glass bottle, are so keen to present themselves as a new category that you'll have to scrutinize the small print on the back label to find the word *tequila*.

"We don't see other tequilas as our competitors," confirms a spokesman for Patrón, which was formed in 1989 by the unlikely duo of entrepreneur Martin Crowley and John-Paul Dejoria, who co-founded Paul Mitchell Systems, the hair-care products that come in white bottles with blocky black print (let's hope they don't get muddled up in the factory). "We compare ourselves with other top-end spirits. We'd expect people to go into a bar and ask not for a tequila but for 'a Patrón.'"

The biggest problem with making tequila from 100 percent blue agave is, they say, ensuring a supply of raw material. The blue agave takes eight years to reach maturity (it used to be even longer, but new propagation methods have helped speed things up), which means a lot of forward planning is required. If demand for tequila increases, as it began to do in the early 1990s, it takes almost a decade for the plantations to catch up. And if there's a blight—as there was in 1997, when millions of Mexico's agave plants were killed by a fungus plague—eight years of production are knocked back in a single blow.

Ways to drink tequila

The tequilas you might want to pour neat over the rocks, perhaps with a slice of lime, are reposado (which has been rested in wood for a few months and has a smoky, spicy quality) and añejo (at least a year in wood, with soft warmth and depth)—and sip, don't slam. A blanco tequila (sometimes also called a *white* or *silver tequila*) is a colorless spirit aged for no more than fifty-nine days before bottling; this also makes an unusually feisty summery drink if you pour a shot into a beaker, half-fill with either fresh pomegranate or grapefruit juice, top with sparkling water, and serve with a lime wedge and a squeeze of lime juice. Patrón also produces a spirit called Patrón XO, which blends tequila with coffee essence: it's dry, forceful, reminiscent of grainy, brain-blastingly strong Turkish coffee, and the combination of caffeine and tequila makes a mean martini or after-dinner sipper—serve it in espresso cups. Then, of course, there is the classic margarita.

Margaritas and what to eat with them

"The American socialite Margaret Sames plied her guests with it at garden parties in Acapulco in the 1940s." "It was created at the bar of a Mexican ranch for actress Marjorie King, who complained she was allergic to every spirit except tequila." "It was first concocted by a bartender as a birthday present for his girlfriend, who had a taste for salt." "It was invented in honor of the singer Peggy Lee. . . ." There are more legends surrounding the birth of the margarita than you could drink cocktails in one evening. Fortunately there is consensus on the ingredients: tequila, Triple Sec or other orange liqueur, freshly squeezed lime juice, and salt for the rim of the glass.

A margarita is good in combination with another Mexican export, the watermelon. You can either serve a margarita with a pile of watermelon slices on the side or put the fruit in the drink to make a watermelon margarita—simply muddle a few chunks of fruit into the spirits, as for a watermelon martini (see p. 134), then follow the recipe below. Otherwise I usually make a bowlful of guacamole, whose creamy avocado and chile heat is a good foil for the cocktail. On a hot day, if drinks look as if they may run on to accompany more substantial food, the cold, limy cleanness of a ceviche starter, pepped up with chile and freshened with spring onions, is delicious with margaritas, and you can follow this up with more seafood, or flour tortillas filled with chicken, sizzling peppers, guacamole, and hot tomato salsa. Not everyone likes a salty glass, and you may want to give it a miss if using a boutique tequila, but margaritas do go with salt, so an alternative is to serve a bowl of super-salty chips on the side.

Classic margarita

First, prepare the glass. Crush a handful of sea
salt in a mortar and pestle or with the butt of
a rolling pin and put the salt on a plate. Rub
the inside of the squeezed-out lime round the
outer rim of a martini glass, then roll in the
salt so it sticks (you don't want salt inside or on
top of the glass—it should be there to give you
a burst of salt on your lips, not to be knocked
into the drink and make the whole thing
taste salty). Pour the tequila, lime juice, and
Cointreau into a cocktail shaker, shake with
ice, then strain into the glass and serve.

1 handful sea salt
2 parts silver tequila
1 part freshly squeezed
  lime juice
1 part Cointreau or
  Triple Sec

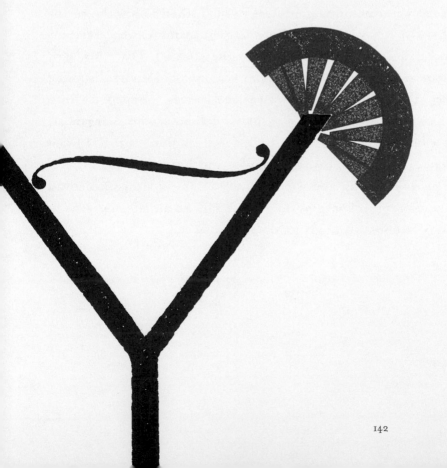

Diabolical margarita

Throaty tequila has an affinity with the heat of chile. You can make a fiery margarita by taking one small red chile and halving, seeding, and slicing it thinly. Using half a chile for each margarita, add the chile slices to the cocktail shaker with the liquid ingredients but no ice and shake vigorously for a couple of minutes to allow it to infuse, and then add ice and continue as normal. For a fire-and-ice margarita, pour the drink over crushed ice to serve.

Guacamole

This makes enough for two or three people.

Blanch the tomato in hot water for 30 seconds, then peel off the skin, cut into quarters, remove and discard the seeds, and chop the flesh finely. Halve the avocado, remove the stone, use a spoon to lever the fruit out of the skin, and chop roughly. Add the garlic and lemon juice to the avocado and mash together with a fork until you have a paste. Stir in the crème fraîche and tomato and season to taste. Serve immediately, as the avocado will begin to turn brown once it is in contact with the air.

1 ripe tomato
1 ripe avocado
1 garlic clove, pressed
2 quick squeezes lemon juice (the juice of less than ½ lemon)
1 tablespoon low-fat crème fraîche
salt and pepper

SULTRY HEAT

Iced coffee for hot days

Coffee is rarely refreshing, unless it is iced, in which case it suddenly becomes two things at once: a caffeine hit and a thirst-slaker for a hot morning. Aside from being a good start to a warm day, iced coffee, like all the best drinks, also contrives to be more than the sum of its parts. Americans often drink black brewed coffee over ice, but what we call iced coffee in Britain is more like the U.S. coffee shop iced latte. There are two ways to make it: the espresso way and—coffee snobs bite your tongues—the instant method. Yes, really. I never use instant granules or even have them in the house, normally, except occasionally when making iced coffee (and tiramisu, but that's another matter). I like it because it reminds me of sitting at small cafés in Greece and drinking Nescafé frappé through a straw while looking out across the sea, but also because, somehow, instant just works when you do it like this. The other thing to know about iced coffee is that even if you never normally sweeten your hot drinks, it often tastes better with a bit of sugar in it.

The instant-coffee method

Fill a tall, thin glass up to about an inch from the top with low-fat milk. Pour the milk into a cocktail shaker or empty clean jar and add one rounded teaspoon of instant coffee and a level teaspoon of sugar (of course, you can adjust the sweetness to taste). Put the lid on the jar or shaker and shake hard until the drink froths up. Add a few ice cubes to the glass, pour the coffee over, and drink through a straw.

The gourmet method

This makes the best iced coffee I've tasted, but it does require some advance preparation. Make some very strong coffee using either an Italian stovetop moka or a French press. Allow to cool, pour into ice-cube trays, and freeze. To make iced coffee, put a handful of coffee ice cubes in a plastic bag, bludgeon with a rolling pin, transfer the fragments to a glass, top with low-fat milk straight from the fridge, and sweeten to taste, stirring to dissolve the sugar.

Rum: the taste of Caribbean sunshine

Of all the spirits we are used to drinking in England, rum is by far the least house-trained. Unlike gin, say, or whiskey, it doesn't belong on the aristocratic sideboards or neatly mown country lawns of our imagination. It is rarely drunk with or even before dinner. If you associate anything with the leaping, near-sickly, vanilla and caramel warmth you get when you raise a glass of rum and its scent curls up your nose like a warm-weather genie, deleting the anxiety from your brain like a tot of sunshine in a glass, it is the promise of unfailing tropical heat, cocktails, and taking things easy.

That's what I like about it, anyway, and why I find myself reaching for the rum when some serious chilled-out relaxation is called for.

You can push it too far—rum (unless you're drinking aged rum) needs some climatic help. It can work psychological miracles in summer and on unseasonably warm days in spring and autumn. In winter, though, it only seems to emphasize the miserable gulf between your imagination and the crawling damp outside the window.

Rum is made in from Mauritius to Madagascar to Guyana, but it is the drink of the Caribbean. Distilled (usually) from fermented molasses, a waste product of sugar refining, it is a legacy of the European settlers who took sugar cane to the West Indies in the fifteenth century and went on to found vast plantations when they saw how much wealth the sweet "white gold" could bring them.

The liquor was viewed by seventeenth-century visitors to the Caribbean with suspicion bordering on hysteria. The British writer Richard Ligon somberly warned it could "overpower the senses with a single whiff . . . it lays [people] to sleep on the ground," and called it "Kill-Divill." Others referred to it as "rumbullion," a word linked to "rumbustious" and "rumpus," both of which are very likely to apply when people have drunk too much rum.

Pirates liked it, though. A barbaric Welshman called Captain Henry Morgan was a seventeenth-century pirate who preferred the description "privateer," on the grounds that his debauched, buccaneering activities were underwritten by the government, which relied on the services of ruthless men like him to protect their foreign interests. He was so keen on rum he used to produce his own in Jamaica and he has a brand named after him to this day. The Royal Navy also took to it, not to mention the locals, who have been drinking it, at home, and in rum shacks, from morning to dusk ever since.

Most tourists in the West Indies first encounter it within three minutes of stepping into the confines of a pampering hotel, when they're handed a bright glass of virulently fruity, sweet rum punch. But on a sweltering day the best way to drink it is to add plenty of water, preferably sparkling, and appreciate the taste.

Rum and soda

I like this on a summer weekend, when it's balmy enough to have the doors and windows open and friends are coming over for a barbecue or an early dinner. It's casual, it's relaxing, and it couldn't be simpler to put together. Just take one bottle of golden rum, one bottle of sparkling water, slosh a bit of each into a large tumbler with plenty of ice, then proceed to sip, while thinking of sun and the melting relief of unfailing tropical heat.

In the Caribbean they take the view that a little bit of rum goes a long way—as I learned the hard way, serving behind the bar at a party at my sister-in-law's home in Trinidad, where the guests took exception to my letting my hand slip. I was told very firmly to measure the spirit in the bottlecaps. "It's hot here," said one, "and we like to drink eight or ten rum and sodas, so they need to be weak. We all know exactly how we like it. Some of us are half-cap people, others like one or one and a half caps. But don't put more in."

If you're eating the right food, you can go on drinking this into the night. Rum and soda goes well with the sweet-savory taste of spareribs (especially if these have been well smeared with molasses to mirror the flavors in the rum), with jerk pork or chicken, corn on the cob rubbed with lime and ginger butter, and with Velma's Stew Chicken—a recipe I picked up while staying with my sister-in-law and have adapted to my own taste.

Velma's Stew Chicken

It took me ages to prise this typical West Indian recipe out of my sister-in-law's Trinidadian house-help, Velma. At first I thought this was because Velma had a hamster cage to clean, dinner to prepare, and two boisterous boys running about, and Catherine was reluctant to allow me to ask distracting questions, such as "But what exactly do you mean by add seasoning to the chicken? What seasoning?" After a while, though, I began to suspect Velma herself was not so keen to part with it. Whatever, here it is, simple, family food, post-school and -office, made mostly with things found in the pantry or freezer. The great secret is caramelizing the chicken pieces in sugar at the beginning, which gives the whole dish its warm, reddish brown color and the sweet tinge that distinguishes it from dreary British comfort food. It makes enough for four people and is usually served with rice and peas, but you can anglicize it by making peas and mash instead.

1 lime, squeezed
1 chicken, cut up
⅓ inch fresh ginger, peeled
*   and finely chopped*
1 garlic clove, peeled
*   and chopped*
salt and pepper to taste
2 teaspoons
*   Worcestershire sauce*
2 tablespoons vegetable oil
2 tablespoons Demerara
*   or granulated sugar*
4 ladlefuls chicken stock,
*   or 1 bouillon cube,*
*   crumbled into the same*
*   amount of water*
2 teaspoons ketchup

Pour the lime juice over the chicken, wipe it with the squeezed-out lime, then rub the ginger, garlic, salt and pepper, and Worcestershire sauce into the skin and flesh and leave for an hour or more. When you are ready to cook, heat the oil in a heavy-bottomed casserole on the stove. Add the sugar and stir it into the oil. Continue to heat gently until the sugar begins to caramelize. Add the chicken pieces to the pan and cook until browned on all sides. You may have to do this in two batches. Return all the chicken to the pan, add the stock and ketchup, and bring to a gentle simmer. Partially cover the pot, and simmer for about an hour, or until the chicken is cooked through. Serve with rice and peas—you can just throw the peas in with the rice when it is almost ready and continue cooking until the peas are hot.

Rum and the British Navy

Sailors have the best words for everything. "Let's splice the main brace" sounds robust and hearty even before you know that it means "Let's have another tot of rum." It originally meant only "Let's mend the big thick rope that's attached to the yard for trimming the sail." The main brace would be several inches thick, and only a long splice (as opposed to a short one) would do the job. Since the ship could not be steered properly with a broken main brace, it called for the skills of the best and nimblest-fingered seamen. In the navy, rum would be issued as a reward to those who had done the hard work. "Splicing the main brace" then became the term used when extra rum was handed out. Now it is reserved solely for special occasions, and only the sovereign or the admiralty can give the order. It is the one time that men can now get their mitts on free service rum. Usually, the form is this: one-eighth of a pint of rum is issued to every officer and man over the age of twenty who wants it. Men who rank below petty officer have their rum mixed with water. Those not taking rum can have lemon-lime soda.

But why rum? How did it become, for about 300 years, the navy's official drink? It was not always so. Before the seventeenth century, the ration of drink in the navy was an astonishing whole gallon of beer or wine a day. But beer at sea was rank stuff. According to one William Thompson, who led an appeal to improve what he called the navy's "pernicious provisions," the beer stood "as abominably as the foul stagnant water which is pumped out of many cellars in London at the midnight hour," and sailors were unable to drink it without holding their breath and their noses. In about 1650, the sailors were relieved of the onerous duty of pinching their noses in order to drink beer. To solve the problem of stowing barrel after barrel of beer, Admiral Blake made brandy the navy's official drink. The spirit was switched to rum in 1687 after the conquest of Jamaica, because rum, made from sugar cane grown in the Caribbean, was cheap and in good supply. When it was first introduced, there was a daily ration of one pint per man. Rum back then was fiendishly strong, sometimes as potent as 80 percent abv—double the strength of the spirits you've got at home. To prevent the sailors from plummeting out of the rigging after taking too much spirit, the habit of dishing out grog—a mixture of one part rum and two parts water—was soon introduced. Since this was the navy, and not some fancy cocktail bar, grog was not mixed to individual order but on deck, in an open-topped barrel, or "scuttled butt" kept for precisely that purpose. The Lieutenant of the Watch stood by to see that no man was cheated out of his daily allowance.

Sadly, the rum ration was stopped in 1969. Some say this was because it made the men sick at sea. (From where else do you think we get the word *groggy*, originally meaning someone intoxicated to the point of nausea?) But really it was just the Royal Navy catching up with the times: these days, navy rations for the over-eighteens consist of three 12-ounce cans of beer "or their equivalent" per day, and the men have to pay for these themselves if they want them.

Different kinds of rum: white, golden, aged, and dark

White rums are transparent to look at and the mildest, lightest, and most innocuous tasting. They are usually bottled straight from the tank, while the other rums are aged for some years in wooden casks that may previously have contained cognac or other spirits. The longer the rum stays in the wood, the more color, complexity, and flavor it takes from it. A golden rum may have been in wood for three years. A "dark" rum often has caramel added to it, to change its color and make it appear grander than it actually is. Aged rums are the ones that make you want to lean back into a leather armchair, inhale very slowly, and take a long, slow, savoring sip. The rum equivalent of a single malt, they have aficionados reaching for words that rival a fine wine taster's vocabulary: think nutmeg, roasted coffee bean, toffee, Demerara, and even banana.

Aged rum with cigar smoke, for late evenings

A sense of relaxation and a stout glass (a whiskey tumbler will do) are all that's required to appreciate a really decent rum. This is no way to start an evening, but an extremely mellow way to finish up, though it can be hard to drag yourself off to bed as the rum dwindles to the bottom of the glass.

There is no reason not to take aged rum as seriously as malt whiskey, though their cheerleaders tend to be very different types. Those for whiskey are likely to be found sipping in suits in St. James (London, not Barbados) or Scotland; rum aficionados in my experience tend to be wilder. Take Edward Hamilton, who runs the Ministry of Rum (www.ministryofrum.com), a website "Dedicated to the Understanding and Appreciation of the Noble Spirit," as he puts it, and which I commend to anyone looking for more in-depth information. Hamilton operates out of a sloop called *Triton* (his first boat, *Tafia*, was shipwrecked in 2001) and also maintains a post office box and office in Culebra, Puerto Rico, an arrangement he admits initially caused problems. "You don't have much credibility looking for a publisher for a book on rum when you're sailing in the Caribbean drinking the best rums you can find in the name of research."

Quite. My own introduction to serious rum came not in the Caribbean but in the unlikely venue of a bar called Trailer Happiness on Portobello Road in London, a shrine to rum, where I once spent a (rather too) happy night; when I decided to leave, I had to question the logic of setting up a place like this in a basement. The stairs were trickier to negotiate than a gangplank.

What's so good about aged rum is the complexity; you find a gravitas often rooted in molasses and coffee, but as the drink opens up lighter scents of vanilla and orange peel might waft through it. It's like smelling a perfume, with earthy, rooty base notes topped out with sunshine scents.

Among the rums I tried at Trailer Happiness was Pyrat Cask 23, a blend of different rums from across the Caribbean, aged up to forty years and made by the Patrón tequila people, who like to compare its smoothness to that of a cognac. The barman had something else on his mind, though. "Notice the farmyard odor," he said. There was a hint of cow sheds, in the nicest possible way, but also a skein of orange peel. That was the first one, I think. Afterward my notes were so illegible I had to conduct a whole series of individual tastings. Here are some of the ones I like.

Hailing from a Jamaican estate that has been around for over 250 years and is famed for the quality of its rums, Appleton 21 has a silky texture, with rich layers of coffee and spice that unwind seductively slowly. The El Dorado range from Guyana is superb, pungent and vanilla-filled. Then there is Gosling's Black Seal from Bermuda, a deep, dark, treacly thing used in the cocktail Dark and Stormy, which smells a little like falling down the sweetest of well shafts—and if you find the ridiculously strong 151 proof rather than the more common 80 proof, you will feel like you have too. Ron Zacapa Centenario from Guatemala is rich, sweet, and dangerously charming, sweeping you off your feet like Bess, the landlord's daughter, was in Alfred Noyes's poem "The Highwayman."

I like a bit of dilution to help the flavors unravel, and because I tend to drink rum in summer, I go with a single lump of ice. Purists can be iffy about cooling down a good drink because it dampens the flavor, but on a sultry evening the heat of your mouth should be enough to remedy that. As with drinking single malt whiskies, a tiny drop of water is good, but you don't need much. If you can persuade someone in the next room to smoke a cigar, a waft of smoke also enhances the experience.

Aged rums are not always easy to get hold of, though as they become more fashionable, it is less of a problem.

Rum cocktails

Perhaps it's because of the circumstances in which I've drunk them, but I always associate rum cocktails with long, carefree evenings. There was the time my cousin and I, then sharing a flat, threw a rum party, made so many strawberry daiquiris and mojitos we got through nearly 11 pounds of strawberries from the market, three huge bunches of mint from the local Iranian shop, forty limes, and two bottles of simple syrup, and still had to spend the hot evenings of the heady week that followed drinking our way through a rum surplus. And the sticky evenings in Brixton, before everyone had babies to look after, when my friend Ros ran a club night and we'd sit drinking rum while the sweat dripped from the ceiling and his tunes floated out into the night. They are drinks that suit not just the heat but letting go.

Cuba libre

It's worth overcoming your built-in resistance to rum and Coke, and all its associations, to try this. Coca-Cola (full sugar, always full sugar) with a thick slice of lemon and a couple of jangly ice cubes is almost more enjoyable than alcohol in hot weather; mixed with fresh lime juice and rum, either white or golden, it's fantastic. The combination is said to have been thrown together in the 1890s by a U.S. army lieutenant based in Cuba, who had a taste for the newly invented cola and the local rum. It was named after the island's struggle for independence. It's better to mix according to your own taste, but as a rough guide I use a couple of shots of white or golden rum and the same quantity of fresh lime juice, and then I top it with Coca-Cola.

Mojito

By now I think we all know what a mojito is. But some people are sadly unaware of what it is not—or at least what it ought not to be.

1 part fresh lime juice
1 part simple syrup
2 parts golden rum
sparkling water
1 spring mint, rolled lightly and leaves bruised

A mojito should not be a green stew, fetid with ragged mint leaves that stick to your teeth like spinach. Argue as much as you like about the rest of it—golden versus white rum; whether mojito gets its name from the Cuban for "little sauce," "something a little wet," or "little mixture"; whether Constante Ribalaigua of the Havana Floridita should get the credit for first mixing it or whether it's simply a take on the American, bourbon-based mint julep. If you really want to get finicky, you might even get into a dispute about the provenance of the mint—the milder strain grown in the mojito's native Cuba makes a subtler, softer drink than the tough, greenhouse-grown mint you find at the supermarket. But please, whatever you do, don't put too much of it in and don't mash it into oblivion.

In Cuba this is a delicate cocktail, nothing more than a dash of rum and a zing of lime, its sourness soothed away with a little sugar, added to sparkling water and stirred with a stem of mint to add a teasing herbaceous skein of flavor. In Britain we have a tendency to overdo the things we like. You may want more of everything—mint, alcohol, and lime—than they do in Cuba, but try to be a little restrained. You can either pick the leaves off the stem and gently bruise them or roll the sprig around a little and pop it in the glass as a stirrer. One is enough.

Mojitos are so easy to make, and so refreshing, that they are perfect for parties, especially outdoors. The only people who tend not to like them are barmen, and that's only because the monotony of mixing hundreds every Friday night for all their admirers makes them want to chew off their own arm the moment they see someone's lips purse to say the word.

Mix the lime, simple syrup, and rum in a tall Collins glass, fill with ice, top with soda, and then stir with the mint, leaving it in the glass.

Daiquiri

In *Islands in the Stream*, Ernest Hemingway writes, "He had drunk double frozen daiquiris, the great ones that Constante made, that had no taste of alcohol and felt, as you drank them, the way downhill glacier skiing feels running through powder snow and, after the sixth and eighth, felt like downhill glacier skiing feels when you are running unroped." Constante Ribalaigua was the legendary bartender of the Floridita in Havana, where Hemingway used to drink during his years in Cuba, who is credited with inventing the frozen version of the daiquiri that Hemingway describes in wistful detail later a few pages later: ". . . as he lifted it, heavy and the glass frost-rimmed, he looked at the clear part below the frappéd top and it reminded him of the sea. The frappéd part of the drink was like the wake of a ship and the clear part was the way the water looked when the bow cut it when you were in shallow water over marl bottom. That was almost the exact color."

2 parts golden rum
1 part freshly squeezed
  lime juice
⅓ part simple syrup

This is the sort of quote that can make you thirsty at ten o'clock in the morning, as indeed Hemingway often was.

They still drink frozen daiquiris, with the ice heaped up like granita, in the crumbling squares in Havana. But it's the original—or a variation of it—that I find most tantalizing. Some say the lime, sugar, and rum drink was knocked together by an American mining engineer called Jennings Cox, who worked for the Spanish-American Iron Company, after running out of gin in the summer of 1896. Others maintain it was already a Cuban specialty, drunk by thirsty men emerging from the mines. Either way, it takes its name from the village of Daiquiri to the east of Santiago de Cuba, it's serious, and it's one of the greatest drinks in the world.

A small warning: considering you can count its ingredients on the fingers of one hand, it's tough to get right. Balance, between the sour lime, sweet sugar, and kick of the rum, is important, but some factions also feel strongly about the rum. The London Floridita in Soho lists half a dozen or so daiquiris (none of them frozen), with deviant ingredients including a dash of grenadine or Curaçao, most of them made with Havana Club Añejo Blanco. I prefer to use Havana Club Añejo 3 Años, though for some reason Pernod Ricard, which owns the brand, is currently trying to push its darker "Especial," which doesn't make nearly such good classic daiquiris (it's a different matter when you put fruit in them). Incidentally, Hemingway is said to have preferred his made with the addition of grapefruit juice and with maraschino liqueur replacing the sugar, which to my mind isn't as good as the classic daiquiri.

I make my daiquiri like this, though of course if you have a sweeter tooth you can always increase the amount of simple syrup, up to a whole part, without losing the drink's structure.

Shake all the ingredients hard, and then strain into a cocktail glass.

Strawberry daiquiri

The giddily sweet smell of fresh strawberries is hard to beat. I use two different recipes for strawberry daiquiris, depending on what sort of drink I want to make. The first is the best for parties, as it makes a lot of rum-flavored strawberry puree drinks very speedily. It's good made with Havana Club three-year aged, but I also like to use a fuller-flavored rum, such as elements eight or Havana Club Añejo Especial, so that the caramel richness of the spirit can fight through the fruit.

3 parts fresh strawberry puree

2 parts golden rum

½ part freshly squeezed lime juice

¼ part simple syrup

Make the strawberry puree by hulling the berries, then blitzing with a hand blender. (You can do this in advance and store, covered, in the fridge.) Shake all the ingredients with ice and strain into cocktail glasses.

The second recipe is more sophisticated and the one I prefer, but also more time-consuming, and I wouldn't attempt it for more than four or five people.

3 ripe strawberries, hulled and diced

2 ounces rum

2 tablespoons freshly squeezed lime juice (about 1 juicy lime)

2 teaspoons simple syrup

Put the diced strawberries in the bottom of a cocktail shaker. Pour in the rum. Use a pestle to "muddle," or partially crush, the berries. Add the lime juice and the syrup, shake with ice, and strain into glasses.

Piña colada

Pity the poor piña colada. Once seen for what it is—a sublime blend of juicy pineapple and iced coconut cream that opens out like a soft breeze in the tropics—at some point around the 1980s it started hanging out in bad company. Suddenly its bedfellows were the slippery nipple, sex on the beach, the long, slow comfortable screw against the wall—all those drinks with names so bad you can order them only by pointing in silent embarrassment to the menu, adopting a hearty slappa-my-thigh guffaw, being so drunk they seem totally hilarious, or, possibly hanging out with Prince William and his crew, for whom this sort of thing seems all in a day's work. Anyway, the piña colada stopped being a drink and became an excruciating razzamatazz of an event, guaranteed to arrive at your table like a carnival float, in an obscenely large glass, decked with thrillingly garish paraphernalia such as a fuchsia paper parasol or six.

Try to forget all that. Think of a curl of sandy beach with palm trees behind it. Imagine heat, an early tropical sunset across a still sea, the humidity that makes you pink and sticky even when you're fresh from the shower, the clack of fan blades turning on the veranda, and someone pressing into your hand a cold glass, filled with pale, sweet snow riven with bright pineapple. That's better, isn't it?

Thanks to the advent of canning and the ease of modern transportation, the pineapple now seems commonplace, but the magnificent fruit did once receive the adulation it deserves. In her biography of the pineapple Fran Beauman calculates that in the late eighteenth century, when adding a pinery to one's country estate was all the rage in aristocratic circles, the cost of a single, English-grown fruit would have reached $7,000 to $10,000 in today's money. To those who could afford it, the expense proved more of an incentive than a deterrent, and the pineapple, with its glorious crest of leaves, would be paraded for as long as possible without being eaten. Beauman tells us that one man claimed to have heard of a "single pineapple going the round of west-end dinner parties for some weeks," and that pineapples became ornamental in other ways, with everything from mirrors and gateposts carved to resemble their knobbly skin.

Time to admire it again. However, having spent a long, sticky time in the kitchen hacking at pineapples, I have concluded it's not essential to use fresh fruit to make a decent piña colada, though it certainly adds to the drama if you do. The more crucial detail is that the drink be thick. The best way of achieving the right consistency is to use crushed ice, which makes it so thick you can practically spoon it into your mouth with a couple of straws. You can vary the rum, using a richer, more aged rum if you like the sunny flavor to show through, or taking it down to a white rum if you prefer the coconut and pineapple to dominate. And, of course, the virgin colada—just pineapple, coconut, and ice—is almost as nice as the alcoholic version.

Whizz the pineapple in a blender so it gets pulpy, but don't overdo it—try to retain some texture without any lumps. Give the can of coconut cream a good stir to mix the watery liquid with the solids before measuring out ¼ cup. Stir the coconut cream and rum into the pineapple puree and pour into an ice-packed glass. Serve with straws.

3 slices fresh pineapple or
*   canned pineapple rings*
¼ cup coconut cream
1 tablespoon golden rum

Caipirinha, the cocktail from Brazil

This is one of those simple but killer summer
drinks that are a specialty of hot countries.
Crabapple-sour and lethally strong, the first
gulp feels like plunging into an icy sea and
coming up for air, gasping but exhilarated.
Unlike a dip in the sea, however, it is likely to
leave you quite incapable of doing much, save
for wondering if another one would be too
rash. This might be the reason Henry Ford
is reputed to have attempted to ban the drink
in Fordlandia, his car-manufacturing town
in Brazil.

1 lime
1 to 1½ teaspoons
   superfine sugar
cachaça

The key ingredient is the Brazilian spirit cachaça. Like rum, it's
a product of sugar cane, though cachaça is always distilled from
fermented sugar-cane juice, whereas rum is more often made from
molasses. Thanks largely to the deliciousness of the caipirinha,
the fame of cachaça has spread in the past few years, but a good one
can still be hard to come by outside Brazil. It's worth searching for
Cachaca 51 in your local liquor stores, because it claims to be Brazil's
best-selling brand.

To make a caipirinha, it's best to use a cachaça that's clear and
colorless, like white rum. You also need good limes. And stout, squat
tumblers. Each drink needs to be made individually and with some care.
They're not difficult to prepare, but, as with a good gin and tonic, the
devil is in the details. Here goes.

Cut the lime in half lengthwise. Score each through from the fleshy
side, cross-hatching so you make a 3 x 3 or 3 x 4 grid of squares and
leaving the skin more or less intact. This sounds complicated, but all

you're doing is cutting into the fruit to make it easier to squash the juice out. Turn the skins inside out so that the cut flesh splays out and drop the lime halves into a tumbler with the sugar. Some like to make it sweeter than this—in the Brazilian province of Bahia, for example, where the local palate is notoriously sweet, you'll see people go at the sugar with a tablespoon, but I prefer to take the edge off the sourness rather than damp it down altogether. Using a pestle, gently work the lime in the bottom of the glass to get the juice out and mix it with the sugar, which, in these small quantities, should easily dissolve. If you make a sweeter version, you may need to leave the lime juice and sugar to stand for a while. Take care, though. I find the pestle business works perfectly well with the first round of drinks; on the second, glasses tend to get smashed. Anyway, next fill the tumbler with as many ice cubes as you can cram in (leaving the lime skin in the glass). You could use crushed ice; I prefer nice, solid clean-cut cubes, smaller ones rather than icebergs. Then pour in neat cachaça until the glass is almost full and stir. Usually I cram an extra couple of ice cubes in after stirring, so the tumbler gets full without putting too much spirit in.

That's it. That's how they make them in the grandly relaxing lobby bar of the Hotel Fasano in Sao Paolo (where Mata Velha Silver is the house brand of cachaça), and nowhere I've been does them better.

OTHER SUMMER SUNDOWNERS

Salty dog

An easy drink that combines bracing grapefruit juice with salt, so it suits those with a savory palate. A salty dog is also, of course, a sailor who's been around a bit.

Take equal parts of grapefruit juice and vodka and shake with ice. Salt the rim of the glass by rubbing a wedge of citrus around the outside edge and rolling it in crushed salt crystals. Once that's done, pour the drink from shaker to glass and enjoy.

The editor's drink: fuzzy navel

For nearly two decades, following an unfortunate adolescent incident, I steered well clear of peach schnapps. Then my editor remembered the drinks she had enjoyed while holidaying in Boston in the late 1980s, and so I made some. And they are strangely irresistible—giddy, sunshiny, dangerously easy to swallow, feel-good things. The name comes from the peaches (the fuzzy down of the skin) and the orange juice (navel oranges). They should probably be drunk to the soundtrack of *Grease*. Or to the Beach Boys. At least in spirit.

3 parts freshly squeezed orange juice

1 part peach schnapps (I use Teichenne)

Mix the orange juice and schnapps and pour into a glass full of ice.

woof

Raspberry vodka

This drink is nothing more than a mixture of homemade raspberry puree and vodka, but it always goes down well, I think partly because it mixes two ingredients that everyone loves and partly because of its color. You can make the puree in the morning (and even freeze it, as bars do, if you like), so the cocktails can be put together at the last minute with little fuss. Do not be tempted to skip the straining stage. This recipe makes enough for four small drinks.

9 ounces raspberries
6 ounces vodka
a few dashes simple syrup

Use a hand blender to blitz the raspberries to a puree, then push through a fine-mesh sieve or strainer, using the back of a spoon, to remove the seeds. Keep the puree in the fridge or freezer until it is needed. Shake the puree and the vodka together with plenty of ice in a cocktail shaker. Now taste it. I prefer to sweeten this drink slightly, just as you would sprinkle sugar on a bowlful of tart raspberries, but some like it au naturel. Add a little simple syrup, shake again, and taste again. Keep going until you're happy with the level of sweetness. This is a matter of personal taste but will also depend on the berries—some are naturally much sweeter than others. Strain into martini glasses.

NONALCOHOLIC REFRESHERS

Lime soda the Indian way

One food writer called it "the supreme quencher of colonial thirst," and along with the smell of wood smoke, sandalwood, and spices, the taste of a fresh lime soda provides an instant mental wormhole back to India. There you are offered it more times a day than you can count, and when you accept there is always a follow-up question: salt or sweet? Thus in the dusty heat, lime soda becomes almost medicinal, replacing salt and sugars as well as liquid. I like it with salt, which, because it reduces your perception of acidity, takes some of the sting out of the lime without sweetening it; some prefer both salt and sugar. The drink barely needs a recipe: simply squeeze the juice of half to one lime into a glass, top with still or sparkling water, and salt or sweeten to taste.

Homemade lemonade

This is what we used to drink at home, all summer long, from a big jug standing on the kitchen work surface. It's got more body and depth than a citron pressé, because the pith and peel are used, and it couldn't be simpler to make. Simply slice up a load of unwaxed lemons, pour boiling water over, add sugar to taste, and leave to stand until cool, when it will be ready to drink. Mum's working recipe was I lemon per pint of water plus I for the pot; in practice this meant using 4 lemons and 3 pints of water. This works out to 4 lemons for about 6½ cups of water.

Virgin piña coladas for children

See piña coladas on p. 160 and try to remember not to put in the rum.

Pineapple and lime

This isn't a recipe so much as a suggestion, but when you're bored with nonalcoholic cordials and water, fill a glass with ice, pour in pineapple juice, and then add the juice of half to one lime. The jolt of the lime works beautifully with the yellow pineapple.

Lapsang Souchong

It may sound hot and wintery, but a cup of smoky Lapsang Souchong tea is a good reviver on a summer afternoon. See p. 52 for more on this tea.

ALFRESCO

It is warm, or at least warmish. Outside, someone is getting hectic with the lighter fuel and the charcoal, and in the kitchen every available surface is covered with ingredients being marinated in bowls. The ideal drink here is easy, long, a little bit sugary (thanks to either its fruit or mixer content) and, most important, not too alcoholic—it's the afternoon, not the evening, so when you're making these, quell the temptation to let your hand slip with the spirits. You want to be able to knock back a few glasses while you mill around, chatting, or lounge in a deck chair with a book, and still be ready to move on to wine or beer later.

I make all the drinks with chilled ingredients and add ice to the individual glasses rather than to the jug—that way you don't have eight ice cubes trying to fight their way out of the jug at once or the ice melting before it gets near anyone's glass.

Drinks to serve from a pitcher

Elderflower fizz

Elderflower and sauvignon blanc have a natural affinity with each other, partly because of the crossover in scent—you find white blossom, citrus, and a gentle gooseberry trait in both. You don't need expensive wine for this; I usually go for something from the Loire or South Africa. The freshness is uplifting and reminiscent of June hedgerows. This makes enough for about ten glassfuls.

Rub the lemons with the back of a knife to release some oils and then cut in half. Tip the cordial, lemons, and wine into a jug and refrigerate until you're ready to drink. When you need it, add the sparkling water and ice, stir to combine, and serve. If you like, you could add a slice of lime or a sprig of mint or borage to each individual glass after pouring.

2 fresh unwaxed lemons
¾ cup elderflower
  (nonalcoholic) cordial
1 bottle sauvignon blanc,
  chilled
3 cups sparkling water

Long Island iced tea

At my university you knew you were at a party if
you had been asked to bring a bottle of vodka
and when you turned up it was poured into
either a bucket or, better (because it prevented
you from finishing the evening with sticky
arms), a watering can, along with everyone
else's vodka and some cheap lemonade.
Meanwhile, in the States, the frat-pack were
doing things more stylishly with Long Island
iced tea, a drink invented in the Hamptons in
the 1970s that takes its name from its brackish,
deceptively innocent tea-like appearance. The
classic recipe also includes a dash of sugar
syrup. I find the drink sweet enough as it is,
but if you have a sweet tooth, add 1 or 2 parts
simple syrup as well. You must use full-sugar
Coca-Cola; otherwise it will taste thin and sour.

1 part vodka
1 part tequila
1 part Cointreau
1 part white rum
1 part gin
2 parts freshly squeezed
　lemon or lime juice
10 parts Coca-Cola

Mix the spirits and the lemon or lime juice. Top with Coca-Cola, stir,
and pour into glasses over ice. If making this in individual portions, you
could shake the spirits and fruit juice with ice, then strain into glasses
before topping with Coke—the result will be colder and slightly more
diluted, no bad thing.

Sangria

Lou Reed sang about drinking "sangria in the park" in his 1972 hit, "Perfect Day," and for me the sight of a glass jug filled with red-wine punch, ice, and floating fruity bits inspires precisely the same lazy, hazy, upbeat mood as the record. There is also more than a sniff of suburbia, the 1970s, and the Costa del Sol, but don't let that put you off. I never do.

The word *sangria* comes from the Spanish *sangre*, "blood," presumably a reference to the color and the fortification factor. There are possibly more recipes for it than the Iberian peninsula has barmen. Some sangria, like the one I tasted at the famous Club 55 restaurant (where Joan Collins is a regular) on Pampelonne beach near St. Tropez, uses spices such as cinnamon that make it taste almost like a chilled mulled wine. That's far too festive for my taste. I prefer the fresh and thirst-quenching properties to dominate, as they do in this recipe, which was passed over the fence to me by my parents' late next-door neighbor. He had gotten it from the owner of a small restaurant near Marbella in the 1980s and was never short of barbecue invitations because everyone he knew always hoped he would turn up early enough to make up several jugfuls. As the drink is very fruity, it doesn't go well with food, so don't bother with nibbles. If people get hungry, they can fish around for some of the fruit salad. It's a movable feast, so don't panic if you don't have all the spirits—one or perhaps even two can be left out without causing

1 bottle cheap Spanish red wine

1 ounce gin

1 ounce brandy

1 ounce golden rum

1 ounce Marsala, Madeira, or Malaga

1 ounce red vermouth

a mixture of chopped fruit—oranges, peaches, and strawberries work well

1½ cups lemon-lime soda

trouble, although it would be a shame to go without the red vermouth. For the wine, I use supermarket plonk—tempranillo is best. Makes six or eight glassfuls.

Mix the wine with the spirits and the chopped fruit—try to avoid pears, which tend to discolor very quickly. Chill in the fridge for a couple of hours, add the soda, and serve in large wineglasses or tumblers with lots of ice.

If you have some sangria left over and are drinking it the next day, do refresh the fruit; the sight of mushy, falling-apart peaches and apples is dispiriting in a glass, though I find the macerated fruit delicious for breakfast the morning after.

Sea breeze

For a while, back in the 1990s, this glowing pink concoction was everywhere, though it was usually made with one ingredient (the grapefruit juice) missing, essentially reducing it to a simple vodka-cranberry and taking away its kick. Just because no one seems to drink it anymore doesn't mean it no longer tastes nice—so rediscover this old favorite.

1 part vodka
1 part grapefruit juice
2 parts cranberry juice
1 slice of lime

Mix the ingredients together, pour over ice, and drop 2 half slices of lime into each glass.

Riesling cup

"I'm drinking wine and—what was the other thing in it?—Grand Marnier," said a friend, glass in hand, bottom on deck chair, as he talked into a cell phone to his wife. He'd come to stay for the weekend with his small son. "Yes," he continued more cheerfully than soothingly, still talking into the phone as he accepted a top-up, "I have remembered that I'm in charge of a child."

Oh dear. On paper, this doesn't look like much. No, I'll go further. On paper, this looks about as appetizing as, say, seafood in aspic—and equally retro.

It does have old-fashioned roots: the family of drinks known as *cups*, which usually consist of a wine base sweetened with fruit and sometimes flavored with herbs, were popular in the nineteenth century. But the waltzy brightness of riesling is in vogue again, and here it makes a dangerously seductive, surprisingly modern-

1 bottle German riesling
3 ounces Cointreau
3 ounces cognac
1 peach, stoned and sliced
handful of strawberries
 or a sliced nectarine
 (optional)
sugar to taste
1¼ cups sparkling water

tasting drink for summer afternoons. The zippy succulence of the wine is streaked with the juice of the peaches and strawberries, the spirit adds depth, and the sparkling water gives it a spritz and lift and also means it's not as strong as it might sound at first. Honest. If you prefer, you can replace the Cointreau and cognac with 5 ounces Grand Marnier, and you could use other white wines, such as sauvignon blanc or unoaked semillon, but I think this tastes better with riesling, whose limy flavors combine beautifully with the peach. It was inspired by an old recipe for peach cup, featuring a combination of still and sparkling Moselle, fresh peaches, and superfine sugar, and a recipe for cider cup featuring Curaçao and brandy that I found in *The Savoy Cocktail Book*. If the wine is off-dry, you probably won't need to add any sugar. Makes about six glassfuls.

Mix the wine, spirits, fruit, and sugar in a glass jug and leave in the fridge for a few hours to blend. Just before serving, add the sparkling water, stir, and pour into glasses over ice.

How to drink well on a picnic

In *Summer Cooking*, Elizabeth David wrote evocatively of setting out on a picnic, feeling very pleased with one's provisions (in her case, olives, salami, anchovies, and bread picked up in the market at Marseilles), only to feel suddenly deflated by the arrival of a far better picnic (friends who set about chopping olive branches to make a fire and unpacking cutlets to grill and potatoes to fry).

It's much the same story with drinks at a picnic: only rain ruins your fun more than the sound of someone else's champagne cork popping. It's a Pavlovian reaction: we've all been successfully trained to think that champagne equals good times, so we assume we must be missing out if we don't have any. Actually, though, few picnics benefit from champagne: it doesn't taste very good out of a plastic cup, becomes either onerous because you feel you have to finish the bottle or disappointing because there isn't enough, and, let's be honest, doesn't really fit into the picnic spirit.

So what to take? Picnic drinks should be like a good cheese board: two or three solidly good things, not too complicated, not too prissy, and plenty of them. One of these should be water. The second should be a good soft drink. Options include homemade lemonade, a stash of cold, shiny cans of San Pellegrino—children like the lemonade and orange flavors while the orange "amara" is good for grown-ups—or a bottle of posh nonalcoholic cordial to perk up sparkling mineral water. The third is alcohol. Bubbles are good on a picnic—they seem to perk everyone up—but they don't need to come from anything as expensive as champagne. Small bottles of lager, cold and clinking in the cooler, that can be drunk straight from the bottle are hard to beat. A robust spread of delicatessen rillettes, cheese, and cured meats is always delicious with old-fashioned hard cider. One of the most perfect picnic drinks I ever tasted was actually a pear cider: Poiré Granit imported by Les Caves de Pyrène, which is made from pears from 300-year-old trees, tastes like biting into juicy pear and soft caramel at once, and has a mere 4 percent abv. As for wine, cava and prosecco still give you that "hurrrah" moment as the cork comes out but are much cheaper, and because they taste lighter and more frivolous than champagne, are far better suited to the occasion. Rosé wine will also work and will do a remarkably good job of pulling together a cacophony of different foods. Try to find one with a screw cap, not just in case someone mislays the corkscrew, but also because it makes taking home an unfinished bottle a less messy prospect.

If I am honest, though, for me a picnic with alcohol is always a battle between my natural greed and the fact that actually I don't like drinking during the day, especially when it's hot, which guarantees a woozy afternoon. If there are, say, squashy plastic bottles of Orangina, which reminds me of French holidays and eating baguettes in the sand dunes as a child, I always gravitate to that rather than the alcohol.

Picnics on the move: walker's rations

No food unwrapped from foil parcels ever tastes as good as it does when you have earned it. I spent my entire childhood being dragged up and down hills in hiking boots, blue slickers, and rustling waterproof trousers and used to love the sugary can of Lilt fruit drink or hot Nescafé sipped from the plastic lid of our red Thermos as I sheltered behind a windswept surveying station. My husband doesn't share this nostalgic view: he is forever pointing at herds of backpack-wearing hikers, shuddering, and muttering, "Think of all the plastic wrap and margarine in there." I do think there ought to be a rule about flasks, though: if ever you use them for coffee, you must never use them again for any other drink, because though it fades and gets stale, the taste of the coffee will never leave them, even after a hundred washes, and will infect anything you later put in there. One thing that is very good in a flask is hot chocolate—hot, milky, and sweet.

SUMMER WINE: TEMPERATURE CONTROL

Ice buckets on outdoor tables, bottles pulled from the fridge and hastily returned after pouring, glasses that instantly begin to bead with condensation . . . when you picture summer wine, the immediate thought is of something white and very cold. I would like to suggest three other things: first, that not all white wine tastes its best when it is sorbet-fresh. Second, that if the weather is at all warm and you have no proper storage place for wine (and few of us do), then the red will probably be as disgruntled and overheated as a dog panting in the noonday sun. Third, that chilled reds can sometimes be as satisfying as whites.

Letting the whites live a little

To some extent the temperature at which you drink a wine is a matter of personal taste. I prefer the sensation of taste to supersede that of temperature, so although I like to drink some wines straight from the fridge, I don't keep my fridge too icy. However, I know that for some half the pleasure of a brisk sauvignon blanc comes from the complementary incision of cold it makes as it carves through your mouth. For wines, such as pinot grigio, sauvignon blanc, or the cheaper grüner veltliner or riesling, for example, that seems fair enough. But whites with more body, breadth, and complexity—I am thinking particularly of white Burgundy, or chardonnay from other parts of the world, aged chenin blanc, or riesling and Rhône whites—need to be allowed to warm (say to 50–55°F) so that they are cool rather than cold. Drink them too chilled and you will catch only half, if that, of their flavor. Allow them to gather a little thermal momentum, and you will feel them bloom into a more expansive, interesting drink.

Calming down overheated reds

Thanks to the old saw that red wine should be served at "room temperature" (a misleading phrase if ever there was one, as it originated in the days when rooms were kept at a relatively chilly 65°F), it rarely occurs to anyone that it might be possible for it to be too warm. Yet red wine loses its form and feels out of kilter if it is even a few degrees too hot. When you taste it, you can feel it becoming bad-tempered: there's more evaporation, so you get a face full of fumes rather than a pure, clear smell, and the wine feels disjointed and uncomfortable, rather like a person who is hot and bothered. The solution is simply to pop the bottle into the fridge or an ice bucket for fifteen minutes or so, until it has cooled slightly—I often ask for an ice bucket for the red in restaurants or pubs when the wine has been stored behind a stuffy bar or in a warm kitchen. The important thing is to rely on your own senses to discern when it reaches the right temperature, then whip it out of the ice bucket and drink as normal.

Enjoying chilled red wine

To some drinkers, chilled red wine is a compromise choice: refreshment for those who would prefer white and the right color at least for those who will not be satisfied unless they have got their mouth around a red. That's a shame, because the sort of lighter-bodied wines that suit fresher temperatures are often just the thing you want to drink, regardless. In winter I like to have Beaujolais, which is made from the gamay grape and has a sappy sort of verve, with a hot coq au vin—the combination is the food equivalent of going for a brisk walk in the cold. It perks you up and makes you feel less stagnant than an afternoon in the house swaddled in central heating and sweaters. In summer I like chilled red—an hour in the fridge is usually enough—with all kinds of food. Though I am fond of Beaujolais, particularly if it is from one of the ten sites awarded cru status—Regnie, Chenas, Julienas, Moulin-à-Vent, Chiroubles, Fleurie, Brouilly, Côte de Brouilly, St. Amour, and Morgon—it often seems to be less good value than other wines. If this is a style you like, you could look for a straightforward gamay from the Loire, which goes very well with the meaty pinkness of seared tuna. In Sicily, a variety called *nerello mascalese* makes good, light reds, best served chilled with barbecued sardines. Cerasuolo di Vittoria is another light- to medium-bodied Sicilian red that suits a light chilling and has so much flavor you could even put it with spicy sausages or marinated meat. Or return to the Loire and seek out a cabernet franc from Saumur, Saumur Champigny, Chinon, or Bourgueil. Their leafiness—they often put me in mind of flowering red currants—and grace suit rare beef and steak tartare as well as leftover meat on the second day of eating.

PURE HEDONISM

Strawberries and demi-sec champagne

A smartly dressed champenois once leaned across the table at an Épernay restaurant and told me a joke: "How can you tell the difference between a champagne grower and a champagne producer?" The answer is that the grower washes his own Mercedes, a gag the locals find hilarious but that might make the rest of us, who pay for champagne, wince over our flutes. I always think of this when I talk about demi-sec champagne, because the idea of drinking wine that is not just fizzy but also sweet can seem like a bilious extravagance. Even Marie-Antoinette, whose husband, Louis XVI, like virtually every other king of France, was crowned in Reims cathedral, which is surrounded by champagne vineyards, was never accused of asking people to drink sweet bubbly.

Demi-sec champagne is more medium-sweet than the literal translation "half-dry," would lead you to imagine, but what few of those who tend to recoil from sugary champagne realize is that a lot of the "brut" champagne we drink is quite sweet anyway. Champagne is the most northerly wine region in France, and in those cool temperatures the wines tend to be acidic to the point of shrillness. This is why it is almost always sweetened, to a greater or lesser degree, when the bottle is topped up with a "dosage" of reserve wine just before it is corked. Sugar makes everything easier to swallow.

"It is also used to hide faults," more than one champagne man has sternly informed me. In pursuit of purity, some of the serious-minded winemakers eschew it, either producing "zero dosage" wines or at least proudly pointing to low dosages that allow more of the true nature of the wine to shine through. But even the best "zero dosage" champagnes aren't always easy to drink. They can be a bit like going down a black diamond run—exhilarating and scenic but pretty damn wild. So if you look at some of the biggest and most fêted names, they will often have a healthy level of sweetness to balance the acidity.

All this is by way of saying that a demi-sec champagne is not such an ungainly beast as you might think. Don't think of it as "sweet" champagne; think of it as "sweeter." Whereas a brut champagne may have up to I tablespoon per quart of additional sugar (last time I tasted it, for example, the Bollinger NV had 1½ teaspoons per quart), a demi-sec will have between 2¼ and 4 tablespoons per quart. In terms of taste, people talk about champagne smelling yeasty, toasty, and lemony, but also like homemade cookies baking in the oven like brioche (imagine walking into a pâtisserie in a small village in France). Those last two words are the giveaway, hinting at the edge of richness you can find in a brut, which in a demi-sec is only amplified—it becomes golden and sweet and luscious.

Like many other sweet drinks, though, it struggles to find its niche. When on earth do you open something as expensive and indulgent as a bottle of demi-sec champagne? Not at the beginning of a meal, when the sweetness would kill your taste buds and send your blood-sugar levels into a frenzy. Yet to save it for the end, when you have already gorged and your taste buds are dulled with other wines, seems profligate.

If you've had a sturdy lunch, it makes a good breaker at about 6 o'clock, before you've really begun to think about dinner. True, there aren't many afternoons in a year that suit this sort of indulgence, but on a sunny day, with a long, light evening stretching ahead of you, there is a blissful luxury in opening perhaps a half-bottle of demi-sec champagne, lolling around the kitchen or the yard and sipping a glass or two while picking at a big bowl of strawberries that will be brought to life by the chill warmth of the champagne. The other option is to factor it properly into a dinner, as I did on holiday once in France: we forwent the gin and tonics, ate a single course of rosemary barbecued lamb with a bottle of Gigondas, and then plunged into a dish of strawberries with a bottle of Billecart-Salmon demi-sec (one of the best) to finish.

Strawberries and moscato d'Asti

It would be unfair to moscato d'Asti to call it a poor man's version of demi-sec champagne. I love the drink, which is made in northwest Italy from the moscato grape, is blessedly low in alcohol (it typically contains about 5.5 percent), is lightly fizzy and a little sweet, tastes of white peaches and Charentais melons, and smells of flowers. It's delightful after a meal, when it seems to bring alive the most jaded palate—you could pretty much lie by a pool and drink it all afternoon. Don't serve in flutes; pour copious amounts into large wineglasses and, if strawberries don't appeal, try it with apricot or mango tart—it's delicious with crème pâtissière.

Peach in a glass of white wine

When I was an au pair in Florence and spent the days running around playing pirates with three-year-old twins, slogging through piles of ironing, and mopping the kitchen floor eight times, just occasionally, as another sticky evening began, I would sneak into a hot bath with a fresh, juicy peach sliced into a small glass of leftover white wine. The wine gets into the peach and vice versa, and eating it all is a blissful way to unwind.

ves me not

loves me

he loves
me not

he loves me

he loves
me not

he loves me

he loves me not

BACK-ENDISH: WHEN SUMMER STARTS TO FADE

There often comes a point in August, supposedly the leonine heart of summer, when the sky turns grey, there's an ominous chill in the air, the trees begin to look jaundiced, and there are more deadheads in the garden than fresh blooms. This is what my mother rather depressingly calls "back-endish," with the implicit message that it's all going to be downhill from here until spring. On a shivery day like this, it feels dismal to go on faking it, pretending it's properly summer and pulling a condensation-beaded bottle of white wine out of the fridge when just looking at it will make you want to run to switch on the heat. On the other hand, it's not autumn yet, so wading into the damson gin would be premature. One drink makes the best of the situation.

Moscow mules for the last days of August

The lime in this has an insistently summery taste, but the heat of the ginger peps it up enough to counter the grimmest weather. The name has very little to do with the Russian capital—Moscow mules were invented in Manhattan in 1941 and named because of the association between Russia and vodka and the fact that ginger beer has an equine kick. It's usually made with ginger beer and lime cordial, but I've replaced those with sparkling mineral water, fresh ginger root, and fresh lime juice for a sharper, more modern taste. The trick is not to let the fierceness of the ginger, which can vary in strength, overpower the lime.

½-inch piece fresh ginger
1½ ounces fresh lime juice
1½ ounces vodka
1 to 2 teaspoons simple
  syrup (adjust to taste)
sparkling water (about
  4 oz)
½ slice lime

This is one of those rare drinks that genuinely tastes just as good with no alcohol in it, which makes it a good, inclusive option for nondrinkers—and pregnant friends always seem particularly grateful to be served something that at least looks the same as what everyone else is clutching. Last time I made Moscow mules we were eating homemade vegetable curry, with proper pilau rice and pappadams shipped in from the nearest Indian takeout. We didn't bother opening wine (rarely a comfortable match with Indian food, in any case) or beer with the food; I just made another round of cocktails and the flavors meshed so perfectly I'd do the same again.

Peel and slice the ginger and bruise using a motar and pestle. Add the lime juice and leave for a minute. Put the ginger, lime juice, simple syrup, and vodka into a cocktail shaker, shake, and strain into an ice-filled tumbler. Top with sparkling water, stir, and add a half slice of lime.

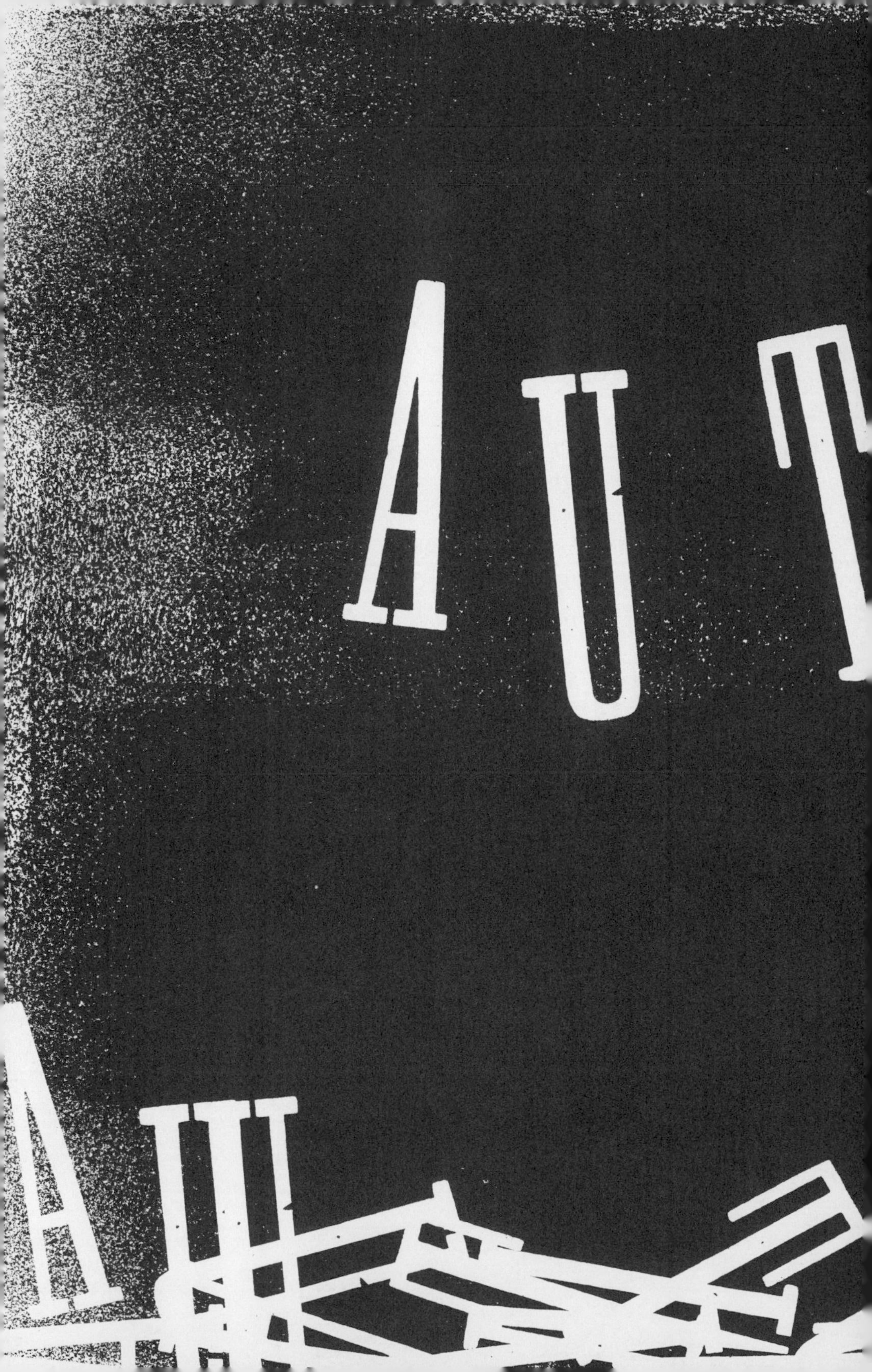
AUT

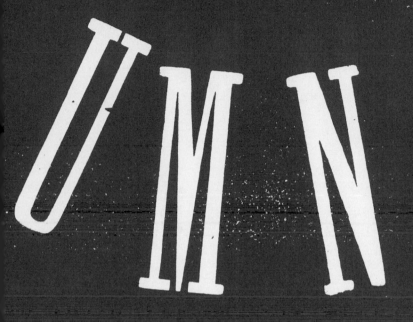

September is the time of year when the season can change most decisively. Suddenly even sunny days may be brought to an abrupt end by a brisk, chill evening. The first frost might fall. The furnace clanks into action, making the house smell of hot metal and baking paint. And all the light food and drink, the salmon and Chablis, the blithe, fruity cocktails featuring watermelon and strawberries and rum seem as out of place as a bikini at the North Pole.

APERITIFS AND DIGESTIVES FOR EVENINGS THAT ARE DRAWING IN

Kir and why it's far superior to kir royale

The mistake that everyone makes when they ask for a kir is to say the word *royale* straight after it. This ensures that a black curranty splash of crème de cassis will be poured into a glass of sparkling white wine, rather than still, which costs more, looks posher, and certainly feels more celebratory, but is also an awful lot less nice.

Kir royale is the drink 1970s hostesses served (the bottle of crème de cassis usually came back to England from France under the front passenger seat of the Morris Marina) to bury the taste of bad fizz, so the taste alternated between stickily sweet, pointlessly carbonated, and thinly metallic.

Kir is the real thing; a cool glass of white wine, which might be a little astringent on its own, but to whose limpid acidity the liqueur adds a lick of heat and the relief of some sweetness. Taking a sip should feel like standing on a frozen lake on a clear day so raw the wind stings your cheekbones and having someone put a black currant candy in your mouth. This is why I like drinking kir as the season tips and the first surprisingly dark and icy nights of autumn set in. I used to order it in the old-fashioned French brasserie down the road, where we'd go to eat coq au vin, demolish the smelly cheese board, and laugh as everyone's spectacles steamed up when they blundered in from the cold. Now I make it at home as a precursor to pork with Calvados or prunes or with crackling and rutabaga-and-carrot mash and roasted beets—the hint of sweet fruit really seems to set you up to eat pork.

You don't need more than a splash of crème de cassis—this isn't about drowning the wine; you're just adding a layer to it. As for what wine to use, crème de cassis is a specialty of Burgundy and even has a protected geographical designation—Crème de Cassis de Dijon must be made using only berries from within the local commune. And the drink kir is named after Canon Felix Kir, a Catholic priest who was elected mayor of Dijon in honor of his work as a resistance fighter during the Second World War. Purists, therefore, will want to make it as he and other locals always have, with a keen-edged Bourgogne aligoté (*aligoté* is the name of the grape, *Bourgogne* because it's from Burgundy). It's not bad with a grassy, stinging sauvignon blanc from the Loire either. The important thing is that the white wine should be bone-dry, light, unoaked, high in acidity (this is necessary to counteract the sweetness of the liqueur), and relatively invisible—avoid at all costs the likes of a splurgy, fat Australian chardonnay. A soave or an Orvieto Classico, or in a pinch a vin de pays from the Gers, if you can find one that's acidic enough, would be fine.

British fruit liqueurs for damp-weather Bellinis

Damson, quince, and sloe are all familiar autumn fruits in Britain and in various parts of the United States, but enjoying them can be hard work. The damson ripens first, from mid-August, and requires bag upon bag of sugar to sweeten its puckering acidity, as well as a lot of patience to deal with the stones. Sloes come later, also grow wild, and it takes a lot of fight to separate them from their thorny tree. Quince, which is actually native to China and Japan, is often cultivated as an ornamental garden shrub, and the industrious in Britain convert it into quince cheese (my family gives its harvest to my grandma, who kindly does the job for them, then redistributes the jars).

Fortunately there is an escape clause for the lazy: all these flavors, and more, can be found inside a bottle made in Devon by the artisan liqueur specialists Bramley and Gage (www.bramleyandgage.co.uk). For over two decades, they have been making the likes of damson gin and greengage, quince, or raspberry liqueur, using fruit sourced as locally as possible, and sometimes even picked wild from the hedgerows. These may look dangerously like the sort of thing you might pick up in the gift-shop area of a garden center on a rainy Sunday, then put in a cupboard to gather dust for the next forty years, but what sets them apart is their integrity: they deliver the comfort of sweetness but aren't sickly stickies. The blackberry liqueur is reminiscent of dusty, rain-soaked brambles; the Dittisham plum liqueur, made with fruit from the Dart valley that has only a fleeting, ten-day season, has a hint of homemade fruit crisp.

The Bramley and Gage website has a link to two distributors that ship around the world, and once you've realized how good all these liqueurs are in sparkling wine, you'll need to order more. I use a half inch or so in the bottom of a flute, then top up with low-rent sparkling wine and serve as an aperitif. If using the quince liqueur, I put out slices of manchego cheese; with the damson, devils on horseback—prunes wrapped in half a slice of bacon, then cooked on a baking sheet in the oven until the bacon begins to crisp. Bramley and Gage has plenty of other suggestions to ensure you avoid back-of-cupboard syndrome, among them a recipe for plum sauce for duck (which unexpectedly uses either greengage liqueur or sloe gin) and one for spiked summer pudding. And, of course, you can always drink them neat, ideally at the end of dinner as the more savory flavors go very well with cheese.

Eaux-de-vie: poire William and mirabelle

At dinners with French winemakers there often comes a point, just as we are finishing, when the waiter is summoned with a small incline of the head and in the quiet exchange I catch a single word, *poire*, before a small glass of clear liquid is brought and consumed with grave relish.

Eaux-de-vie are spirits distilled from the alcohol of fermented fruit, or fruit brandies to put it more simply. Alsace is famous for the purity of its eaux-de-vie, but there is a strong tradition of making these bolts of firewater in Germany, Austria, and also Switzerland. Kirsch, scarcely seen now that we have put the Black Forest cake days of the 1970s behind us, is just a cherry eau-de-vie. They can be made with any fruit, from raspberries to blueberries, apricots, or quince, but to my mind the two really worth having are poire William and, even better, mirabelle, a kind of yellow plum. The best I have yet tasted were made in Villeneuve-sur-Vère in the Tarn by Maison Laurent Cazottes (currently imported by Les Caves de Pyrène); they are quite extraordinary in their purity—as they should be at hovering around $75 for a small bottle. The poire William tasted so precisely of the fruit it was made from you could almost feel the sweetness and textured scrape of the coarse pear flesh dragging across the tongue, so that it was a surprise to find only liquid in your mouth. The Goutte de Reine Claude Dorée Passerillée (greengage) also yielded an incredible clarity of flavor. "We take all the stones out of the fruit by hand," explained the producer when I commented on this. "All 300,000 of them. We do everything by hand so as to avoid bitter or dirty tastes. The quince are the toughest to deal with because they are very hard, but we have a very big sharp knife."

Such painstakingly handmade versions are not within many people's budget, but a bottle of poire William or mirabelle is a worthy addition to anyone's liquor cabinet, and the smallest glassful is a pleasing digestive after a heavy meal.

MIDAFTERNOON: SOMETHING TO INVIGORATE WEEKEND COOKS AND GARDENERS

Sloe gin and vodka and how to make your own

This old-fashioned drink is regaining popularity in Britain, where sloes grow wild. In
America you are likely to find them only in the
northeast, but for those who are interested,
I have included my recipe here. Perhaps
because of its medicinal taste, sloe gin is one
of the few alcoholic drinks it seems not just
acceptable but even obligatory to have on one's
own in the middle of the afternoon. I'm not
talking about settling down for a long, solitary
session, but a nip peps up dinner preparations
after a strenuous morning in the garden or
an afternoon run. Sometimes I sneak just a
teaspoonful, which reinforces my idea of it
as a very pure, light kind of cough mixture.
Of the two commercial brands I know well—
Gordon's and Plymouth—the Plymouth is
infinitely superior, prickly and authoritative,
while the Gordon's is too sticky and confected,
reminiscent of boiled sweets. The homemade
stuff is more satisfying, though. It's easy enough
to make; the tricky bit is gathering the fruit of the blackthorn. Its Latin
name is *Prunus spinosa*, and the sturdy bushes are as painfully prickly as
the name suggests, so take gardening gloves and a walking stick to pull
apart the branches; in Britain the fruit usually ripens in September
and October.

1 pound sloes

3 cups gin (or vodka)

1⅓ cups sugar

This is how my mother makes sloe gin. She uses Gordon's.

First you need to break the skin of the berries so their flavors can infuse the gin. The old-fashioned way of doing this was to prick each berry several times with a darning needle; it's much quicker and easier simply to spread them in a single layer on a baking sheet and freeze overnight. The skins will then burst, and you can avoid the lengthy pricking process. Then immerse the sloes in the spirit, add the sugar, and stir to combine. Distribute this mixture evenly between sterilized glass jars with an airtight seal and leave to macerate for—well, ages.

The sloe spirit will be drinkable after about three months. But I finished the last of my mother's 2006 vintage eighteen months after it was made, and it had vastly improved since its early days, increasing in gravitas and taking on a more earthy, better-melded taste, so do save it if you have the patience. Some people like sloe gin made with no sugar at all; I enjoy the contrast of syrup and rasping warmth, but I think if you're planning on drinking the sloe gin young, you could afford to reduce the sweetness.

Sloe gin is at its best drunk out of small dessert-wine glasses, secretly in the kitchen or lounging on a rug with the Sunday papers by the fire. Sloe gin and tonic is also good, but don't add lemon, which will spoil the flavor. Once you have finished the sloe gin, don't throw away the sloes; you can spread them, ginny, pure, and unadulterated across a loin of pork, which you then roll, roast according to your normal recipe, and serve with Hasselback potatoes and red cabbage. You won't want to eat the stony sloes, but they transfer a pleasing medicinal flavor to the meat.

A glass of Madeira
In his book *Beyond Nose and Tail*, Fergus Henderson, the chef at St. John in London, writes, "Eleven o'clock and still two hours until lunchtime.

Something to keep you steady—nothing finer than a slice of seed cake washed down with a glass of Madeira."

His dignified words are a lone voice of succor in a vast, dark wilderness: these days, Madeira is so far out of fashion it does not even have the status of being unfashionable.

It was not always thus. Madeira once had such standing that in 1776 Thomas Jefferson used it to toast the Declaration of Independence, and according to legend a fifteenth-century Duke of Clarence, allowed to choose his own method of execution after being convicted of treason, plumped for drowning in a barrel of the stuff. However, you only have to listen to the lecherous, stamp-collecting old man keen to accrue some more notches on his cane in Flanders and Swann's "'Ave some Madeira, M'Dear" to see that by the music-hall era it was already falling out of favor.

Madeira is a curious drink with a curious history. Several hundred miles off the coast of Morocco is the tiny, steep island, the remnants of a spent volcano, where it is made. Madeira was a natural stopping-off point for ships working the old trade routes, and they used to pick up barrels of the local wine, fortified with a little brandy to help them survive the long days and nights of pitching, rolling, heat, and cold. Instead of destroying the wine, the long sea voyages were found to improve it; before long great quantities were being sent as ballast so they could benefit from the effect of passing through the tropics. When they were unloaded, the casks were stamped with the words *Returned Wine* and commanded much higher prices than the untraveled versions. Today the process of creating Madeira owes less to happenstance. The wine is no longer sent on improving trips abroad, but it is left to stretch out in warm rooms, sometimes using sauna-like heaters known as *estufas*, until it has softened and enriched.

Cheaper Madeira is often reliant on a grape called *tinta negra mole*, the better ones on sercial, verdelho, bual, and malmsey (malvasia), which make, in that order, dryish through to caramel-sweet yet still refreshingly acidic Madeira.

The best of the vintage wines do not just have longevity; they are almost immortal: I once tried a Madeira from the 1930s that, instead of tasting like a once grand but now faded and withered duchess, was fresh and bright with orchestral complexity and length.

Look for producers such as Henriques & Henriques, D'Oliveiras, and Barbeito.

As for the wines, the drier styles are the easiest to handle: sercial (typically very alert and tastes of spicy dried pears and almonds) and verdelho (dried apricots, candied orange and lemon peel, with some nuts) are both tangy and lively, while bual (baked apples stuffed with raisins and honey) and malmsey (caramel, roasted nuts and figs) are for the sweet of tooth.

They make a delicious pit-stop nibble with roasted almonds, mince pies, panforte, or manchego. And Fergus Henderson is right: they are also very civilized with a slice of seed cake, or even the buttery, densely textured Madeira cake with its crispy, sugar-crusted top. I would only quibble with the timing: for me elevenses is still too early—far better the lull of afternoon, say tea-time, between lunch and late dinner, when a small pick-me-up is required.

MADEIRA

1900

THE APPLE HARVEST

The stories of apples and their juices

Granny Smith, Braeburn, Cox's Orange Pippin, Golden Delicious . . . these are some of the names most familiar to us, but there are thought to exist around 8,000 named varieties of apple, all with their own distinctive taste and bite. The nature of each sings out with great clarity and purity in its juice, so if you have a juicer that can handle apples, you can slice them up, fling them in, and enjoy the virtues of each variety as it ripens. If not, you can try the apple juice that is now sold in farm shops and at farmers' markets all over the country, which is often pressed and bottled as a single variety. Both liquids are superior to and have a world more character than the generic stuff the color of cold tea that you can get at the supermarket, as well as being a great way of getting better acquainted with some of our more tasty and obscure varieties, many of which are on show at the National Fruit Collection at Brogdale Farm in Kent.

There, on 150 acres of land, besides cherries, gooseberries, and other fruits, is one of the most comprehensive, authenticated collections of apples in the world—around 2,400 different apple trees. It must look spectacular in spring, when white and pink-tinged blossoms fall on the orchards like drifts of snow. By summer, there are already hard little balls clustered behind the leaves; some, like the Skovfoged from Denmark, are long, almost purple fruit; others are dappled pale green with a gentle blush of red. And in autumn, when most ripen, the branches arc and bow under the weight of the harvest.

Each apple has its own story. The most ancient in the collection is the Decio, thought to date to the time of Attila the Hun, which was brought over from Lazio by the Roman general Ezio. The most unattractive apple could well be the Knobby Russet, with its khaki, reptilian skin. The most flirtatiously decorative trees are the Japanese, with their almost violet-colored leaves. Then there is the Blenheim

Orange, which was discovered in Woodstock in Oxfordshire in 1818 and is fêted for its nutty flavor. "It's the king of the Pippins, large and showy," said Jonathan Fryer, my guide for the day, as we wandered through the orchards, neatly set out in rows behind high alder hedges, planted to give shelter from the gusting winds.

Not all varieties can boast a lineage measured in centuries because, as Jonathan explained, "The great period of development for apples began in the 1850s, when breeders all began trying to make apples that were bigger, better, and juicier to eat." Discovery, the earliest ripener they have at Brogdale, is one of these relatively new apples: it dates back only to 1949. Its fruit is just tinged pink, can sometimes be picked as early as July, and its juice is delicious: medium-sweet, as delicate yet vivid as a Mosel riesling—the kind of thing you would want to have in your fridge to quench your thirst at any time of day and that would go especially well with a runny Camembert.

Some trees are fabulously named—Molly's Delicious, for example. "And very handsome her apples are too," remarked Jonathan. Then there is Chorister Boy, so called because its skin is bright red like a choirboy's cassock, and Ananas Reinette, which is gold in color and said to taste of pineapple.

At Brogdale they bottle seven different varieties of juice each year. Bramley's Seedling was as tartly acidic, sharp, and dry as you might imagine, a real livener that you could use in the kitchen as a substitute for verjuice, knock back to wake you up at breakfast time, or mix with sparkling water for a longer, thirst-quenching drink. The Howgate Wonder is "a huge American apple," I was told, as the man in the shop spread his hands ever wider like a fisherman telling tales, "almost as big as a Charentais melon, and dual purpose: pick it early when it's acidic and it's a cooker; later and you can eat it." Its juice is medium-dry, and tastes, on the finish, like the soft bite of a red apple. Both of these would be lovely with a hard, sour cheese such as Wensleydale or

Christopher Boy

Cox's Orange Pippin

Egremont Russe

Braeburn

Blenheim Orange

Howgate Wonder

Granny Smith

Ananas Reinette

Brogdale

Bramley's Seedling

Golden Delicious

Skovfoged

James Grieve

Molly's Delicious

Decio

salty Caerphilly. James Grieve, an English apple from 1893, tastes of baked apple and rhubarb. Egremont Russet, a traditional English apple (and a good pollinator) first recorded in 1872, makes a sweet, nutty nectar of a juice, like liquefied apple strudel, streaked with sweet raisins and honey. Put with a blue-veined cheese like Cambazola or creamy Cropwell Bishop Blue Stilton, it would make a feast of a picnic lunch.

Brogdale sell their juices at their on-site shop in Faversham, Kent, and you can also visit for guided tours of the orchard, or the autumn apple festival.

One final thing: if you are juicing the apples yourself, for variety you could throw in a handful of some of the other late summer/early autumn fruits that marry so well with apples—plums, perhaps, blackberries, or black currants. Only the last are tart enough to make you consider extra sugar. If you do, think about pouring the juice into a mug, adding a teaspoon of superfine sugar, then warming it in the microwave, which will help the sugar dissolve and also make a more comforting drink.

Cider at the kitchen table

A gently fizzing, stout tumbler of amber liquid, a sweet-sour smell of apples, and a vestige of the nostril-twitching, feral scent of a stocky workhorse as it walks past you in a muddy lane. Cider—proper cider, not the industrial-tasting hangover-in-a-pint-glass stuff—is one of the few alcoholic drinks that makes you believe it might almost have a rosy-cheeked goodness to it. It is also a wonderful match for all kinds of autumnal food, including, of course, if you are not drinking beer, the British classic ploughman's lunch. Actually, when it comes to cheese, it is hard to go wrong here, because most ciders drink beautifully with most cheeses. If you have a cider with a particularly noticeable, funky farmyard smell, it will find its equal in the pungent aroma of washed-rind cheeses. Salty cheeses go well with drier, more acidic ciders, while a soft, sweet drink, such as a cider made from dessert apples, needs either something mild or a blue cheese—Stilton would be perfect—and is also good against nutty Emmental.

A few bottles of cold cider can transform the remains of a large ham, brought out again for lunch with a hearty farmhouse loaf, into a real occasion. It suits onion tarts, pork pies, cold sausages . . . in fact most things porky. And for dinner, too, given that stewed apples go so well with pork, what better than a roast of it, complete with crackling, red cabbage, roasted turnips and other root vegetables, and perhaps pommes boulangère with a few apples sliced into it, to accompany the hearty glassfuls of apple-scented alcohol beside everyone's plates?

FOOD AND DRINK TO GRAZE ON

Beer at home with food

In a good, old-fashioned British boozer, there is really only one thing you can order without feeling out of place: a pint. This ought properly to be accompanied with companionable near-silence, the occasional nod, a few dry comments, in-jokes and jibes, and, possibly, a bag of pork rinds. At home in England, beer typically comes out when bums are parked on sofas ready for the football starting on telly, when some poor, shivering soul is trying to light charcoal outside in the rain, or just as the delivery many arrives with chicken rogan josh, pappadams, and rice from the local curry house.

Lager sluices back an Indian takeout very nicely, especially one that has a subtle sweetness that takes the edge off the chile. But there are many other foods that beer suits just as well, if not better than, wine. The idea of drinking beer with food sounds a bit like reinventing the wheel, but it is something the brewing companies have been trying to push now that wine has established itself as the natural choice of drink with any dinner. And with good reason: the combination of barley, converted into drowsy, sweet-smelling malt, and hops, which give beer its tension, a citrus tang, and bitterness, is too good to sell short. An impressive beer can always find food that goes well with it.

It was Rupert Ponsonby, one of the founders of the Beer Academy, the "Beer Education Trust" of Britain's Institute of Brewing & Distilling, who taught me that putting beer with food is no different from matching the wine. "You can either choose one that complements the food, in terms of style and intensity," he said, "or look for one that cuts across it." He illustrated his point by suggesting a hoppy, edgy pale ale with spicy shrimp. The pair are delicious together: the citric freshness of the ale acts like a lemon wedge, and it sashays through your mouth with the boisterous shrimp. Proving the other part of the rule, the delicate, floral, grassy scent of a pale golden beer glides up gently against fish pie without crashing and overwhelming it.

That said, one of the most brilliant beer-and-food combinations is completely counterintuitive. I can't think of any reason why stout or porter should go with oysters. The reverse: the heaviness of the drink should obliterate the taste of the delicate bivalve. And yet it does not. They drank pints and platefuls of these in Dickensian times. But some of my favorites are the most obvious: bangers, mash, and a sludge of onion gravy loves a good bitter. Refreshing Pilsner-style lagers cut perfectly through the fat of peppered salami and play against the clean spice of rye bread. English cheeses are also good suitors for traditional English beers. With a hard, mature, tangy Cheddar, try the richness of a strong amber or brown ale. And my mum is a great fan of blue Stilton with barley wine.

You can also drink beer with sweet afternoon pick-me-ups. An oak-aged beer (Innis & Gunn's is available in the New York area) has a caramelized warmth that sits well with apple crisp or tarte tatin. And for those who like to drink with chocolate (in cake, mousse, or any other form), a cherry beer demonstrates why Black Forest cake is such a good idea.

Sherry: the professionals' favorite drink

Sitting at my desk one gloomy morning, I opened an email that sounded like coded instructions for a mission impossible during the Spanish Civil War: "Providores has got Fernando de Castilla," it read. "I think we should go." The two of us to whom it was addressed agreed instantly. By 7:55 that evening we were converging on a Marylebone restaurant, and moments later each of us was cradling a wineglass containing a couple of inches of pale, cool liquid that smelled of sourdough bread and sea spume on a dank day when you walk along the beach and it blows into your face and hair and makes them sticky.

Sherry—it doesn't have to be Fernando de Castilla, although I do have a soft spot for that particular bodega—is a magical drink, yet it's unusual to find devotees outside of a bridge club or the Senior Common Room of an academic institution. The exception is among those who work in food and drink, including some of the trendiest chefs around, many of whom are so obsessive that when you talk to them about sherry it almost sounds as if they belong to a cult.

The prospect of a cold glass of fino gives me more thirsty focus than the promise of champagne. One wine writer I know has a "sherry cupboard" stuffed with sherry vinegars as well as vials of rare, aged palo cortado that he guards as jealously as some men do their wives. You can see his eyes monitoring it across the kitchen, and he becomes quite twitchy if anyone moves within its range. I once spent a few days in Jerez, in the southwest corner of Spain, the home of sherry (if you aspirate the J, you can see where it gets its name), when Heston Blumenthal happened to be judging a sherry-and-food-matching competition. After walking around the old frontier town, where on the surrounding slopes the albariza chalk soil reflects bright sunlight even on the coldest January day, I joined him for a glass of fino (or three) and he kept muttering about how sherry was not taken seriously enough.

Sam and Sam Clark, the husband-and-wife team who run the London restaurant Moro, are mad about it too. "It's the romance of drinking something with history," Sam (male) Clark once told me, a faraway look in his eye.

Sherry is matured in a solera: rows of barrels in which wine for drinking is taken from the last, but never more than a fraction is drained off at once. The last barrels are then topped up with wine from the barrels preceding them, and so on, with new wine topping up only the first in the series. This blending process allows each sherry bodega to maintain its house style. And because the barrels in the last row are never emptied, in theory they still contain a tiny proportion of wine from when the solera was first set up, so in your glass you may have a drop, or a few molecules, of wine that is tens or hundreds of years old.

The mainstay of sherry is the palomino grape, although sweeter sherries also have a portion of molasses-tinged pedro ximénez. Sherry comes in a variety of styles: the lighter manzanillas and finos are salty, tight, and stingingly refreshing, while the more oxidized amontillados, palo cortados, and olorosos have layer upon layer of nutty flavor (more detail follows). It is almost insanely good value: there can be more complexity in a $10 bottle of sherry than in any other similarly priced wine from any other part of the world.

So why don't we drink more of it?

The disgrace that passes for sherry in most households is one reason it is held in such low esteem. I'm thinking about the sorry bottles hoarded, open, from one Christmas to the next as if they're as indestructible as turpentine, when fino and manzanilla should be drunk, like any ordinary white wine, within a day or two of being opened, a week at the most. Most people in Britain never recover from the aversion therapy of being fed this stuff every Christmas as adolescents, just as Americans wonder how a grandmother or great-aunt can swallow the stuff kept for cooking, which now smells more like turpentine than wine.

Nor does it help that we drink the wrong kind of sherry. A lot of the sherry bought in the UK and U.S. falls into the cream or pale cream variety—a distressing muddle, though doubtless they would prefer to call it a blend, of different sherry styles mixed with your great-grandmother in mind—whereas the Spanish sensibly down enormous amounts of brisk, dry manzanilla and fino, which together make up around 80 percent of their intake, and hardly any cream at all.

Converting sherry-haters is easy: all you have to do is give them an ample glass (I pour sherry into wineglasses, which show it off much better than the thimbles our grandparents used) from a freshly opened, chilled bottle and lay on a spread of chewy ham to nibble with it. But I'm not so sure I should be writing this at all—the fewer sherry drinkers there are, the more of the good stuff there will be left for me.

How to tell your oloroso from your manzanilla and what to eat with them

The following sherry styles are listed, in order, from the lightest through to the richest and most intense.

Manzanilla

Manzanilla and fino are both protected from oxidation by a white yeast, called a *flor*, that grows across the surface of the liquid, so it does not come into contact with the air. This is why they are lighter in color and taste. Do not, however, confuse the two. Go into a bar in Jerez, ask for a manzanilla, and you will be treated as if you have just walked into the club shop for the Spurs soccer team and asked for a North Londo archrival Arsenal shirt. This is because manzanilla is made 15 miles to the northwest of Jerez in coastal Sanlucar de Barrameda, and there is no rivalry more intense than that between neighbors. Manzanilla is the most elegant, the bone china of sherries. As primed as the racehorses that thunder up and down Sanlucar's broad, long beach every August, it is dry, with a lean, palate-cleansing vigor, and a salty taste. Drink it chilled. Salted roasted almonds make a good manzanilla nibble. It's also perfect with seafood—shrimp fried in garlic and lemon, sardines smothered with chopped tomatoes, sliced onions, and torn basil leaves and shoved under a hot broiler until the skin blackens, or chile squid.

It makes a good "first drink of the evening" and if friends are coming over, I make scallops with prosciutto to eat with your fingers like a canapé as everyone sips. You need about half a slice of prosciutto or jamón ibérico per scallop, and three or four scallops per person is usually enough. Just wrap each scallop in prosciutto, put on a baking sheet, and cook in an oven pre-heated to 375°F for 7 to 8 minutes, or until the scallops are cooked through.

Fino

In inland Jerez, where it's hotter, the flor grows less vigorously, with the result that fino has more guts than manzanilla. It's richer, with a deeper, bready taste, a more pungent yeasty character, and, very often, a smoky crackle on the nose. It is the perfect foil for a fish soup, breathing saffron, tomatoes, and garlic rouille, it also goes well with gazpacho and with oysters—or could be drunk with tapas.

For a good tapas spread, charcuterie is essential. You might also add a bit of tortilla español, artichokes, and manchego cheese with membrillo. If you have some of the dry chorizo that supermarkets sell like salami, you can slice it, fry it in its own fat until its shrivels and is hot almost all the way through, blot the grease off with paper towels, and put it out on plates too. I also like to griddle Belgian endive leaves until they are charred and juicy—the bitterness of these is great with fino. Either all of this can make a meal on its own, or you could move on to paella, or a slow-cooked leg of lamb with a good bottle of Rioja.

Amontillado and palo cortado

This is where the real confusion starts. Both of these begin life like a fino, but in each case the flor dies away, exposing the sherry to the air, and the process of oxidation then begins. The difference between the two is a question of timing. In an amontillado the flor hangs around for longer, so the sherry becomes an aged fino before the yeast dies. A palo cortado is the style that sherry aficionados crave almost more than any other. It is one of the rare, one in a thousand, barrels of fino to lose its flor, entirely naturally, very early, and with longer exposure to the air sits somewhere between an amontillado and an oloroso. Both have more intense, complex flavors than a fino—you taste almonds and hazelnuts, coffee beans and caramel (I sometimes also taste penicillin, but that doesn't sound so romantic). If I'm going to be eating cured hams with these two styles, I always ask for the meat to be sliced a little thicker, so you have something to chew and sink your teeth into. Both are also good after dinner if you've got something hard and pungent, like a washed-rind pecorino, on the cheese plate.

Oloroso

Dark in color, and reminiscent of mahogany sideboards, old leather trunks, gnarled bowlfuls of uncracked nuts, dried figs, and walnuts, an oloroso is made by fortifying the sherry so it is too alcoholic to sustain any growth of flor. These wines are made dry, but sometimes sold in sweetened styles. Perfect after dinner, they are very complex and intense, and if they're any good, the finish feels like it lasts for years. In *The Perfect Marriage: The Art of Matching Food and Sherry Wines from Jerez*—a treasure trove of quite complicated recipes from sherry-loving chefs, Heston Blumenthal suggests putting a sweet oloroso with foie gras.

Pedro ximénez (PX)

There are three grapes used in sherrymaking—palomino (by far the most widely planted), moscatel, and pedro ximénez (known as *PX* because no one can pronounce it), which is used for sweetening. In pure form, PX looks like engine oil—black and viscous—and tastes so sweet you can almost feel your teeth melt as you sip it. Think of molasses, mixed with molten dark and golden raisins, and that's what this tastes like. The only way to drink it is to pour it over vanilla ice cream.

Cream sherries

Cream sherries come in all shapes and sizes because they are blended from the styles listed above to produce wines that may be sweet, dry, or in between. According to Harveys, which makes Bristol Cream sherry, this is how the name arose: "Our sherry was known as Bristol milk, because it was given to young children to give them vigor. On tasting a series of blends one day, an important lady said, "If these are milk, then this one should be cream, because it's the finest." Well, it's a good story. I'm no fan of cream sherries, unless they have been chilled right down and poured over a bowlful of sliced oranges or stuck in a trifle. Christmas isn't Christmas without a large helping, or six, of my late Grandma Moore's fabulous old-fashioned sherry trifle, with its luminous layers of pink blancmange, Bird's Eye custard, and sprinkles leaking their color into the double cream on top. Sounds a trifle odd? The recipe comes from the era of corned beef and tongue sandwiches, but I promise it's gorgeous, especially after a turkey sandwich supper. It makes enough for a hungry family of four to eat twice.

Grandma's trifle

Break the ladyfingers into the bottom of a large glass bowl. Add the sherry bit by bit, sprinkling it across all the sponges—they should be sodden but not afloat. Now, add the jam, stir gently until it resembles, as my mother puts it, "a soggy mess," and spread it evenly in a layer across the bottom of the bowl. Make up the blancmange, cool slightly, then pour over the sponge mixture to form a second layer. Leave to cool and set. Now make a pint of custard following the instructions on the package, but adding a fraction less liquid, so it is slightly stiffer than usual. Allow the custard to cool as much as you dare before it sets, then pour it over the blancmange to form the third layer. Refrigerate, and when ready to serve, whip the cream and spread over the custard to form the final layer of the trifle. These days we no longer cover with sprinkles, but if you do use them, only add them at the last minute as the color will bleed into the cream.

1 package ladyfingers

6 to 7 ounces pale
  cream sherry

1 tablespoon good red
  jam—raspberry is best

1 pint pink blancmange,
  made from a mix

1 pint custard

1 cup heavy cream

213

DINNERTIME

Wines for autumn: opulent whites and reds that give succor

As the sunlight turns golden and the evenings start to bite, wines that gave so much pleasure in summer—the sauvignon blancs and simpering pale rosés—begin to feel flimsy and inappropriate and seem to offer no protection against the cold.

This is when it is pleasing to pull out more opulent whites that may be toasty or riven with vanilla after months or years lying in oak, or richer and more thoughtful after spending some time maturing in the bottle. Head to Burgundy for whites made from chardonnay, which have a graceful roundness, like the chiming of a bell. Nutty Montagny is good with seafood cooked in butter. If you like Chablis, look for one that is old-fashioned in style and slightly aged, as opposed to a steely young one with a lemony kick. The New World is also expert at supplying chardonnays that glow with sunshine. Australia and Chile make some of the fatter versions, while New Zealand tends to be more restrained— for my money the chardonnay from Cloudy Bay is usually far tastier and certainly better value than its iconic sauvignon blanc. All these are delicious with nothing more complicated than a good roast chicken.

Chenin blanc, the white grape used to make Vouvray in the Loire, is also good when the days shorten. Very cheap wines made from chenin blanc for drinking almost from the moment the cork is placed in the bottle are characterized by a crisp, appley simplicity. Spend a little more, give the wine a couple of years to broaden, and it begins to generate a lanolin-like texture, a rich glow and an intensity that can sometimes give the impression it may have had the slightest bit of oak aging, even when it has not. I like Vouvray sec with fish pie, because its texture melds perfectly with the creamy, fishy sauce and clouds of mashed potato. You can also use chenin blanc from South Africa, the other part of the world that has had particular success with this grape.

As for reds, pinot noir begins to come into its own in the autumn. A simple Bourgogne Rouge or a Passetoutgrains, light in body with a stream of red-berry flavors, is ideal with classic roast pork. If you can afford more expensive, aged red Burgundy, with its characteristic perfume of mulching leaves mingled with primary fruit that meet at the rim of the glass, like smelling life and death at once, then do it.

I also like Tuscan wines as the days shorten—but then I like them all yearround. As I write this, it is October. I am sitting at the kitchen table in a clifftop house at the edge of a small village near Orvieto, working during the day as the wind pulls leaves from the olive trees and whirls them around and around, then stopping in the evening to stand out on the veranda, smell the wood smoke from the farmers' fires on nearby hills, and open a bottle of wine. I have drunk Rosso di Montepulciano with pumpkin, mozzarella, garlic, and sage pasta. There have been feasts of pasta amatriciana, crostini di fegatini di pollo, and chickpea soup with Chianti Classico, which with age acquires a haunting smell reminiscent of truffles, dust, orris root, sour cherries, and mushrooms and takes on the ancient elegance of old mahogany furniture. Perhaps best of all, that grand wine Brunello di Montalcino, from the magisterial vintage of 2001, whose decaying scent is like a concentrated essence of the one I find when I put my nose outside in the evening air, and which I have drunk with a thick-cut steak, simply dressed with olive oil, salt, and pepper.

Italy does autumnal wines very well. Barolo and Barbaresco from Piemonte are dry, austere, and tannic beasts made from nebbiolo, which at its best is always said to smell of dried rose petals and tar, though I often find the scent of black tea in there too; they are delicious sipped with onion tart, truffle risotto, or a mixture of dried and fresh mushrooms cooked with pasta or on toast.

And last, consider a Rioja from Spain, which mellows beautifully with only a few years of age and is perfect with a pork roast cooked with fennel seeds and served with garlic and saffron mashed potatoes.

Alcohol in the kitchen: Marsala and apple brandy

I tend to use alcohol in the kitchen more in autumn than in any other season. I know that autumn has truly arrived the first time I decide to sauté pork tenderloin and then use Calvados or apple brandy to deglaze the pan, mix in some crème fraîche, and serve it with slices of eating apple caramelized in a bit of butter and sugar. Actually, I often make this dish just as an excuse to buy Calvados or its English alternative, Temperley's excellent Somerset Apple Brandy (the ten-year-old is best), because a glass of it is so good after dinner.

One thing I would never be without, particularly at this time of year, is Marsala.

You can find the Sicilian fortified wine at most supermarkets (Pellegrino is the very respectable and widely available brand), usually the "dolce," its sweetest form. For cooking, many recipes specify using dry Marsala, which gives a sharper, cleaner finish, but it is not always easy to find. Even with savory dishes it's generally not a catastrophe to make do with sweet Marsala, though if you make this substitution, do remember that you are adding sugar and taste accordingly, rather than letting your hand slip with the bottle.

The classic Marsala recipe is zabaglione, the very eggy, foamy dessert.

Zabaglione

Beat the egg yolks with the sugar until they
turn pale, then put the mixture in the top of a
double boiler and heat it gently while beating
in the Marsala. Continue to beat for 10 to
15 minutes, until the whole thing rises like a
cumulonimbus, at which point you can pour
it into small glasses and serve.

4 egg yolks
¼ cup superfine sugar
½ cup Marsala

I use my Marsala most often, though, for saltimbocca alla romana.
I actually prefer to use sweet Marsala in this recipe, because I like the
viscosity and gloss the sugar brings, and then I add a squeeze of lemon
just as cooking finishes to counteract the sweetness. There's no need to
add lemon juice if your Marsala is dry.

Saltimbocca alla romana

If your butcher hasn't done this already, place
the veal between two thin sheets of plastic wrap
and beat and roll it until it is thin. Season,
cover with a slice of prosciutto, and put the
three sage leaves on top, securing them with a
toothpick as if you were sewing with a needle.
Now sizzle the veal in a frying pan with a little
butter for a couple of minutes on each side.
Add a good slug of white wine and another of
Marsala, and leave to simmer for a couple more
minutes, scraping the bits from the bottom of
the pan into the sauce as you would if making
gravy. Melt an extra knob of butter into the
sauce just as you are about to serve it and eat
with cooked spinach.

1 veal scallop
3 sage leaves
1 slice prosciutto
2 teaspoons butter
white wine, a good slug
Marsala, a good slug
lemon juice (optional)

Marsala also goes well with chicken livers. It's essential to the Tuscan crostini di fegatini di pollo to which I am addicted (I have never been able to improve on Claudia Roden's recipe, which you can find in *The Food of Italy*). You can also make a delicious pasta starter by frying finely chopped shallots and garlic until both are soft, adding chunks of chicken liver and cooking until they are brown on the outside but still pink in the middle, then deglazing the pan with Marsala (this time it must be dry), mixing the whole lot with a small amount of cooked egg tagliatelle and finishing with chopped flat-leaf parsley.

Tawny port and manchego cheese to end dinner

There are certain topics that must always be addressed when you visit a winery. You have to admire the winemaker's barrels, talk at length about yeast strains, and over a long lunch discuss fermentation temperatures and the difficulties of when to pick the grapes; then, by about the coffee course, you may be able to ask him which of his wines, or which of the local wines, he drinks at home and actually get an honest response.

In the Douro valley, where port is made, everyone I tried this on gave me the same answer. What all the port shippers seemed to be drinking most of wasn't the lightest, white port, which is refreshing in the scorching Portuguese heat, or one of the many red styles, from ruby to late bottled, crusted or vintage, of which, naturally, they were proudest. They were all swigging tawny port, which they drank chilled, either as an aperitif or instead of dessert after dinner.

Tawny is the port I find most versatile and easiest to drink, too. *Mellow* is the best word for it. It has a seductive opulence, and the combination of its sweet viscosity with the coolness of it straight from the fridge is highly seductive. Beware, though, because it can be made in one of two ways. The name comes from its tan hue, but this may be achieved very cheaply, by mixing red port with white and fiddling with the color to give it a brownish tinge, which results in a vapid and best-forgotten drink. Far better if the port has been aged slowly, in oak casks, until the tannins in the wine, along with the color, naturally begin to fade and the wine takes on a mellow, hazelnut glow. You can identify these tawny ports because the label will boast about their age—say, ten or twenty years old. And when you drink them, you'll see how different they are: the good ones (Ottima twenty-year-old, Quinta do Noval, Sandeman, Niepoort, Fonseca, and Warre are reliable) taste of nuts, golden raisins, and dried figs. The older they are, the more detailed and profound they get and the more the dried-fruit flavors give way to brazil nuts, walnuts, macadamias, and roasted almonds.

I don't tend to drink tawny port as an aperitif because it's sweet, which makes it more soporific than an appetite-whetter. Instead I like a small glass of it after a single-course dinner, ideally with some creamy manchego cheese, which really seems to sing against tawny port, making the port taste creamier and the cheese more caramelized. On occasion an embarrassingly small number of friends and I have gotten through an entire bottle as well as a huge block of cheese. It's also good with blue-veined cheese, ice cream, almond tart, almond cake, polenta cake, and tarte tatin.

OTTIMA QUINTA DO NOVAL SANDEMAN NIEPOORT FONSECA WARRE

There are two sides to winter. First there is the festive build-up to Christmas and the season itself, all the way through to the New Year, when cold is a novelty, and warming casseroles with red wine, as well as rich food and drink with a tang of celebration to them, all seem entirely at home. This is when cognac, Armagnac, champagne, and cocktails are thrown about. Then there are the dismal months that follow, with still-dark days, an endless trudge of grey, when anything that reeks of seasonal merrymaking feels tired and drab, like half-empty bottles the morning after a party. This is the time of year when it is hardest to find food and drink for which you can work up an appetite. Some give up altogether and detox. Alternatively, a famous chef once told me that in January he gets around this by filling his menu with everyone's favorite comfort food; I find that a complete change of pace in January, into clean-tasting vodkas and sake matched with food from the frozen North (blinis and pickled herring) and Asian-inspired noodle rice paper wraps do the trick. There are also certain wines, such as albariño from Spain or rosé, that don't at first seem to belong in winter, but provide a welcome respite from heaviness and, rather than being disgruntled by the damp, dark cold are almost lit up by it. Then, when all else fails, you can just retreat to the armchair by the fire and pour a large tot of your favorite whiskey.

CHRISTMAS IS COMING

From the gleam of pomegranate seeds to the luxurious opulence of brandy and champagne combined in the classic champagne cocktail, there is a distinctly festive quality to all these drinks.

Champagne cocktails

If you are going to mix champagne with anything, there ought to be a rule: the finished drink must be better than the unadulterated champagne. This might seem obvious, but you only need think of a weak mimosa—insipid, apologetic, limp—to realize the rule is seldom followed and actually, unless you have such a bad champagne that disguising the taste entirely is the only way to get it down, almost nothing will improve it.

1 brown sugar cube

7 or 8 drops angostura bitters

cognac

champagne

1 strip of orange zest

The champagne cocktail is a glorious exception. The patrician scent of the cognac conspires with the luxury of the champagne and the tang of the orange peel to make a drink that is heady, celebratory, delicious, and totally and utterly lethal. Even so, I wouldn't waste anything special on this—certainly not vintage and not even a special nonvintage. They're easy enough to make:

Soak the sugar cube with the angostura bitters and place in the bottom of a champagne flute. Pour just enough cognac into the glass to cover the sugar, then top with champagne (be careful; the champagne will froth like fury the moment it hits the sugar) and add the orange zest. Drink at once.

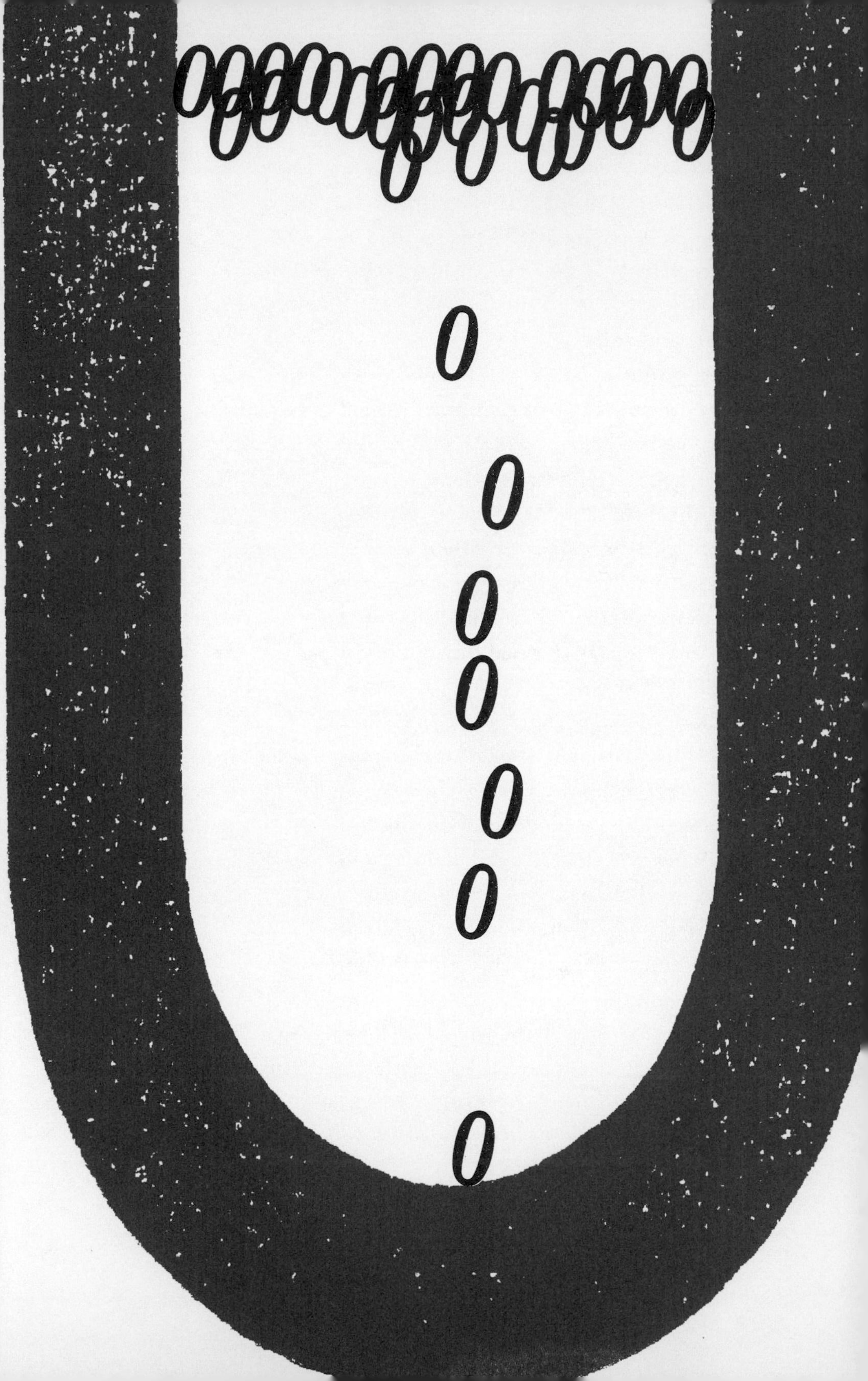

Gasconomic orange: Armagnac champagne cocktail

Where cognac is refined and urbane, and smells almost softly soapy, like continental men's aftershave, Armagnac has throat and rustic fire. Mixed with fizz, it makes a more feral, jagged version of a classic champagne cocktail. This drink is a take on one they make in Gascony using Pousse Rapière (literally, "rapier thrust"), a liqueur made from Armagnac macerated with oranges, and champagne. The ridiculous yet irresistibly pleasing name "Gasconomic Orange," was dreamed up by my friend Sally when she handled the public relations account for Armagnac in this country. They are so good that when we drank them together we got a little carried away; by the end of the evening, when we remembered to be sensible, we sagely decided to dilute the drink by adding more champagne.

Pour the first two ingredients into a champagne flute, top with champagne, and garnish with the orange zest.

1 brown sugar cube

7 or 8 drops angostura bitters

cognac

champagne

1 strip of orange zest

Vodka with pomegranate seeds

Jewel-bright, translucent pomegranate seeds look stunning mixed in with ice cubes in a tumbler and then topped with vodka (straight from the freezer, of course). I use a couple of teaspoons of seeds per person and supply cocktail picks so you can pick at them when the vodka has gone. Beware, though. Pomegranates have become a very fashionable ingredient, but no one tells you they are also very messy. The first time I tried this, digging into the halved pomegranate to excavate the seeds, I spattered indelible crimson juice in a 360-degree sweep around my friend's immaculate kitchen. She emailed the next day to say the pristine spines of her cookbooks had been "improved by the Pollocking," but I am not sure she meant it.

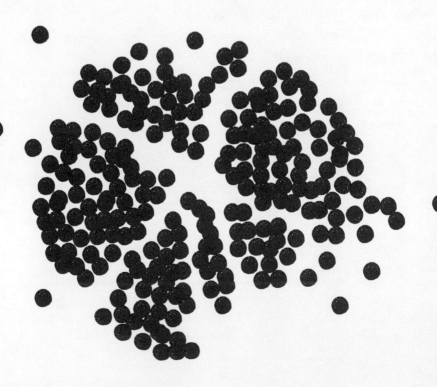

Pomegranate fizz and cheesy wafers

This isn't too potent, which makes it useful for larger parties. You need to use real pomegranate juice, not a pomegranate "beverage" or "made from concentrate," because as well as the deep fruitiness, the taste depends on there being a touch of astringency that you find only in the fresh stuff. The liquid equivalent of a red party frock, it's not sophisticated, but it's fun and has a sense of festivity. You can use the cheapest sparkling wine—its taste will more or less be drowned out by the pomegranate. This makes enough for about ten glassfuls.

1 bottle sparkling white wine
3 cups fresh pomegranate juice
8 ounces vodka

Mix all the ingredients in a jug, pouring the sparkling wine in first because it will go crazy when it hits the sugar of the pomegranate juice. Then serve in either large wineglasses or tumblers filled with ice.

Cheesy wafers

Everyone has his or her own variation on the classic cheese-straws recipe. This is mine, adapted from Nigella Lawson's recipe for cheese stars, which uses red Leicester in place of the Gruyère or Cheddar. I have also added hot red pepper flakes, because I like the sudden burst of heat when you hit one, and thyme. It goes so heavy on the cheese it almost feels as if the flour is there just for propriety's sake, but you get away with it by using self-rising, which helps to puff the wafers out. How many it makes obviously depends on the size of the cutter you use, but it's about right for four to six people. If you like, you can make the dough the day before and leave, tightly wrapped, in the fridge overnight.

1½ tablespoons unsalted butter, cold from the fridge
⅓ cup self-rising flour
2½ ounces Gruyère or Cheddar, grated (a generous ½ cup)
1¾ ounces fresh Parmesan, grated (about ¼ cup)
½ teaspoon hot red pepper flakes
2 teaspoons fresh thyme leaves
1 to 2 teaspoons cold water, if you need it

Preheat the oven to 400°F. Cut the butter into cubes with a knife and rub into the flour and grated cheese with your fingers, as you would to make pastry, until the mixture resembles fine bread crumbs. Sprinkle the hot pepper flakes and thyme over the mixture and stir. Once they are thoroughly distributed, use your hands to squeeze and then knead the ingredients into a dough. If necessary, you can add a tiny amount of water, but you shouldn't need it. When you've got it pressed into a ball, wrap the dough tightly in a plastic bag or plastic wrap and leave to rest for 15 minutes in the fridge. Roll the dough out on a floured surface until about ⅛ inch thick. Cut out the wafers and spread on greased baking sheets lined with wax or parchment paper. Cook for 10 minutes or so, until golden, transfer to cooling racks, and serve just as soon as you can touch them—they are delicious hot.

Brandy and ginger refresher

There is something very Christmasy about the combined smell of brandy and ginger. The other beauty of this drink is that it's long, so you can take slightly more thirsty sips than you ordinarily might from another brandy cocktail.

1 part cognac

3 parts ginger ale

Pour both ingredients into an ice-filled tumbler, stir, and serve.

HOT DRINKS FROM THE STOVE

In deepest winter the sight—and smell—of a large saucepan full of fumy alcohol simmering gently on the stove, waiting for someone to ladle a drink out of it, makes a house feel like a home. Hot punches and wassail cups aren't just good for pre-Christmas parties. They are comforting to come back to on cold January weekends when you've been freezing on the sidelines of a sports match or tramping across icy fields and want to mill around the kitchen feeling your cold fingers come back to life. Like turkey hash, they can also be a useful way of turning leftover dribs and drabs into something that's more than the sum of its parts.

Mulled wine

There seems to be a snooty anti—mulled wine
movement gathering pace, which is a shame
because this is a drink that says to me the
holiday season has arrived. I never deviate
from the recipe my mother has been using for
decades, which is repeated here. There's no
point in using anything other than cheap wine,
but it should still be something you would be
happy to drink cold. Tempranillo from Spain
is one good option, and Chilean merlot works
well too, because it's sturdy and fruity but not
so distinctive that it can't make a good canvas
for the spices. Don't just open the wine and
pour it directly into the pan. Check that it's
not corked first (see p. 24) or you will ruin the
entire drink. Serves six.

1 bottle red wine
1 glass brandy or port
5 cloves
1 orange, sliced
1 cinnamon stick
1 pinch apple pie spice
sugar to taste (optional)

In a saucepan, gently heat the wine and
spirit. Stick the cloves into the orange slices.
Add the cinnamon, clove-spiked orange
slices, mixed spice, and sugar. Simmer for 15
minutes, and then serve.

Robbie's wassail cup

I first drank this one grey, rain-soaked evening between Christmas and New Year. Essentially a sort of mulled cider, it's a refreshing and perhaps more sophisticated alternative to mulled wine. The recipe was put together by my friend Robbie by the simple process of looking several up on the Internet, taking all the bits that seemed essential to a wassail cup, leaving out the ones he didn't like the sound of, and adding a few extras that he did.

The word *wassail* comes from the Old Norse *ves heill*, "to be in good health," according to the *Oxford English Dictionary*, and has a variety of interrelated meanings, all of them full of goodwill. It may be a "toast or salutation," a "festivity when much drinking takes place," a drinking song, a drink, or the practice of going from house to house singing carols.

Wassail cup used to be made in celebration of the apple harvest and thus contains cider and baked apples. It smells very good—a noseful of wintry spices that somehow avoid the nasty tendency some of these drinks have to reek of potpourri. It tastes great, too—hot and appley, with a pleasing nip in the throat. Fino is the best sort of sherry, but no need for fancy stuff. Again, with the cider, the general rule is that if you'd drink it cold it will be fine hot. As with most recipes of this type, there's no need to be too precise about ingredient quantities—keep tasting and adjust to your own palate. What you must be careful about, though, is the spice element—too much and you will overpower the drink. Makes ten glassfuls.

Heat the oven to 340°F. Put a spoonful of sugar in each apple, then place them in a roasting pan with the water and bake for 20 to 30 minutes, until soft but not too collapsed or mushy—you don't want them to disintegrate into the wassail. Meanwhile, place all the other ingredients except the brandy in a large saucepan. Bring to a boil, then turn down the heat and simmer gently (with just a few bubbles coming to the surface every so often; if it's too hot, the alcohol will boil off) for about 20 minutes. When ready to drink—taste it to check that the spices have infused into the cider—add the apples and cook for 5 more minutes. The idea is that the apples should add flavor to the drink, much as a bay leaf does in stock, but not fall into it. Finally, just before serving, add the brandy and continue heating until the mixture is piping hot again. Use a ladle to fill glass cups or generous wineglasses. This is good with hard cheeses, and the hot apple taste goes well with mince pies too.

6 teaspoons brown sugar

6 eating apples, cored

⅜ cup water

1 cup sherry, or more to taste

8½ cups hard cider

1 orange studded with cloves at approximately ¾-inch intervals

a 1-inch cinnamon stick, no more

5 or 6 allspice berries

¼ teaspoon freshly grated nutmeg, no more

1, or even 2, wineglasses cooking brandy

HIBERNATION

Drinks to chase away a cold

Look at the small print on the bottles of cough syrup on the drugstore shelf and you'll find many contain little more than glucose, sucrose, honey, and alcohol. So why bother when you can take the fresh ingredients and make a cheaper, more delicious, longer drink at home?

Lemon, honey, and hot water

Just mix the freshly squeezed lemon juice and honey in a glass or mug, then top with water that's recently boiled but just cooled a little. My taste is generally quite sour, so you may need to double or even triple the quantity of honey. The result feels throat-repairing (even if only temporarily) and easily does instead of tea at breakfast time.

juice of ½ to 1 lemon
1 teaspoon honey

Hot toddy

Of course, lemon, honey, and hot water is even more "medicinal" if finished off with a tot of whiskey. The vitamin C for health, the honey to soothe, the alcohol to numb . . .

Hot buttered rum

This has a real security-blanket feel to it. Mix the butter in a glass with the brown sugar and add the rum, then top with hot water and drop in the cinnamon. Add a tiny grating of nutmeg to finish if you like.

1 thin slice of butter
1 teaspoon brown sugar
1 generous tot of dark rum
1 cinnamon stick
freshly grated nutmeg (optional)

Eggnog

It was snuffling round the leftovers on Boxing Day that got me into this. I'd eaten a few cold sausages and a couple of potato croquettes, but what I really had my eye on was the brandy sauce left over from the pudding. Would it be acceptable to drink it straight from the jug? Well, no one was looking . . . That's when it crossed my mind that eggnog—at its simplest a combination of raw eggs, brandy, milk, and perhaps some cream—is nothing more than raw custard spiked with alcohol. Why had I always been so put off by the idea? It is particularly suited to cosseting you through the sort of sniffly, dark weekend afternoons when you're in a robe pretending to be far more under the weather than you actually feel, not eating very much, and not intending to leave the house again until Monday. It is also good when there is present wrapping to be done.

Americans are big on eggnog and have dozens of variations on the theme. I like mine with brandy best and prefer to beat the yolk and white separately, as it gives a better texture. They have a comforting nursery feel, probably because they're reminiscent of the mug of hot milk with sugar and an egg stirred in that parents used to feed children before they went to bed, and, perhaps because they feel nourishing, they are dangerously easy to gulp back.

This recipe makes two restrained or one very greedy portion, so serve either in a pair of small tumblers or wineglasses or in a tall Collins glass.

Beat the egg yolk with half the sugar until pale. Beat the egg white until stiff, add the remaining sugar, and beat to glossy soft peaks. Combine the milk, cream, spirit, and egg yolk mixture. Fold in the egg white, pour into glasses, and top with nutmeg or cinnamon if you feel like it (I never do).

1 egg, separated
scant ¼ cup superfine sugar
scant ¾ cup milk
3 tablespoons heavy cream
1 ounce brandy or rum
freshly grated nutmeg or ground cinnamon (optional)

Brandy Alexander

Cream cocktails are not everyone's bag, but sometimes, after a cold-turkey sandwich supper, say, the sweetness is just what you need. The only bad thing about this classic is that it calls for crème de cacao, cocoa bean liqueur, which all too easily becomes one of those nuisance bottles that fills your cupboard and is taken out only once or twice a year, so make sure you really like it if you make the investment.

1 part brandy
1 part crème de cacao
1 part heavy cream

Shake all the ingredients with ice and strain into a cocktail glass.

Baileys

No one likes Baileys. That's what they all say, anyway. Yet oddly when I had a bottle at home once, a former flatmate admitted: "I hope you don't mind, but we drank a bit of your Baileys last night. And the other week too . . . " A bit? They had finished it. And I hadn't had so much as a glassful. I also notice that Baileys—creamy, sweet, and unctuous, and poured over lots of ice to give it some edge—is what women begin to buy toward last call in the bar when they think no one is looking. I don't know why everyone should be so embarrassed about it. Baileys is like a whiskey version of the brandy Alexander cocktail—it's made with cream, Irish whiskey, cocoa nibs, vanilla, and caramel—and though it feels as if it has been around forever, was only actually launched in 1975. As well as being a great end-of-evening drink, it is also delicious in ice cream. If you have an ice-cream maker, just make a white-chocolate or vanilla ice cream and chuck in a few good slugs of it.

IN FROM THE COLD: WARMING UP AFTER WALKS ACROSS FROZEN FIELDS

Chile aside, and disregarding temperature, ginger is one of the most warming things you can eat or drink. If you are the riding, shooting, or fishing type, a ginger wine or a whiskey mac—the British counterpart of the American bourbon and ginger—would be the best thing you could put in your hip flask. And even if you are not, it is probably worth taking yourself off on a long, lonely walk across some frozen, frosty fields to enjoy the vigorous spread of ginger's heat either while you're out or as a reward once back home.

Ginger wine

Ginger wine is made by fermenting currants or raisins, then adding various spices such as cloves and saffron and, of course, the eponymous ginger. People often talk about "green ginger wine," which has nothing to do with its color (though it is usually sold in green bottles) and everything to do with the old culinary habit of referring to fresh ginger as "green ginger." The name has stuck, even though ground ginger is often used to make it today. The two biggest and best-known brands in Britain are Crabbie's, which has some of the sharpness of biting into crystallized stem ginger, and Stone's (which uses ground ginger), which by comparison tastes more like baked gingerbread.

This traditional British drink is lovely neat, but it is also famously used in a whiskey mac.

Whiskey mac

This is one of those cocktails that, by virtue of a   *2 parts blended whiskey*
cosy name and warm demeanor, somehow have   *1 part ginger wine*
honorary cup-of-tea status and are considered
harmless enough to drink before the sun is
quite over the yardarm.

Just mix the whisky and ginger wine and
pour over ice into a small tumbler.

A SIP OF SOMETHING BY THE FIRE

A word on whiskey

Whiskey is a spirit to which I always come with a sense of reverence. This is not just because of the taste, in which you find hints of the icy sea spume and peat bogs of the wild landscape in which it is made. It's also because, of all drinks, this is the one I associate either with hard drinking and hard men or with serious conversation and contemplation. No doctor I have spoken to has ever been able to confirm the suspicion many of us hold that different drinks affect our brain in different ways, so perhaps the reverse is true: we turn to certain drinks according to our mood. If you were hoping to set the world to rights over a late-night drink, a decent scotch might well be something you would pour. It certainly feels appropriately intellectual: a drink you can wrestle with, linger over, and appreciate with all its nooks and crannies.

There is a historical association between whiskey and thinkers and writers, many of whom drank to excess. Dylan Thomas's last words are said, apocryphally perhaps, to have been "I've just had eighteen straight whiskeys, I think that's the record." Winston Churchill and Graham Greene were also keen whiskey drinkers. Greene wasn't always persnickety about flavor, though. In his novel *The Human Factor* he has the double agent Maurice Castle drink J&B whiskey, the better to be secretive about the level of his alcohol consumption. "He always bought J&B because of its color," writes Greene. "A large whiskey and soda looked no stronger than a weak one of another brand."

Whiskey drinkers are usually more precise in their likes and dislikes. They know exactly what mood will suit a blend (which is composed from both barley and grain whiskeys, are precise about when they will have a vatted malt (made only from malted barley but a blend from several distilleries), or when only a single malt (a whiskey made from malted barley in a single distillery) will do.

They will also have run their palates across the heather-covered hills, the glens, and the craggy coastlines of the Scottish landscape and worked out which area makes malts that please them the most. They will be aware that Islay, the southernmost island of the Inner Hebrides, is famed for the pungent, iodinelike, smoky peat smell of its whiskeys; that the Lowlands produce some of the most delicate and floral; that Speyside in the east of the mainland is said to produce some of the most complex. And they will know about the imprint that the oak, whether it is an old sherry cask or a bourbon barrel, will leave on the spirit.

For the whiskey drinker, there is very much to consider—it is a subject that requires an entire volume of its own. Suffice to say that when you are drinking whiskey, one of the choices you will have to make is how: straight up, on the rocks, or with a little cold water. I usually go with water, which I serve on the side in a small milk pitcher so that people can pour their own, because woe betide you if you get it wrong in someone else's glass. The reason is that water, not being as cold as ice, allows you to taste the spirit better, and diluting it slightly does seem to make the flavor bloom and express itself more eloquently.

A handful of my favorite whiskeys, a list that grows longer every time I taste more, would include the following: Highland Park 12 years old, a heathery, sophisticated, beautifully defined Orkney single malt; Ardbeg 10 years old, an Islay with a smoky, marine tingle and satisfying sense of completeness; and the Macallan Sherry Oak 10 years old, for the spicy, panforte-like, Christmasy feel the sherry casks bring to the spirit.

Cognac versus Armagnac

Brandy is a spirit distilled from fermented grape juice (though the word is often applied to spirits made from other fruits, such as apples). It can be made anywhere in the world—I have had some pretty decent stuff from Spain—but the finest comes from France, from two neighboring regions.

Cognac and Armagnac are like the town mouse and the country mouse of the brandy world. Cognac has sophistication and finesse, as suave as a man in a Savile Row suit, all neatly pressed and ironed into shape. Its smell is smooth and sweetly woody, like continental aftershave, and it seems burnished, like a finely polished piece of old mahogany. Armagnac, the country mouse, is not such an elegant fellow, but he has a lot of character. If he were a piece of furniture, he'd be a solid oak kitchen table, sturdy and beautifully carved, that has been in the family for years, seen a lot of spillages and a lot of raucous dinners, and come out of them intact but not unmarked. Armagnac is not just more rustic; it is throaty. You can feel its guts, the hot fire, almost hear the stories that would be told over a glass of it. You can probably tell that's where my heart is, but the consensus is that cognac is the finer, leaving Armagnac looking just a little too yokel to compete.

The reasons for the differing taste are several. Cognac is mostly made from the ugni blanc grape, which is known in Italy as *trebbiano* and makes quite undistinguished wine (its distillate is clearly a different matter). The cognac vineyards are in western France, north of Bordeaux, in the Charente and Charente-Maritime, and spill into the Dordogne and Deux-Sèvres. And the spirit is double distilled, a batch at a time, in a copper-pot still, before being matured in oak, which soaks through the spirit, filling out its flavor.

Armagnac is made among the narrow lanes and quiet hills of Gascony, to the south of Bordeaux, very often in tiny quantities by small family producers. It is also made from ugni blanc, but significant amounts of two other grapes, colombard and folle blanche, are also used. It is distilled just once, in a number of different ways, sometimes like cognac, sometimes in continuous or semicontinuous stills, through which the wine can keep running before it goes into barrels. Armagnac needs years before it gives and softens enough to show its true pedigree, but when you do sip an old one, with its distant flavors of prunes and forests, the extraordinary thing is that it never tastes its age.

Finally, forget about those ostentatious and cumbersome balloon-shaped glasses: brandy likes to be drunk out of a glass that allows some, but not too much, of the drink to evaporate. As ever, you can buy the ideal shape from a specialist, but a good wineglass that curves in at the top will do.

Regarding labels, here are a few pointers. Cognac must have been aged in oak for two years before it's released and, in ascending order of quality, it may be marked *three star* or *VS* (*Very Special*, meaning its youngest spirit is at least two years old); *VSOP* (*Very Special Old Pale*, meaning the youngest element must be at least four years old); *Napoleon*, *XO* or *Hors d'Âge* (youngest element at least six years old). For Armagnac, three star must be more than two years old, VSOP over five, and XO over six, but you will frequently come across much older spirits than that.

erry Christmas Merry Christma

SOMETHING DIFFERENT

After the gluttonous feasting of Christmas and New Year, Thai, Chinese, and Japanese food provide a change of pace and a fillip of interest, and they aren't stodgy or rich. The drinks that go with them are similarly refreshing.

Lychee "martinis"

In his *Oxford Companion to Food*, Alan Davidson tells us that in China in the first century A.D., "a special courier service with swift horses was set up to bring fresh lychees from Canton north to the Imperial Court." Later, during the Ming dynasty, special lychee clubs met in temples to gorge themselves silly on the fruit so prized that it has moved countless Chinese poets to rhapsodic verse. We don't quite seem to appreciate the lychee in the same way. It is an odd creature: pocked brittle skin that seems to belong to a prehistoric reptile, and slippery, pale flesh that looks a bit like an eyeball torn from its socket. It's the smell that gets you—haunting and fragile, like a nightingale's song. Or at least that's how you start to think after a few lychee "martinis." (Strictly speaking it isn't correct to use the term *martini* for fruit vodka drinks, but it's become common practice to do so, and I've stuck with it because it sounds more appealing.) The concept here is simple: take the fruit, peel, stone, blend, strain to remove bits of shell and lumps, add about the same amount or slightly more vodka from the freezer, shake with ice, and strain into cocktail glasses. You could use canned lychees, but though they give a more robust drink, there is no refinement. Fresh ones (available in Asian markets) have much more fragrance and produce a more ethereal, "homemade" taste. I like to drink this before eating a bowl of noodles or a fresh stir-fry—or the Thai wraps detailed opposite.

Lemongrass vodka

Vodka infusions are easy to make, and this is no exception. Take one stalk of lemongrass (the size you buy in the supermarket, not the longer ones you find at Thai grocers) for every quarter bottle of vodka, bash it a couple of times with a rolling pin to break the skin, and drop into the vodka. Leave to steep for about three days at room temperature, then pop the vodka into the freezer. You can either pour it into a tumbler over ice or shake with ice and serve martini-style in cocktail glasses. I sometimes make this if I'm eating chicken marinated in nam pla, lime juice and chile, or a Thai salad.

Thai wraps

These are the perfect thing to eat after lychee "martinis" or lemongrass vodka. I like communal food that can be eaten with your fingers, and as most of this can be prepped in advance and the wrapping up is done at the table as people eat, it leaves plenty of time for making drinks and chatting. Before cooking the meat, you should mix the dressing and chop up all the accompaniments, then you can put the hot ingredients on the table as soon as they are done and let people get on with it. Two different animal proteins will usually be enough, but if you're cooking for larger numbers, you could introduce more variety. The quantities here will feed four hungry people—I usually bank on each person eating three or so wraps. When

1 package Thai rice paper
  wraps

For the Thai dressing:
2 tablesoons nam pla
juice of 2 limes
1 stalk lemongrass, finely
  chopped
1 tablespoon olive oil
1 small red chile, finely
  chopped

rolling my wraps, I never put all the fillings in each one—I love to have chicken with basil and mango, for example, and beef tenderloin with spring onions and cucumber.

Thai rice paper wraps are made, as you'd imagine, from rice, water, and salt. They come in hard, round sheets that become pliable and sticky when soaked briefly in water and can be found at many Asian markets.

Thai marinated beef or chicken

Combine the marinade ingredients, mix with the meat, making sure that all surfaces are well coated, and then cover and let stand for 3 hours. When ready to eat, heat a small amount of vegetable oil in a frying pan. The chicken should stir-fry in 5 minutes or so. Let the steak have a couple of minutes on each side, less if it's not very thick, then let stand for 5 minutes before cutting into slices.

For the marinade:
1 red chile, seeded and
    finely chopped
2 stalks lemongrass
    (or 1 long one if bought
    at a Thai supermarket),
    finely chopped
2 garlic cloves, pressed
    or finely chopped
juice of 1 lime
1 tablespoon nam pla

10 ounces beef tenderloin,
    left whole, or 2 skinless,
    boneless chicken breasts,
    cut into strips

Sesame chicken or pork

Heat the oil in frying pan or wok. Throw in the chicken or pork. Cook, stirring occasionally, for 5 minutes. Add the sesame seeds and ginger and continue stirring until the seeds turn golden and the meat is cooked. Turn into a warmed dish and serve.

1 tablespoon dark
    sesame oil
2 skinless, boneless chicken
    breasts, or 10 ounces
    pork fillet, cut into strips
2 tablespoons sesame seeds
3 thin slices fresh ginger,
    peeled and finely chopped

Shrimp with garlic

Stir-fry the shrimp and garlic in olive oil until the shrimp turn solidly pink. Turn into a hot dish and serve.

20 raw shrimp, peeled
2 garlic cloves, pressed
olive oil

Accompaniments

Put all the vegetable ingredients in separate bowls and lay out on the table, together with the rice paper wraps and a bowl of warm water. Let the guests make their own packages. It's easy once you get going: just dip the wraps in the water for about 30 minutes, shake dry, put on a plate, fill the center with a selection of protein and vegetables, and spoon on a little Thai dressing. Fold over the bottom of the wrap, then roll up and eat with your fingers.

½ cucumber, washed but not peeled, cut into 2-inch-long batons
2 large carrots, cut into slim batons
1 bunch spring onions, coarsely chopped
1 bunch Thai basil leaves
1 bunch Thai mint leaves
1 bunch cilantro
1 package rice vermicelli, soaked in hot water for 20 minutes, then drained
1 handful kumquats, halved (optional)
2 large handfuls baby spinach leaves, washed and cut into shreds (optional)
1 unripe mango, peeled, sliced, and cut into pieces (optional)

Coming to grips with sake

Never ask anyone how sake used to be made if you are just about to sip it. I made this mistake. "They didn't know about yeast in Japan two thousands years ago," sake expert Wakana Omija told me. "But they did know that if you chew rice and spit it out, then leave it for a while, it becomes a drink."

Two things, Wakana: Why would anyone chew rice and spit it out? And if they did, why in the name of ten thousand wave paintings would anyone come along and think, my, that saliva-filled basin of semi-masticated grain looks tasty—I think I'll have a glassful? Wakana looks taken aback. "I don't know, but according to all the ancient literature that is how it was made. It was considered a very special drink that was offered to the gods and drunk by royals and emperors."

It certainly puts squeamishness about people with corns, warts, and cheesy-smelling feet treading grapes to make wine into perspective. This information could cause a serious sake setback, particularly for those whose first or perhaps only experience of the drink has been in Chinese restaurants where they feed you small, unwelcome cups of something warm and brown that is curiously redolent of lamp oil. So I had better say right now that quality sake is an altogether different and quite delicious thing, which you would be more likely to compare to bitter almonds, lychees, cypress, or, because both have that strange character known either romantically as umami or censoriously as MSG, a glass of sherry.

Sake varies enormously in style, as Wakana points out. She was born in Japan but now lives in California, where she works for a (very good) sake brand called Akashi-Tai. "Back in San Francisco they can handle the traditional hardcore sakes like honjozo genshu, which is rich and ricey and also popular in Japan. In Europe people tend to prefer the lighter, more floral ones that are best drunk chilled, like white wine. Daiginjo is a good place to begin."

Sake terminology can seem impenetrable when you first encounter it but is not that difficult to come to grips with. Premium sake is graded according to how much the rice has been "polished," a word that conjures up a Grimm Brothers-go-to-the-Orient vision of tens of thousands of enslaved geishas rubbing painstakingly away at individual grains of rice until they acquire a satisfactory sheen. Actually, *polished* in this case really means "milled." In the strains of rice used in sake production, the starch tends to be concentrated at the heart of the grain, while the fats and proteins are toward the periphery. The more the rice is polished, the more fat is shed and the purer the starch content becomes. Sake made from highly polished rice may taste intense, but its character will also be more delicate, floral, fragrant, and refined.

To make honjozo, the rice must be milled so that no more than 70 percent of the grain remains. In ginjo there must be no more than 60 percent and in daiginjo—the style recommended by Wakana for sake beginners—no more than 50 percent, although sometimes the rice will be milled so that as little as 35 percent remains. Some of these daiginjo sakes are so soft and peachy they remind me of creamy silk lingerie. There is often also a refreshing hint of lemon.

I once tasted a sake that claimed to have broken polishing records: gently, gently, for fear of its collapsing into dust (for truly good sake it is important that the grain not break, though it's rumored that some commercially minded producers mill the rice down to earn the classification and then throw in the bits they have ground off to save money), the rice had been reduced to a mere 19 percent of its original size. The resulting sake, called Isake 19, was butterfly-wings delicate but had detailing worthy of a grand master and a taste that lingered for ages after you had swallowed. It was mind-blowingly expensive, though—the equivalent of hundreds of dollars a bottle. The price, its producers explained, was the result not only of the high waste of rice but also of the intricate milling process. "It takes five days to reduce rice to 50 percent of its initial size. But to get it to 19 percent, you need not eight days, as you might presume, but ten, because it must be done so carefully."

Once it has been milled, the rice is washed, soaked, and steamed, and then two things happen at once. Rice harboring a microbe called *koji-kin*, apparently similar to that used when making blue cheese, is added, which releases enzymes that convert the rice starch to sugars that can be fermented. And sake yeast is added, along with water, so that fermentation can happen at the same time.

Finished sake will generally have an alcohol content of around 20 percent abv. If it is bottled neat, it is termed *genshu*. I prefer those that are diluted with water to take them down to about 16 percent abv. Just to make things even more complicated, some sake has extra alcohol added— this is called *honjozo*. A sake that has no added alcohol and is made only from rice, koji, and water is known as *junmai*, while a "regular" sake, one that does not fall into any of the special designations, is known as *futushu*.

How to drink sake

The temperature at which a sake is served is not an indication of quality or lack of it, but a matter of style and to some extent preference. I like to have a lighter, daiginjo straight from the fridge, much as you would a white wine, while a heavier, fuller, richer sake can taste better either at room temperature or slightly warmed. The label on the bottle will usually offer some advice. You could drink sake out of small wineglasses—the light, chilled styles work particularly well this way—or invest in shallow clay cups similar to those you might see in a Japanese restaurant. The cup is usually placed inside a lacquered wooden box and filled so that it overflows—traditionally a sign of the host's generosity. You then drink the sake from the cup, before tackling the liquid in the lacquered box.

What to eat with sake

Sake is becoming better known in the West thanks to the popularity of sushi bars and the ever more fashionable Japanese restaurants. I forced myself to try the more refined incarnations of sake, despite the scalding experience of those early lamp-oil forays, after a friend with a knack for alighting on the latest genuinely good thing said that when he goes to Manhattan on business the first thing he does after getting out of his taxi from JFK is to get some sushi and a glass of sake.

It is important to drink sake in context, though this need not always mean having it with Asian food. One London department store added a sake (Isake Classic, specially designed for learner palates) to the menu in their oyster and champagne bar, and the combination works well as long as you steer clear of lemon juice or vinaigrette, whose acidity throws the whole thing awry. It's nice to see the drink stepping beyond the ethnic ghetto. But sake is never going to taste good with shepherd's pie, or boeuf bourguignon. This makes it a tricky thing to have at home, so I asked Wakana for some easy food suggestions to eat with sake.

She said that she often makes a bowl of ricey soup. "It's very simple: you just take three parts of water and two of ponzu, a kind of citrusy sauce, heat them, and pour them over a bowl of sushi rice. It's a great hangover cure." For lazy Saturday afternoons she suggested a stir-fry made with anything that's leftover in the fridge and throwing in some raw spinach or bok choy, onions, and perhaps some chicken or thinly sliced beef. Or, she added, "I might grill some salmon and instead of hollandaise serve it with a wasabi vinaigrette." (Her recipe follows.)

Chicken marinated overnight in a teriyaki sauce, grilled and served with edamame, is a delicious combination with a peachy glass of sake as well. And, oysters aside, there are some Western foods that sit beautifully next to it, in particular cured hams—hardly surprising when you think how nice a plate of serrano is with a glass of sherry, which shares the same salty umami quality. Tuna tartare, or carpaccio of tuna with olive oil and spring onions, is also good.

Wakana had one final word on Japanese table etiquette. "We never pass food directly chopstick to chopstick," she says, observing me passing someone a piece of food to try. "That's because after a cremation it's customary to take a piece of bone out of the ashes and pass it around the table, stick to stick." I won't be doing that again.

Wakana's broiled salmon, wasabi vinaigrette, and rice salad

The vinaigrette is best made with Japanese soy sauce, rather than the stronger Chinese version. Serves two.

Cook the rice according to the instructions on the package, allow to cool, and mix it with the other salad ingredients. Broil the salmon for 10 minutes or until cooked, turning halfway through. Shake the vinaigrette ingredients together and serve on the side. Eat with a glass of chilled daiginjo.

For the rice salad:
1 small red onion,
  thinly sliced
5 ounces sushi rice
1 handful fresh cilantro,
  chopped
3 handfuls baby spinach
  leaves, shredded

2 pieces salmon fillet
  or red snapper

For the vinaigrette:
1 teaspoon wasabi
1 tablespoon rice vinegar
1 tablespoon light soy
  sauce
2 tablespoons olive oil

Saketini

This is one of those magical drinks that is just so much more than the sum of its parts. Aromatic, herbaceous, and with a real edge where the gin and the sake meet and spark off each other, it's strangely hard, unless you know, to tell what you are drinking. When I order it in Zuma in Knightsbridge, I always ask for salt chile squid to go with it. It's a great combination, but it's also one I can't be bothered to make myself, so at home I settle for store-bought spring rolls.

Shake both ingredients with ice and strain into a cocktail glass.

1 part Tanqueray Ten, from the freezer

2 parts daiginjo or ginjo sake, chilled

ICE AND SNOW

How rough do you like your vodka?
In November 2006 the BBC's Russian affairs analyst reported that Osman Paragulgov, head of Russia's union of wine and spirit producers, was lobbying for the introduction of something he called "social vodka," a regulated spirit to feed the appetites of those too poor to buy the real thing.

If this sounds like a dipsomaniac's approach to welfare provision, behind it lay a brutal reality. The previous month a clutch of Siberian towns had announced a state of emergency after nearly 900 people were hospitalized with liver failure after drinking counterfeit vodka. The annual death rate across the country for those poisoned by industrial solvents passed off as vodka was estimated at around 42,000. The question you might ask is why the pungent smell of window cleaner or antirust solution as a glass is raised to the lips does not give the game away. Part of the answer is that often it is not drunk for pleasure but to facilitate obliteration.

The writer Vitali Vitaliev once spent an evening showing me how to drink vodka "the Russian way," as he put it, a procedure that involved exhaling, gulping back a shot, and downing a mouthful of gherkin or pickled cabbage before inhaling again. This was, he said, the best method of getting the spirit, all too often ferociously harsh, down without tasting it. I couldn't quite decide if he was putting me on when he said that if no pickles were available, it would be acceptable to pick up a scraggy alley cat and bury your nose in its matted fur instead. He also became quite passionate when it was suggested that some of us drink because we actually like the flavor of the stuff we are swallowing. "Your taste buds have been perverted by the Western drinking culture!" he cried.

No doubt Vitaliev would have got on splendidly with Prince Harry, who was once photographed by the tabloids snorting vodka up his nostril, a method of ingestion that ingeniously bypasses the taste buds, thus dispensing with the need for an old tabby. I take the old-fashioned view that if you're going to have a drink, you may as well enjoy it.

Even real vodka can be pretty rough, though. Vodka is a white spirit that is distilled, in some places, from the by-products of oil refining or wood-pulp processing, neither of which sounds delicious. Fortunately EU regulations require it to be made from "alcohol of agricultural origin." Complaining that they did not think the drink ought to be an "alcoholic wastebucket," three countries—Finland, Sweden, and Poland—from the so-called "vodka belt" recently attempted to have this definition restricted to the traditional but not traditionally desperate ingredients of grain and potato. They were unsuccessful: today you can buy vodka made from all sorts of ingredients, from grapes (for example, the French brand, Cîroc, which many argue ought to be a brandy or grappa) to molasses or soybeans.

I think you can sometimes taste what a vodka has been made from: rye, for example, gives a particularly savory, caraway-like taste, while the molasses used in many cheap store brands gives a more throaty spirit with little nuance or precision. But unless the vodka is flavored, what makes arguably the biggest difference is its purity, achieved by redistilling (and sometimes redistilling again) and filtering. Precisely what it is filtered through has a big impact; it is commonly passed through activated charcoal (*activated* here means chemically treated so it is more absorbent). This is why vodka people make the most enormous fuss about purity. The word *vodka* is suggestive of cleansing—it comes from the diminutive of the Russian word for water. And with expensive vodka the emphasis is never on taste, always on lack of taste. You hear a lot of "Distilled three times, then washed in spring water," "Made using water from an ancient sandstone aquifer," "Filtered through quartz sand," and so on. I expect if you had a mind to drink vodka made using liquid from a freshwater spring in the crater of a subaquatic volcano five miles beneath the waves of the Atlantic, distilled seven times and then further purified by passing it through the Dalai Lama's small intestine, you would probably find someone prepared to sell you it somewhere. At a price.

Up to a point it is a good idea to create vodkas so refined that they don't attack your palate like a pitbull with a man's arm between its teeth, or taste so horrible they are, literally, indistinguishable from industrial solvents. But unless you're going to be drinking the spirit neat, either as a shot or in a martini, very pure vodka is not only an expensive way of doing things; it's not even always the best.

Vodka began its fashionable ascent in the West only after the Russian Revolution of 1917, when distilleries were confiscated by the Bolsheviks and many vodka distillers fled, with the intention of carrying on their trade in the West. One of these was Vladimir Smirnov, who, on arrival in France, changed the spelling of his name to *Smirnoff*. The first Smirnoff-branded distillery was set up in America in 1934, but it was not until after the Second World War, when the colorless, clean-smelling drink began to be seen as something attractively modern, that it really caught on. Vodka's lack of flavor made it an ideal mixer in cocktails of all kinds.

In some ways, our method of drinking vodka is not so different from that described by Vitaliev: we merely substitute cranberry juice for cat fur to mask the taste of the alcohol. But vodka brands have become a fashion statement for which some are willing to pay extortionate prices. Some bars exploit this, topping up their expensive, branded bottles with cheap spirit, safe in the knowledge that none of their customers will be able to tell.

When making cocktails at home, I use brands such as Smirnoff, which might not be exciting neat but are more than good enough for the cocktail job, because they don't have off-flavors that might spoil the balance of the drink and aren't ludicrously expensive.

If drinking it with tonic (which I rarely do), I go even further and say, almost heretically, the cheaper the better. With tonic water—and I will accept only the best tonic water—I will actually drink the cheapest vodka you can find. Vaguely reminiscent of petroleum? No problem. A slight hint of old potatoes? Perfectly fine. A scraping, fiery texture with a good old burn on the back of the throat? Bring it on. Unless you have something you can taste through the quinine and sweetener in the tonic, what on earth would be the point?

How to taste posh vodka

Tasting vodka is a little like tasting bottled mineral water: it's all about texture and nuance, and it's surprising how much your palate can discern when you are drinking it neat. Some vodka feels very precise and hard-edged, like a diamond; others feel more splurgy and fluent. Some are silkily soft; others rasp. Some taste like the alcoholic equivalent of tap water that's not obviously chlorinated. That is, you think, "Yes, it just tastes like vodka; there's no other tasting note."

The two unflavored vodkas I keep in my freezer for drinking neat or as martinis are Russian Standard, which is made from wheat grain and "pure glacial water from the frozen north" (this stuff is unavoidable). It has a smooth texture but a pleasing viscosity—fat and oily, in a good way—and some breadth. It is extremely good with raw or smoked fish and, because of the mouthfeel, works well with fatty fish such as tuna belly. If in the mood for something lighter, sharper, and fresher, I also have Belvedere. This is distilled and bottled in Poland, made from 100 percent rye grain, which gives it a sharp, caraway breeziness, and it has the softness of finest angora.

Flavored vodka

A new era for flavored vodka was ushered in by the Swedish firm Absolut back in the 1980s, when it launched Absolut Peppar (a spicy flavored vodka that tastes of chile, herbs, and green tomatoes), which they followed with Absolut Citron, a lemon-flavored vodka that became instantly fashionable. But flavoring vodka is not new. It will come as no surprise to hear that, to mask the clumsiness of early distilled spirits, the Russians and Poles have been doing it for centuries, using a range of natural ingredients that included acorns, horseradish, and watermelon. I sometimes add my own flavorings to vodka (the method follows if you would like to make cranberry or lemongrass vodka). The one commercial flavored vodka that stands out from the rest and that I usually have in my freezer is Zubrówka, from Poland. Made from rye, it is infused with bisongrass, otherwise known as *sweetgrass* because of its intense perfume, and as Holy Grass by the American Indians. The stuff used to flavor Zubrówka is harvested by hand from the Bialowieza Primeval Forest, a stretch of ancient woodland still relatively undisturbed by humans, and it gives the vodka a sweet, meadow scent, as if freshly cut grass and dried grass have been mixed together.

Zubrówka with apple juice

When herbal Zubrówka meets apple juice, an *3 parts fresh apple juice*
extraordinary fusion happens: it's almost as *1 part Zubrówka*
if you can smell cinnamon, or an apple crisp
baking in the oven.

Pour the apple juice and Zubrówka over
plenty of ice. You can also make a longer
drink, by mixing 1 part Zubrówka with 1½
parts apple juice, then topping with sparkling
water. This time a more herbaceous character
comes through—all tarragon and apples—which
is lovely with smoked fish if you're looking for
a nibble.

Making your own cranberry vodka

Fresh cranberries are always around in the supermarkets just before
the holidays, and nothing is simpler than making your own cranberry
vodka. Just use the butt of a rolling pin to lightly crush a large handful of
berries (they should be split but still hold their shape), slip them into a
bottle of vodka, leave them to steep for a few days at room temperature,
then put the bottle in the freezer. This makes a surprisingly strong-
flavored, pleasingly astringent drink that is delicious drunk icy cold in
shot-sized portions.

Scandinavian inspiration: aquavit

Aquavit, the Scandinavian spirit, is like an herbal vodka: strong,
colorless, imbued usually with caraway and sometimes with other herbs
such as dill and cumin. With its lethal alcohol and herbaceous bite, it
tastes as if it were made for fortifying the soul on serious expeditions,

across plains of ice, through landscapes where the only noise is the howling of the wind and the creaking of the snow. Look for Aalborg Akvavit from Denmark and keep it in the freezer.

Food to eat with neat vodkas and aquavit
With a glass of vodka kept at subzero temperatures so that it is not only cold but also viscous, a smorgasbord is delicious. There would have to be blinis—with wild smoked salmon, cod's roe, and caviar if you have a wealthy Russian for a friend. There would be herring, crispbread, sliced egg and gherkins, and perhaps other kinds of smoked fish and meat. If you are drinking aquavit, the gamy, savory taste of bresaola marinated in juniper and dill goes brilliantly—ditch everything else and simply make a bresaola, lemon, and arugula salad as a starter in the ordinary way. If you are going to move on to a main course, then look at recipes that use allspice (a Finnish favorite)—say, meatballs flavored with allspice and served in a creamy sauce.

GLAMOROUS WINE-AND-FOOD COMBINATIONS FOR DARK DAYS

There are certain wines to which we always turn when the days shorten—reds that seem hearty and full of fire, the liquid equivalent of pulling on a sweater against the cold. But here are another couple that are not quite so obvious and that I find leaven the long gap before spring.

Atlantic whites with seafood: albariño and muscadet

The Bibendum Oyster bar lies at a very expensive set of crossroads in South Kensington. Every day for the first eight months of my working life, I walked through it, en route to the upstairs offices of the publishing company where I worked, quite disastrously, as a publicity assistant. I used to love the way the vegetal smell of the cut stalks and pristine blooms at the flower van just outside mixed with the scent of cold seawater from the pink lobsters and fresh oysters at the entrance. Crossing the mosaic-tiled floor of the lobby, headed for my place beside the photocopier, I longed to sit down at a table there, especially in the winter, when the gleam of light off the cutlery, the marble, and the crushed ice piled with fruits de mer seemed to make a virtue of the greyness outside. Though many associate seafood and white wine with summer holidays, they have seemed to me a glamorous thing to eat and drink in the gloom ever since.

Besides champagne and Chablis, which everyone knows, there are two whites that seem made to be drunk with a plate of crustaceans. Atlantic wines, you might call them, and they have an equanimity—a quiet sense of calm with no attention-seeking gusts of shrill flavor—that suits dark, cold months.

Albariño has an affinity for gloom. The grape thrives in Rias Baixas (pronounced "ree-ass by-shass") in Galicia, in the northwest corner of

Spain, where storm clouds come scudding in from the grey ocean to drop their heavy load of rain. Known as *alvarinho* over the border in Portugal, where it is used to make vinho verde, it is veined with refreshing acidity but doesn't screech. It has a fragrance of peach and almond blossom, but instead of reeking, as viognier sometimes does, it has the subtle smell of a garden or hedgerow after rainfall at the beginning of June. It is crisp, but rounded and gloriously aromatic, and sometimes it carries just a vestige of stony minerality and a little bit of quince to ground it.

Albariño has become highly fashionable in the past few years, but it's not until you put it with food that you see how good it can be to drink. Its white fruit character and fragrance go beautifully well with pink prawns and crab claws. The seafood, whether a rich crab tart or hot creamy pots of crab containing the odd little accidental shard of shell, or griddled shrimp with a simple squeeze of juice, benefits from the delicately invigorating wine and in turn blots out any of its sherbet-like edges, making it seem more profound.

With muscadet, it's the yeasty taste, bracing salinity, and texture that marry so well with shellfish. Made from a grape called *melon de Bourgogne* (though muscadet, the name of the wine, has become the grape's synonym) and grown around the mouth of the Loire several hundred miles to the north in France, where the Atlantic also exerts its choppy influence, muscadet is much more of an everyday drink than albariño. Cheap, and with a forthright plainness, it is also a remarkably good value, and much ignored, perhaps because of its prevalence during the 1970s; even at the very bottom end of the price range, it remains a true wine, rather than a manipulated, tweaked piece of commerce. The better (and scarcely any more costly) examples are labeled *sur lie*, indicating that the wine has been bottled directly from its lees, the sediment of dead yeast cells, which gives it more depth, body, and a yeasty flavor. Muscadet can seem very ordinary, but when drunk with a dish of seafood something happens: it carves out a space for itself and you begin to see its focus, minerals, and salt. Just like albariño, against seafood it acquires more stature. In both cases, the result is a simple feast that lights up a dark evening.

A rosé in winter

When it comes to rosé wine, most people drink with their eyes. Or don't drink, in the case of the late Scottish newspaper editor John Junor, who, famously, once had conniptions when he noticed this item on the expense report of one of his correspondents. The issue was not that he felt it improper for a reporter to use expenses to satisfy his thirst—au contraire, he was first of all furious that the journalist in question had ordered a mere half carafe, then livid when he noticed the pinkness. "Only pooves drink rosé," shrieked Junor, at the summit of his rage.

Junor's behavior may have been bizarre, but the idea that rosé might not be very manly was widespread, and it persisted. Among oenophiles, rosé had other difficulties too: it was not—indeed, is still not—considered serious, the ultimate putdown in this snobbish world. In fact, to be seen twirling a glass of salmon-colored liquid by its stem was for a long time considered the height of poor taste.

The long, hot summer of 2003 scorched those cares into oblivion. Suddenly, all anyone wanted to do after a day of sun was sit around slaking their thirst with summery, feel-good glasses of rosé. To general amazement, rosé didn't just catch on for a season; it became more popular every year, even in darkest December.

The first thing most look at is the color, which might be any hue from the very palest vin gris of France, whose ghostly pink is so light as to be, as the name suggests, almost grey, to peachy salmon, lucent red currant, or a strident fuchsia deeper and darker than some wines officially classified as red. Of course not everyone sees it quite so poetically. A colleague who writes for the *Yorkshire Post* describes shades of rosé variously as "ballet shoes, faded ballet shoes, old greying granny underwear . . . ," though for some reason these descriptors never seem to make it out of her personal notebook and into print.

In Provence, where rosé accounts for almost 80 percent of the region's vinous output, at the Centre de Recherche et d'Expérimentation sur le Vin Rosé, color is studied intently, with special kits produced so that winemakers can match up their rosé shade for shade, like interior decorators do with paint and Pantone charts.

Rosé wine takes its color from the skins of the red grapes from which it is made. Virtually all grapes, whether red or white, have clear juice, so the depth and shade of color depends principally on two things: the pigmentation of the particular grape variety and the amount of time the winemaker lets the grape skins macerate. There are still mysteries about how exactly one wine ends up the color of a squashed raspberry, another more like a cherry stain. As Nathalie Pouzalgues, a technician at the Provençal research center, explains, "We've made the same process of vinification with the same type of grapes—but you end up with different colors of wine. We know there's a link between color and acidity. We also think that soil must make a difference. But we can't explain all the things we observe."

So much for the practical side of it. John Junor aside, the psychology of wine color is even more peculiar. I would hardly believe this unless I had tried it, but if you drink the same rosé out of two glasses, one transparent, the other opaque black (such glasses are made to sharpen the palates of blind tasters by removing the clues offered by color), the rosé that you can see tastes . . . I can only describe it as pinker. It seems more fruity, and the red currant, strawberry, or wild cherry notes appear more emphatic. It's all in the mind, of course, but the effect is there nonetheless.

But it is not only the grapes that are affected by terroir. So are humans. Some winemakers know their customers so well that they deliberately make different colors of rosé for different markets, and the worse the

weather, the darker people seem to like their wine. "We've certainly found that in the north of France they seem to prefer deeper colors of rosés," Nathalie says. Well, that figures. In the summer sunshine I love nothing better than a rosé from Provence that's so pale it is barely there and has a gentle smell of sandalwood and damp hay. Actually, in terms of taste those are my favorite rosés anyway. But in the cold, grey drizzle of most English seasons I am drawn to a color that is more cheery and robust—something with a bit more red in its cheeks. The most appealing winter rosés are the deepest-colored—geranium hues that stand out against bleak, icy weather. It's not all about color either: the flavor tends to be more strident, too, with a little more tannin and grip, thanks to the longer skin contact. When it's cold and damp outside, this chunky slice of chilled wine is a real pick-me-up. Look to the Languedoc for midcolored, fragranced rosés made from negrette and caladoc. For real verve, the New World has all the answers: malbec rosé from Argentina, or the leap of a pinot noir rosé from the antipodes, for example, though I also like the sour-cherry, savory tang of rosé blends from Italy.

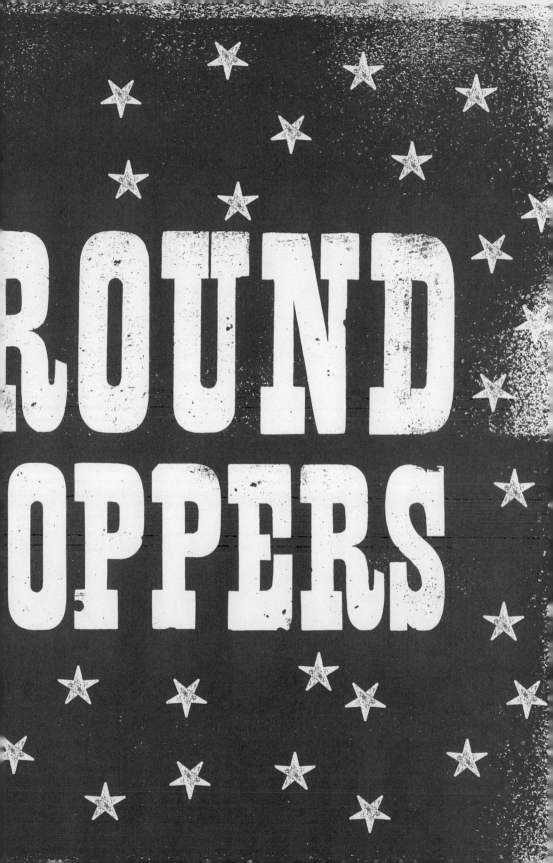

This chapter contains all those drinks so iconic they transcend seasonal drinking and in all cases so damn good that you want them for their own sake, never mind what the weather is doing. I could have added more (it was with many pangs that I allowed sherry to be contained in the autumn chapter and prosecco in spring), but these are the ones that made the final cut. Madame Bollinger, one of champagne's grande dames, used to say of that French sparkling wine, "I drink it when I am happy and when I am sad. Sometimes I drink it when I am alone. When I have company, I consider it obligatory. I trifle with it if I'm not hungry and drink it if I am. Otherwise I never touch it—unless I am thirsty." You might easily be moved to say the same about any of the drinks in this chapter.

THE MARTINI

Debates on strength

If there were only one cocktail, it would have to be the martini. The name alone glints with hard-edged glamour, and the image of its straight-sided glass, flaring out from a single point, is evocative of an evening ill spent.

No other drink has inspired such reverent-to-the-point-of-absurdity loyalty, and no other causes feelings to run so high. Here, for example, is the essayist Bernard DeVoto: "You can no more keep a martini in the refrigerator than you can keep a kiss there. The proper union of gin and vermouth is a great and sudden glory." People have managed to write entire books on what is, after all, no more than a two-ingredient drink, served very cold, sometimes with a bit of lemon peel or an olive floating in it. I even have a book that charts the history of the martini by presidential era, though that seems marginally less strange when you

consider the controversy that arose during Jimmy Carter's presidential campaign in 1976: he complained about the businessman's habitual "$50 martini lunch," a phrase that soon reported as the "three-martini lunch"—and hundreds of outraged Americans wrote in to the papers to take issue with him.

I'm with Jimmy Carter on this, though. Three martinis? Who could walk, let alone work, after that? As the not-exactly-drink-shy Dorothy Parker famously remarked, "I like to have a martini/ Two at the very most./ After three I'm under the table,/ After four I'm under the host!"

And so we come to the heart of the matter. You can dress it up any way you like. You can talk about a "dry martini" (that's drinkers' code for homoeopathic quantities of vermouth and lots of spirit, please). You can quote Winston Churchill and decree grandly that merely glancing across the room at the bottle provides the requisite amount of vermouth to make the cocktail. But you have to work hard to get away from the fact that asking for a martini today is merely a socially acceptable way of asking for a bottle of gin—hold the brown paper bag—and could it come direct from the freezer, rather than its hiding place in the corner of the wardrobe, please? And drinking virtually neat gin is an act that tends to be frowned upon otherwise in most middle-class circles. I'm not saying a martini isn't a wonderful drink. But it is somehow elevated by the ceremonies we perform around it and, as if to excuse ourselves for drinking something that comes so close to being neat white spirit, we seem to have spent the past century talking away its lethal potency.

One of my favorite pieces of writing on the martini is found in David A. Embury's *The Fine Art of Mixing Drinks* (first published in America in 1948; I have the revised British edition from 1958). Embury is not convinced the drinks he calls the Vermouth Rinse and the Vermouth Spray are actually martinis. (The first is made by rinsing a cocktail glass with vermouth, then pouring it back in the bottle before adding gin; the second by using an atomizer to add a mist of vermouth to a glassful

of spirit.) But he does engage in a vigorous, full-page discussion on "When Is a Martini Strong?" With more precise mathematics than most would be able to deploy after drinking a martini, he seeks to explain the difference in alcoholic strength of a martini made with 3 parts gin to 1 part vermouth compared to one made with 7 parts gin and 1 part vermouth. Consider the problem for a moment and see what you think. The initial reflex is to assume that a 3:1 martini is roughly half as strong as a 7:1 martini, but wait: in the 7:1 you are not doubling the proportion of gin, only upping it from three-quarters to seven-eighths, which is far less of a shift. Then you must consider that the vermouth is not alcohol-free. "I have asked dozens of my friends how much difference they thought there was," writes Embury. "Two classes of people—chemists and accountants—give the correct answer: practically none." I won't reproduce his calculations here, but he works it out as a difference of 2 to 2.5 percent abv—nothing!

Embury's words underscore another point: don't expect anyone to agree about how dry a martini should be. He tells us that "the usual recipe book specifies one-third vermouth and two-thirds gin." However, in Hemingway's *Across the River and into the Trees*, the colonel, drinking in Venice with his nineteen-year-old girlfriend, orders, in typically macho style, something rather more ginny: "Two dry martinis. Montgomery's. Fifteen to one." This is a reference not to the way Field Marshal Montgomery took his martini but, apparently, the ratio by which he liked his troops to outnumber those of the enemy when going into battle.

The trick, as always, is to know how you like it and either mix, or ask for it to be mixed, accordingly.

Your own martini: how to make it

You can decide for yourself which gin you prefer (see p. 300 for a discussion of different gin brands) and how much vermouth you wish to add. The real key is that it should all be arctic. Put the glasses in the freezer half an hour before you wish to drink. The spirit should already be in there. For a super-dry martini, it is enough to run a few drops of vermouth round the rim of the glass—so you catch its scent with each sip—and then shake or stir the spirit with ice to loosen its flavor before pouring into the glass and adding, maybe, another drop of vermouth.

Take a paring of lemon rind, snap it (yes, if your lemon is fresh, it should snap) so that it almost breaks in half to release the oils in the skin (you could wipe this around the edge of the glass, too), drop into the drink, et voilà. Some prefer to leave out the lemon and add an olive instead, though I've never got on with this idea.

My martini

My perfect martini is Plymouth gin, stirred with ice, Noilly Prat smeared around the rim but none in the drink, and a twist of lemon. I also like a vodkatini made with Belvedere vodka, an almost perfectly soft spirit—its texture is quite incredible, like goose down, again stirred, with a lemon twist and Churchillian quantities of vermouth.

007

James Bond's martini: the Vesper

Never mind the shaken or stirred business, 007's drink of choice was an unusual concoction of vodka and gin, which he named after Vesper Lynd, the only woman who ever melted his heart. I include it here more for interest than anything else. Kina Lillet is a brand of white-wine-based liqueur.

3 parts Gordon's gin
1 part vodka
½ part Kina Lillet

Shake with ice until the drink is very cold, then strain into a glass with a large, thin paring of lemon peel.

Other classic variations

A Gibson is a martini dressed with a small pickled onion in place of the lemon peel. This is popular in America but has always seemed quite revolting to me. A dirty martini is an ordinary martini to which you add a small amount of the brine from a jar of olives.

A true martini is always made with gin, but over the past few decades vodka has become such a popular substitute that many have forgotten it is actually an interloper. Like a gin martini, though, a vodkatini, or "vodka martini," is a great drink.

SIMPLE APERITIFS

Negroni

One-third red vermouth, one-third Campari, one-third gin, and nothing else (though watch out, because sometimes when you order this bartenders inexplicably decide to spray soda into it): this is an aperitif that never seems out of place. The negroni is a beautiful thing, garnet in color, sweet-astringent to taste, and decisively highbrow. Drinking it feels like taking a sip of Florence, Renaissance frescoes, students swooping about on scooters, palaces built like fortresses with impenetrably thick walls and crenellations and all. The tight, shadowy streets of that city are, according to one legend, where the negroni was invented in the early twentieth century; it was named after one Count Camillo Negroni, who used to drink it at the Casoni Bar on Via Tornabuoni (the place is now a Roberto Cavalli outlet, selling dresses in brazenly violent prints).

Negroni drinkers are like a secretive Masonic sect, so proud of their affiliation that when they mention it by name, a certain knowing look, recognized only by other negroni drinkers, darts across their face. Thanks to the fact that it is quick and easy to make, it travels well (waiters who don't know the drink are often happy for you to get behind the bar and make your own). And it is just as happy at home as it is in a bar.

For a while I used to make a negroni by shaking the ingredients with ice and then straining into a small glass and drinking it martini style. Now, like most people, I prefer it on the rocks. You can either mix the vermouth, gin (Gordon's is fine), and Campari, pour into a large, ice-filled tumbler, and throw in a slice of orange (blood orange looks good in winter, when it is in season) or pour each ingredient separately over the ice and then stir. This way, because you are adding lukewarm alcohol, you get a small dilution as the ice melts, so the drink keeps changing, just slightly, as you move down the glass, becoming increasingly refreshing, which is a good thing with something so powerful.

Another variation on the negroni, which some argue is actually the authentic drink, is to replace half the Campari with another Italian bitter called Punt e Mes, which has a stronger orange flavor, is fruitier, sweeter, and gives a drink with more breadth and texture.

Black olives and slices of prosciutto are good to pick at when drinking a negroni. But remember: it means business, so should be made only when dinner is reasonably imminent.

Americano

This is similar to the negroni, but considerably less ruthless. Simply mix equal parts of sweet red vermouth and Campari in a tall Collins glass or cup filled with ice, then top with soda and a slice of orange.

Whiskey sour

I skirted around the whiskey sour for a long time before trying it. Whiskey is a serious matter, a drinker's drink, and in a cocktail it exudes an even greater air of caution than it does drunk straight. The more rounded, booming American whiskey, so fat you can almost take a knife and fork to it, seems not just potent but also filling. As far as I was concerned, the prospect of drinking it with lemon juice and egg white—like a sort of raw whiskey lemon meringue pie—felt exhausting.

1 tablespoon plus
2 teaspoons freshly
squeezed lemon juice
1 tablespoon plus
2 teaspoons simple syrup
1½ ounces whiskey,
either bourbon or
scotch—blended will do
1 tablespoon egg white

But, with the siren call of duty and research and all that . . . one tired night I made a whiskey sour in my kitchen, and within a sip I was addicted. This drink is not what it appears. The recipe looks ferociously strong, but shaking with ice dilutes it considerably, to about the level of a G&T. The melted water slows the attack of the whiskey and turns it into something you can almost sluice down as well as sip, while the acidity of the lemon gives it a bit of cut.

If you switch the traditional American whiskey to something Scottish—I have become obsessed with sours made from Chivas Regal 12-year-old, a smooth blended whiskey—you get an even more unexpectedly refreshing, acerbic drink, with a kind of transparency that lets the heather and peat gleam through. It's utterly gorgeous as an out-of-the-office come-downer—even with the scotch it still has an American feel, as if your perfect 1950s housewife should be "fixing" it for her honey when he gets home from work. (Indeed, when the friend I had invited over for my tasting session arrived, I told her, "Put down your bags, take off your coat, we're going to make you a whiskey cocktail,"

and she did say, "Victoria, if you were a man, I'd definitely marry you.")
But the drink is so sparky and pleasing, you could also return to it for
a pep-up after a long dinner. The tricky thing is getting the balance
between sugar and lemon—it does need some sweetness; otherwise it
just feels like flavored whiskey, and I tend to drink it sweeter than I'd
generally like because it seems to hang together better that way.

You need a lot of ice to get this right.

Put the ingredients in a cocktail shaker and shake hard. Add ice and
shake again. Strain into a tumbler filled with fresh ice.

A note on egg whites in cocktails
Several of the recipes in this chapter use egg whites, an ingredient that
seems to put some people off their stride. Salmonella scares have made
us squeamish about raw eggs and unaccustomed to using them as an
ingredient, but it wasn't always so. Some of the earliest classic cocktail
recipes, from Peruvian pisco sours to white ladies, call for egg white,
which acts as an emulsifier, giving a creamier, fluffier texture to the
drink. It's perfectly straightforward to deal with and doesn't make the
drink taste at all "eggy."

White lady

A white lady occupies its glass like a phantom, glimmering faintly, barely seeming to touch the edges, as if in defiance of gravity. Once sipped, the apparition becomes a stingray, fragrant with gin botanicals, its sourness undercut only slightly by a smear of sugar from the Cointreau, each shivery mouthful delivering a lethal lemony nip.

2 parts gin
1 part Cointreau
*1 part freshly squeezed
   lemon juice*
1 teaspoon egg white

Perfect before dinner (but make sure you drink only one), this is a cocktail that inspires lifelong fidelity. It was invented soon after the end of the First World War by the great Scots bartender Harry MacElhone, after whom Harry's Bar in Paris is named. I use a recipe passed on to me by the right-wing commentator Simon Heffer, who in turn got it from the Conservative minister Ian Gow, who was killed by an IRA car bomb in 1990. Apparently Gow used to make it in the officers' mess of his old regiment, the 15th/19th King's Royal Hussars, and was adamant that every bartender he ever encountered should learn to make it according to his precise instructions. I like to use a gin with some weight—Tanqueray is ideal; try to avoid Bombay Sapphire or Miller's, which don't have enough of a juniper anchor.

Put all the ingredients in the shaker (you don't need to whisk the egg white beforehand), shake hard, add ice, shake again, and strain into martini glasses.

A white lady without egg white

With albumin, a white lady takes on a milky opacity. It feels smoother and silkier in your mouth, and its surface looks as if you could ski across it. I include this version for those who cannot or dare not eat raw egg white. This is a white lady made as Errol Flynn liked to drink it in the 1950s, when he lived in Rome with his third wife, Patrice Wymore. The recipe was passed to me by Petronella Wyatt, who in turn got it from the Countess of Wilton, a famed beauty who in her youth worked for Errol Flynn and was trained to make the cocktail to his precise instructions.

1 part gin
1 part Cointreau
1 part freshly squeezed
 lemon juice

Shake the three ingredients with ice and strain into martini glasses.

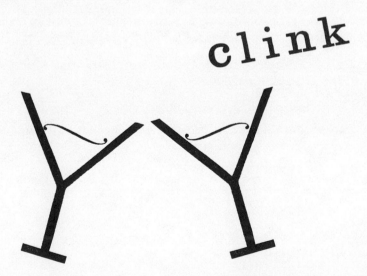

clink

Sidecar

This is named after a captain whose name is sadly lost to barroom history, who apparently spent much of the First World War stationed in Paris, tootling, or rather being tootled, around in a motorbike sidecar. As fighting in the trenches worsened, he did his bit by making frequent excursions to a certain bistro, where this drink was created and named after his mode of transport. Apparently the original contained six or seven ingredients. These have since been reduced to three—cognac, lemon juice, and Cointreau—usually mixed in equal parts. David Embury, to whose book, *The Fine Art of Mixing Drinks*, I am indebted for the sidecar story, objects to this recipe on the grounds of sweetness, though he does allow (somewhat alarmingly) that this is "not a bad formula for a midafternoon drink." I beg to differ. My version of this cocktail uses a little more brandy than is traditional, but nothing like the quantity Embury suggests, and I find it quite savory and strong enough for the evening. The presence of brandy makes it particularly suited to winter, and firesides, but it is too good not to make in summer as well. It's important to use a spirit of drinking quality, but there's no need to go expensive.

1 part freshly squeezed lemon juice
1 part Cointreau
1 ½ parts cognac

Shake all three ingredients hard with ice, then strain into martini glasses.

Between the sheets, long version

This is supposed to be a short drink, but when I was introduced to it as a student, in the Maypole Pub just round the corner from the ADC theatre in Cambridge, it was always served long, presumably to discourage too much bad behavior, and I still prefer it made with soda. It's also useful to have something like this up your sleeve for parties or larger gatherings, when anything finished too swiftly would be disastrous. It's still pretty punchy.

Mix the first four ingredients, pour into a tall, ice-filled glass, and top with soda.

1 part Cointreau
1 part white rum, such
  as Bacardi
1 part brandy
1 part freshly squeezed
  lemon juice
sparkling water

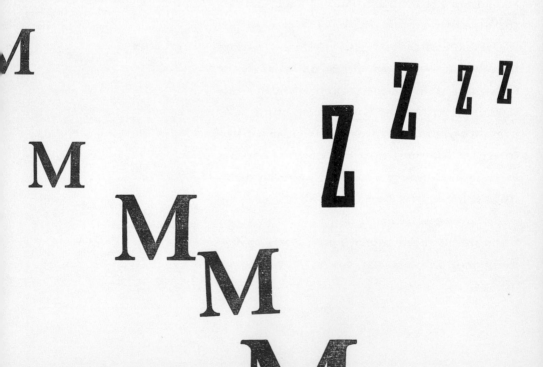

GIN AND TONIC

The dangers of becoming a G&T obsessive

Some people think there is no need for instruction when it comes to making gin and tonic. Those people are wrong.

A G&T is the most dreadfully traduced of drinks, all too often made too flat, too weak, with one lonely ice cube sweating itself to an early grave and a slice of old lemon floundering on the surface like a corpse, whereas it should be effervescent and bright and so busy with ice that the bubbles have to fight their way up to burst with a splash and a hiss on the top.

To make a good gin and tonic you do not just have to care about every ingredient, you have to be anguished about them.

I never appreciated my husband more than the time he arrived in Italy proudly carrying his own tonic and a set of tumblers (hand-blown, heavy Irish glass) imported from the cupboard at home, because I had warned him that the Schweppes produced under license and sold in the local shop was virtually flat and that he might deem the glasses in the rented house inadequate.

The lemon (or lime, which I do sometimes allow in my drink) matters too. There was once a nasty moment at home when Mum handed me a G&T: I took a sip and said accusingly, "Has this lemon been in the fridge?" Even though it still looked firm and juicy and the flesh hadn't begun to shrink away from the segment walls, its smell reminded me of clothes that haven't been washed often enough. I kept catching whiffs of unclean air. And as it turned out, I was right; the lemon had been cut into and refrigerated.

I wrote about the incident at the time in a newspaper column, which apparently caused much hilarity among another group of relatives holidaying together in Portugal, who read it online and spent the next fortnight shouting across the villa pool, "Has this lemon been in the fridge?" But I also received quite a mailbag from readers who appeared to share my insanity. A few, I was pleased to see, took it further. Among them was an editor who had offended countless barmen with his regular G&T ordering routine, which involved shouting, "We'll have one tonic between two. ONE between TWO," then wrestling the bottle out of their hands before they could make a mess of it by daring to pour it for him.

Another reader, a professor in a university mechanical engineering department, confessed he was so anxious about running out of fresh lemons that he kept some, sliced "on day of purchase" and stored between plastic (he was particular that this should not be plastic wrap but something thicker, such as a freezer bag), in plastic containers, in the freezer. "To be very exacting in extracting the flavor from the fruit," he wrote, "simply pour the gin into the glass, add the frozen lemon/lime slices, and allow to marinate for 10 to 15 minutes before putting in the ice and tonic."

As I said, precisely how you make a gin and tonic is important. So here is a brief guide to each ingredient.

The gin

As a confirmed juniper addict, I like my G&T made with Tanqueray or Gordon's Export (47.3 percent abv, as against the 37.5 percent abv of the ordinary stuff, which makes more of a difference than you might think). See p. 300 for a more detailed comparison of the different gin brands. The bottle of gin should be kept in the freezer so that the drink is as cold as possible.

The ice cubes

The more ice the better, in my view, and I have recently moved up from three to four cubes. See p. 17 for further instructions on ice.

The tonic

Now please pay attention. The tonic must be fizzy, and that means using individual cans; large plastic bottles are not good enough, even if they have only just been opened. As for the brand, for me Schweppes is king. I prefer the original Indian Tonic Water because it contains less artificial sweetener than the lower-calorie tonic (even in nondiet Schweppes the sweetness comes from a combination of sugar and sodium saccharin). Serious G&T aficionados go nuts about artificial sweeteners. The problem is not the health controversies about the likes of aspartame, but the slightly bitter, synthetic aftertaste a finely tuned palate can detect on the finish of the drink. Thus they are the ones you see in the booze warehouses at Calais homing in, not on cases of wine and crates of beer, but on trays of tonic water, because the original Schweppes sold on the continent, unlike the stuff we get here, contains no artificial sweeteners.

I also like Fever-Tree tonic, which contains no artificial sweeteners (or preservatives) and is expensive but good: in a G&Fever-Tree you have a much less interrupted view of the gin.

G&T cognoscenti in England often go on about Waitrose's house-brand tonic water, also free of artificial sweeteners, but I don't like it as a tonic—it's confectionery sweet and lacks the requisite astringency. A friend who swears by it cuts it with soda water. Last time I used it, I ended up compensating for the tonic by rattling the gin in a cocktail shaker with the juice of half a lemon, a lot of ice, and the scored rind of the lemon shavings, just to get some acidity and bitterness back. I can't help feeling that making such a production (in fact, virtually making a Collins, not a G&T) may be a step too far.

I scarcely need to mention that the tonic must be chilled.

The citrus fruit

Lime, lemon, or both is fine. I tend to prefer limes in summer, or if I'm about to eat aromatic food such as Indian or Thai. As I have said in the liquor-cabinet section, you should buy lemons and limes that are heavy for their size. I use thick-hewn half slices or wedges.

The glass

A heavy tumbler is best. I like ones made from uneven glass. The glass should look as if it understands the gravity of the drink, and it should have plenty of space in it. A G&T needs a bit of room. One friend has now finessed his G&T making to the point where he puts the glasses in the freezer for twenty minutes before making the drink. Not strictly necessary, but good, somehow.

Assembling the G&T

Ice goes in the glass first. Then a hunk of citrus fruit, which you should squeeze slightly to release some juice, perhaps even rubbing it lightly round the rim of the glass. Gin goes in next—don't stint. And finally top with tonic to taste.

What gin is

Gin and romance do not exactly go hand in hand, skipping off into the sunset together. Gin, like whiskey, but without the drama of the windswept peat moor, is seen as a drinker's drink, a means of blotting out life's ugly daily routines.

This is partly a cultural hangover from the eighteenth century, when consumption of low-grade, fiercely potent, cheap gin was rife, particularly among women; it was blamed not only for the birth of infants made sickly by their mothers' prenatal addiction but also for child abuse (and in some cases mortality) on a grand scale. In 1751, in his *Enquiry into the Causes of the Late Increase of Robbers*, Henry Fielding denounced it as "that poison called gin, which, I have great reason to think, is the principal sustenance . . . of more than 100,000 people in the metropolis." The same year, Hogarth issued his now infamous, highly politicized print, *Gin Lane*, depicting squalid scenes of gin-induced corruption in the midst of which a woman with syphilitic ulcers on her splayed legs is too woozy to notice her baby slipping out of her arms and down a flight of steps. Small wonder the spirit became known as "mother's ruin."

Until recently, gin has never affected any mystique; it comes across like an industrial product, made for a purpose (to effect inebriation) but given respectablity by an air of the medicinal (the juniper and all that quinine in the tonic), though the medicinal effects of quinine are not always positive. One of my favorite gin stories concerns Clarissa Dickson Wright, one of television's *Two Fat Ladies*, who once went to see a doctor about her problematic metabolism. Because she had "sticky blood," a condition associated with those who have damaged their adrenal gland through long use of antimalarial drugs containing quinine, the doctor asked if she had spent time in Africa.

"Oh, it's not that," retorted Dickson Wright. "It'll be all the gin and tonic."

Gently the doctor explained it was simply not possible to drink enough G&T to damage her adrenal gland in such a manner. "Would ten pints a day—four of gin, six of tonic—for twelve years do it?" said Dickson Wright, and the doctor was then forced to concede it probably would.

At the height of its popularity, in the eighteenth century, gin was drunk uncut from the still, at roughly twice the strength at which it is sold today, and was closely related to the pot-distilled genevers from the Low Countries, whose pungent flavors derived as much from the alcohol as the herbs, and was usually heavily sweetened to mask the terrible taste.

Today its legal definition sounds almost as bleak as that early gin must have tasted: basic "gin" must simply be made with ethyl alcohol, cut down with water to a minimum strength of 37.5 percent abv and flavored, artificially or otherwise, so long as the dominant flavor is juniper. (In many gins, premium and otherwise, the dominant flavor, to my palate, is not juniper, which begs the question: where are the gin police?)

This helps to explain why the store brands can taste as if they belong in a flame-thrower's act. It scarcely feels like good news to learn the alcohol cannot be petrochemical in origin; it must have been made from an agricultural product, usually grain, sometimes molasses, but in theory also possibly grapes.

Fortunately "distilled gin" gets you something a little better—the neutral alcohol has to be redistilled, and with natural flavorings, though artificial flavors may still be added later. For "London gin" (a dry style that evolved when the taste of gin improved to the point where it didn't need to be drowned out with sugar, but which, confusingly, doesn't have to be made in London), only natural flavorings known as *botanicals* are permitted.

And botanicals are where the magic lies. The plant material may be berries or roots, seeds or peels, barks or leaves, gathered from around the world to impart their scent during redistillation to the spirit that will become gin. Orris root, from certain species of iris, which smells of wood and violets (it is used in Chanel perfume and found in the Middle Eastern spice mix ras-el-hanout), comes from Florence. The bark of the cassia tree, an evergreen closely related to cinnamon, is harvested from the forests of Indochina. Almonds are plucked from their trees in Spain. Coriander is grown in Bulgaria and Russia (or comes, like the stuff in your supermarket spice jar, from Morocco, where the seeds are bigger and taste more peppery). There are dozens of other botanicals, from the Shetland Islands sea pinks used in Blackwood's to licorice and angelica.

The most important ingredient of all is possibly the most elusive.

"The juniper used in gin is not cultivated," says Desmond Payne, the master distiller for Beefeater and, before that, Plymouth. "It grows wild in Umbria and Macedonia. The locals are as secretive about the exact spots where the shrubs are found as the French are about the whereabouts of truffles, and when the berries are ready, they go out into the hills with stout sticks, whack the branches off the trees and collect the juniper berries as they fall."

Not just any old sackful of juniper will do. A gin distiller receives as many as 150 samples each autumn, and after crushing and sniffing, squeezing and measuring the amount of oil in each (and sniffing again), he makes a selection as careful as that of any perfumier. The juniper not only has to be good; it has to be blended and matched so that the gin brand has consistency from one year to the next.

Acquisition of botanicals is taken very seriously. Sometimes master distillers, meeting each other at trade events, will lean across the table and ask each other anxiously, "How are you finding the coriander seed this year?"

An urgent phone call from a juniper dealer over the Christmas break may have them hastening to their offices to place their orders before prices rise or the particular parcels in which they have expressed an interest are sold to a rival.

Once assembled, the quality and particular mix of the botanicals and precisely how they are introduced to the spirit determines the nature of the finished gin. (Beefeater, for example, steeps everything together for twenty-four hours, while Bombay Sapphire merely allows the vapors of the spirit to pass over the botanicals, which are wedged into the stills in a kind of wire basket.) Alcoholic strength also has a profound impact on flavor. "Alcohol carries the botanicals," says Beefeater's Payne. "Which means that it carries flavor. A lot of gin brands have been tempted by duty rates down to 37.5 percent, but I think that at that level you begin to lose some of the impact of the botanicals. The fresher, citrus notes are more volatile, and they disappear first."

Indeed. Britain's Waitrose stores stock the 47.3 percent version of Tanqueray because a series of blind tastings had convinced them that the flavor is better. And my own taste tests of Beefeater's 40 percent gin against the 48 percent export version suggest that the one with more alcohol has managed to preserve the freshness of the botanicals better— it smells and tastes more vivid (and also has a history of performing better in competitions when samples are tasted blind). This despite the fact that both are made in the same way, cut to different strengths immediately before bottling, and then cut again with water so they can be tasted at the same alcoholic strength, for fairness.

So why not make all gin export strength? The issue is, of course, duty; on spirits it is calculated according to the precise alcoholic strength of the drink—a certain amount for every 1 percent of strength per 100 liters—rather a fixed amount per bottle. This means a bottle of gin with a lower abv would attract a lower duty than one with a higher abv. From a budgeting perspective, then, the gins you should avoid when buying in Britain are those with a lowish abv, of say 40 percent or below, selling at the highest prices. In America, only the export strength will be available.

Gin brands: what's what

Gordon's: London Dry (37.5% abv) and Export Strength (47.3% abv)

Gordon's London Dry (green and white livery) is the default gin option in most British households, and many gin drinkers (until recently, me included) are thus programmed to consider it a benchmark. Alas, it's not as good as you'd hope. Juniper and a rather sad, lemon-liquid-detergent sort of citrus predominate, and next to Tanqueray, whose flavor profile it most closely resembles, poor old Gordon's looks ragged and puling. The export version (clear plastic or glass; mustard label garlanded with juniper leaves and berries), the only one sold in the United States, is a different matter—more fragrant, strong and true and rather good.

Beefeater (40% abv)

Made to a recipe put together by James Burrough, a trained chemist, in the 1860s, Beefeater is the only large make of London Dry gin still distilled in the capital. A connoisseurs' choice, its nine botanicals (juniper, angelica root, angelica seed, licorice, coriander seed, orris root, lemon zest, Seville orange rind, and almond) are allowed to steep for twenty-four hours, giving it a powerful, complex but very smooth taste. It's the bitter, marmaladey Seville (most other gins that use orange peel use a sweet orange) that catches you, strongly, when you first take a sniff, then the juniper makes its entrance. The Beefeater London Dry (47 percent abv) version sold in the United States is even more vivid and vital; both have a long, rounded finish. I sometimes drink Beefeater and tonic with a slice of orange instead of lime or lemon.

Tanqueray (43.1% abv, or the superior 47.3% abv from Waitrose for those in the UK)
This is a superb gin, aimed squarely at juniper addicts, because it delivers a gloriously emphatic, pine-needlish hit of spice right up front, then follows it up with more juniper. And a bit more. Anchored in root and earth rather than peel and perfume, it has a soft mouth-feel and finesse that matches its not inconsiderable bluster. This is the gin that Gordon's lovers flock to once they discover it, and it's one of my favorite all-arounders.

Tanqueray Ten (47.3% abv)
A great drink, and completely unlike its sibling. I don't know what they put in Tanqueray Ten, because the manufacturers make a great mystical secret of it, but the predominant smell is of sweet lime, backed up with fragrant coriander seeds and juniper somewhere in the middle. Lively, invigorating, and textured, it reminds me of lime zest mixed with spices rustling and jumping in a frying pan as you heat them to release the flavor before smashing into them with a mortar and pestle. Despite the spice notes, it's more aromatic than earthy.

Hendrick's (41.4% abv)

The juniper is so delicate one tends to think of this as being its own beast rather than a gin, which is probably exactly what its makers were aiming for when they created the quirky brand in 2002. Distilled in Ayrshire, Scotland, and put in brown, apothecary-style bottles, it sells on its point of difference: infusions of essences pressed from the petals of Bulgarian roses and cucumber pulp mashed into cold water, which are added after distillation. In fact it's the floral notes that dominate, making a Hendrick's and tonic a quintessential summer drink (see p. 130), though for me it would always be an additional gin, never the main one in the cupboard. It's also expensive.

Miller's Gin (40% abv)

Miller's doesn't say it uses cucumber in its gin, but somehow this smells far more cucumbery even than Hendrick's: it reeks of the stuff. The gimmick here is that once distilled, the spirit is sent to Iceland to be cut to bottling strength not just with any old H_2O but with "glacial waters" that are "the purest, softest water on earth." To my taste, the botanicals aren't well balanced—it may smell smooth, but to drink it's a bumpier ride, and the juniper doesn't mesh with the other flavors.

Bombay Sapphire (40% abv)

The distinctive, square-cut cyan glass bottle has earned this a remarkable following, yet it's the only big brand I will refuse to drink even when it's the only gin on offer. Why? I've never been a fan of its somewhat lame, citrus-oriented botanicals; once you've smelled and tasted this without tonic, you don't want to go back: when it should be pure and fresh, it is often fustily reminiscent of a stale lemon just rescued from the back of a fridge, or "an old lady's net curtains," as a fellow taster once put it. It's also expensive considering the low abv.

Plymouth (41.2% abv)

The juniper in Plymouth is quite delicate, but this is still a good gin. Gentle without being weak, and fragrant without being flouncy, its elegant florality can get a bit lost when mixed with tonic but is fabulous in a martini or in cocktails where soda is the mixer. A gin with a pristine, unruffled, fresh linen-jacket feel to it; unlike London gin, Plymouth may be produced only within a protected geographical limitation. Good value and a good all-arounder.

Whitley Neill (42% abv)

Whitley Neill's point of difference is that it contains two African botanicals—cape gooseberries and baobab fruit—which gives it a warmer, rounded, more orangey taste. I like it, but as a "variation" gin rather than a stalwart.

Gin and Dubonnet

Among the royal memorabilia hoarded by Billy Tallon, the late Queen Mother's favorite page, and auctioned in 2008 after his death, was a small, handwritten note from the QM herself detailing arrangements for a summer picnic. "I think," it said, "that I will take 2 *small* bottles of Dubonnet and gin with me this morning, in case it is needed." I am not sure which I prefer, the use of "needed," suggesting that Dubonnet and gin might have some urgent medical purpose, like bug repellent, iodine, or Band-Aids, or the emphasis on "small," so self-conscious it appears to contradict itself like a double negative.

Dubonnet is a wine-based aperitif flavored with herbs and quinine and with an abv of 14.7 percent. The royal family are probably the only people in Britain who still fondly believe it is some sort of mixer. Gin and Dubonnet is a favorite at Buckingham Palace, apparently mixed three parts gin to one of Dubonnet, poured over ice, though the late QM's private secretary loyally gasped at the idea of such proportions and said he "would have thought it ought to be the other way around; otherwise it would be awfully powerful." The late QM, quite rightly, used to confide that she wouldn't be able to get through all her engagements "without a little something," and her daughter Queen Elizabeth II is partial to it too. It probably doesn't qualify as a show-stopper anywhere beyond the gates of Buckingham Palace, but I include it here as a curiosity. If you do make one, I suggest plenty of ice and pouring it over a blade of orange zest rather than the half-slice of lemon that is preferred in the royal household.

ALL-NIGHT DRINKS

The two drinks that follow are traditionally made with American whiskey, usually bourbon. Made from fermented mash using a minimum of 51 percent corn, which gives it its sweet, sunshine flavor, bourbon is aged in charred barrels. Technically it can be made anywhere in the United States, but virtually all of it comes from the state of Kentucky. Jack Daniel's, for the record, which comes from Tennessee, is not considered a bourbon because the charcoal filtering process gives it a different character. The alternative to bourbon is intense-tasting rye whiskey.

Old-fashioned

1 brown sugar cube
few dashes of angostura bitters
bourbon
1 large paring of orange rind, 2 to 3 inches long

Those who know about old-fashioneds don't order them when they go out: they ask the barman if he has time to make one, a courtesy almost unheard of in this consumer age. This is because an old-fashioned is to the cocktail bar what a risotto is to the kitchen: an apparently simple concoction of so few ingredients that it barely seems to merit a recipe, but that requires a great deal of care, not to mention stirring; making one raises so many points of contention that explaining precisely what sort of old-fashioned you would like could easily involve a ten-minute discussion.

Considering the lineup of its constituent parts—bourbon (or rye whiskey), sugar, angostura, ice, and possibly a slice of orange or strip of peel—it's hard to see what all the fuss might be about. This, surely, is merely sweetened whiskey, served on the rocks with a citrus garnish? One sip is all that is required to see that it is not. The way I make it, you get a mouthful of bourbon, as rich and dark as Demerara sugar, loosened with a touch of melted ice, almost imperceptibly complicated by the sugar and bitters and riven with the fragrance of essential oils from the orange rind. It demands that you make an earnest appreciation of it, but aside from that, it is remarkably versatile—cozy in winter, refreshing in summer, quite a serious start to an evening, and just as good after dinner too.

The old-fashioned has pedigree, and not just because Cole Porter wrote a song about it ("Make It Another Old-Fashioned, Please"). Some say that it was the earliest cocktail of all, in the sense that "cocktail" was for a while the name of this particular drink, and that it dates back almost to 1800. Another story has it that it was created for a Kentucky bourbon distiller by the bartender of the Pendennis Club in Louisville in the last decade of the nineteenth century.

It's what you put in it that counts, though. White sugar or the richer brown? Should the cube be replaced with sugar syrup? Rye whiskey or bourbon—and if so, what brand? And, most controversially of all, should the drink contain any fruit at all? To my mind this last is the most important point. Some think it heresy to put any part of an orange anywhere near an old-fashioned; others say that without it you're just drinking sweetened whiskey, take an entire slice of orange, and squash it up at the bottom of the glass. I am firmly on the side of those who think an old-fashioned should contain orange (I like a strip of rind pared without any pith), and this is how I make the drink at home. My version goes heavy on the stirring, which I find quite sociable anyway. Think of it as slow drinking. Or at least, slowing-down-your-drinking. Just don't pour something else to keep you going while you make it.

Woodford Reserve, Maker's Mark, and Buffalo Trace all make good old-fashioneds. The glass to use has the same name as the drink—an old-fashioned glass—which is a short, heavy tumbler, often beautifully engraved.

Put the sugar cube in the bottom of the glass and soak with the bitters. Add ½ teaspoon water. Crush the sugar cube with the back of a teaspoon and mix it into the liquid so that it starts to dissolve. Add the orange to the glass and use a pestle (or the teaspoon again) to bruise it to release the essential oils from the skin. Now start stirring. And keep stirring. The idea is to dissolve as much of the sugar as possible before you begin to add whiskey, and as you do this the citrus peel will slowly release its flavor into the drink. After about five minutes, add about ¼ inch of whiskey. Keep stirring until all the sugar is dissolved, which will probably take another 10 minutes. Finally you can start dropping in the ice—as many cubes as you can fit. Continue stirring as you slowly top the glass up with whiskey. Drink with gravitas.

An alternative old-fashioned

This drink also tastes good when made with another aged, toffee-colored spirit that turns amber and releases a panoply of scents—molasses, coffee, and bitter orange—when slightly diluted: rum. Try it with Gosling's Black Seal (80 proof—there is a 151-proof version that's almost too intense to go near) for a dark taste of a drink that makes you feel you should be aboard the *Black Pearl* with Jack Sparrow.

Manhattan

The Manhattan has been called the drinking man's drink. Made originally with rye whiskey, and now usually with bourbon, it is one of those cocktails that you had better take as seriously as you do a martini. My own Manhattan consumption has never been enormous, so for tips I am indebted to my friend Anna Colquhoun, a raging foodie who spent eighteen months with her husband living in San Francisco, going to cooking school, bread school, slaving in the kitchens at Chez Panisse, and, as far as I can make out, filling in all the gaps in between drinking Manhattans. As she says, "Every bar in San Francisco will do a Manhattan without blinking, even grimy dive bars—they'll just want to know if you want it "up" or "on the rocks.'"

A Manhattan essentially consists of whiskey mixed with sweet vermouth in varying proportions starting at 2:1 and going up to 5:1 in extreme cases; with a couple of dashes of bitters, it is stirred with ice and poured over a stemmed preserved cherry into a heavy whiskey tumbler that's been chilled for a few minutes in the freezer. Never shake a Manhattan— the dilution from the melted ice and the coolness are what you are after, but the frothing and shards of ice produced by shaking it are nothing short of catastrophic.

Just to complicate matters, there are two variations on a classic Manhattan: a "perfect Manhattan," in which you use half sweet, half dry vermouth; and a "dry Manhattan," in which you use only dry vermouth.

As a general rule I like Manhattans just to be Manhattans; if the drink is too sweet for you, then in my view it is better to up the proportion of whiskey rather than to substitute some dry vermouth for the sweet. Why? Well, with dry vermouth, to my taste the Manhattan tastes more like a spiced whiskey and less like a cocktail, though there are rare times when I will make an exception.

As for which whiskey to use, I love the taste of Buffalo Trace, but I somehow feel that Woodford Reserve, which is fatter and louder, makes a better Manhattan. According to Anna, "Rye is becoming much cooler than bourbon among SF's hipsters. Old Overholt seems to be the most popular with good barmen; SF's own Old Potrero is good too. We tried making Manhattans with rye and thought they were pretty good, nicely grassy."

Cherries can be tricky here—the best are the black amarena cherries that grow near Bologna, but just try finding them . . . I settled for a jar of stemless sour cherries I found, and at most American bars what you'll get is a maraschino cherry.

My Manhattan

Put all the liquid ingredients in a cocktail shaker filled with ice and stir carefully until the drink is cold. Strain into a chilled heavy tumbler containing a single cherry. It's fine for the Manhattan to sit in the bottom of the glass occupying half an inch or so of space, as long as the glass is a good one.

3 parts Woodford Reserve bourbon
1 part sweet red vermouth
2 dashes bitters
¼ tsp syrup from the cherry jar
1 cherry

AFTER DINNER

Irish coffee

Arriving in the dank, rainy port of Foynes in County Limerick after crossing the Atlantic in the early days of aviation, American travelers apparently felt so down-hearted that mere caffeine was not enough to perk them up. One creeping winter's evening the chef, Joseph Sheridan, was moved to spike the drink with whiskey and present it as "Irish coffee," which was received with gratitude by the desperate passengers and rapidly caught on. That, anyway, is the commonly told story of how we came to drink hot coffee, sweetened with sugar, lifted with alcohol, and with a pillow of cream floating on top.

It's seldom seen these days, which is not surprising, considering its inauspicious beginnings, its associations with struggling to keep warm and the need to be cheered up, not to mention the way it looks a bit like half a pint of Guinness in a Paris wine goblet and just makes you think of having flambéed shrimp in a steak house in the 1970s. What is odd is that in my experience the people who really get the point of liqueur coffees are those who live in the sun. I've sat in bars in Madrid at 2:00 A.M. with everyone around me sipping them as if it were the only proper and civilized thing to do with that slice of the night. My own moment of revelation came on a Greek island-hopping holiday when, on Mykonos, we found a gay piano bar stuffed with men with enormous muscles and the smoothest, most perfect skin, all sitting quiet as pussycats, listening to Nina Simone songs and sipping liqueur coffees—no one drank anything else—from sunset till sunrise. Suddenly a creamy coffee, black underneath, its bitterness sluiced with sugar and spirit, sipped through cream, seemed the pinnacle of refinement.

To make a liqueur coffee, make fresh coffee in the ordinary way. Pour into a tall glass; add a spoonful of sugar (sweetening it helps the cream float) and a tot of spirit. Then, separately, whisk some heavy cream just a little, so that it is still runny but has taken in some air, reduced in density, and acquired a subtle froth. It must still be pouring consistency. Put the cream into a pitcher, then take a teaspoon, and hold it upside down at a gentle angle just over the surface of the coffee. Now pour the cream very gently down the back of the spoon. This way it won't hit the coffee at speed, and it will already be spreading sideways, so will float out across the surface.

True Irish coffee is made with Irish whiskey, but you can use other spirits and liqueurs too. Cognac, Armagnac, and scotch are all good, as are coffee liqueur, Grand Marnier, and Baileys.

PS...
FIVE
USEFU
LISTS

FIVE USEFUL LISTS

Alcohol-free drinks that don't feel abstemious

Some don't drink, some can't drink, and sometimes you can drink but don't want to. Fruit juice always seems to me to belong to breakfast, though if you feel otherwise turn to p. 73 for some ideas. Nonalcoholic cordials are always welcomed by drinkers as well as nondrinkers, especially if you have sparkling water to dilute them as well as tap. Those who miss alcohol because they like a sipping—as opposed to gulping—drink should look for acidity, bitterness or gingery heat, all of which slow you down.

For sunny days: strawberry grog
Fresh strawberry puree, ginger beer, and lemonade: lots of flavor and a bit of fiery bite. See p. 105 for the alcoholic version and simply omit the gin.

For any time: citron pressé
Sharp and reviving, and the business of putting it together makes it almost feels like drinking a cocktail. See p. 117.

An early evening aperitif: elderflower and tonic
The marriage of sweet nonalcoholic cordial and bitter quinine is attractive, and the tonic means you drink it more slowly than you would an ordinary cordial. See p. 121.

For thirst-quenching in heat: lime soda
The buzz of freshly squeezed lime, diluted with a little soda and either sugared or salted. See p. 166.

For something to kick ass with steak: fresh, homemade
Virgin Marys

The flavors in a Bloody Mary are similar to those in steak tartare, only here you put the tomatoes, Tabasco, and Worcestershire in a glass and serve the meat on the plate. Using fresh tomato juice gives it more delicacy, so go easy on the seasoning. You need the best tomatoes you can find as the drink depends on their tasting of something.

4 medium tomatoes
5 drops Tabasco sauce
pinch salt
1 very small dash
   Lea & Perrins
   Worcestershire sauce
about 1 teaspoon freshly
   squeezed lemon juice

Blanch the tomatoes for 30 seconds in a bowl or pan of boiling water, use a sharp knife to score a cross in the skin at the base of each, and slip the skin off. On a plate (rather than a board, because you are going to need to recycle the juice that runs off), halve the tomatoes, cut out the stem, and discard. Seed, coarsely chop the flesh, and put it in a jug. Now hold a strainer over the jug and tip the debris from the plate into it so that the runny juice goes in the jug and you hold out the seeds. Blitz the tomatoes with a hand blender until smooth. Now season with the remaining ingredients, tasting as you go. Stir and serve. See p. 82 for more on the Bloody Mary.

To drink with curry: vodka–free Moscow mule
Lime and ginger go well with coriander and cumin, which is why this drink is a hit with pappadams and chutney, and curried vegetables and rice. See p. 184.

For the click moment: placebo G&T
Part of the pleasure of alcohol has to do with the ritual of the day, separating the bit where you have to make an effort from the bit where your shoulders can go down. I think far too many of us have a Pavlovian response to the noise of the fridge door closing and a cork being pulled or the *pfft* of a can of tonic being opened. This is why, on nondrinking days, I often make myself a tonic with no gin (or vodka). The trick is to be every bit as careful with it as you would be with the real thing: good lemon, fresh tonic, lots of ice. It really seems to do the trick, and it's a convivial way of not drinking because the nonalcoholic drink looks just the same as everyone else's.

A sundowner for hot, sticky days: virgin Cuba libre
Coke, rum, and freshly squeezed lime—minus the rum. It still works, and you get a buzz from the sugar. See p. 155.

For after dinner or with dim sum: infusions
Whether avoiding alcohol or not, virtually everyone seems to like fresh mint infusions (see p. 122). You can also buy teas with such delicate, complex flavors that they are just as interesting as any wine. Green, white, and oolong teas are lovely with dim sum. (See p. 53 for sources.)

Drinks for sunny large gatherings

2 My criteria for drinks to be served to more than, say, eight people is that they should be easy to make, and also long. Start serving martini-strength cocktails at a large party and you are asking for trouble. I have put drinks suitable for such occasions in the Friends Over section in the Spring chapter, and in the Alfresco section in Summer. In addition, you could consider the following. It goes without saying that all of these would be suitable for smaller gatherings too.

Moscow mules, p. 184
Mojitos, p. 155
Cuba libre, p. 155
Between the sheets, p. 290

Nostalgia: drinks that recapture lost youth

3 We drank the most appalling things when I was a teenager: Malibu and lemonade, endless pints of industrial cider, snakebite and black (black currant liqueur added to a mixture of beer and hard cider). So I am not quite sure why, but there are some decent drinks whose very smell reminds me of the best bits of being young.

Fuzzy Navel

This peachy drink takes me straight back to being seventeen. It tastes blithe and innocent. See p. 164.

Melon–vodka

The smell of honeydew melons reminds me of the long summer holidays and lying on the beach getting irresponsibly brown. And burnt. See p. 134.

Piña colada

A great cloud of snowy pineapple and coconut ice. Perhaps it's the link between sweet coconut and Malibu that reminds me of adolescence, or perhaps it's just the retro feel. Either way, this is delicious on a hot day and can be nonalcoholic too. See p. 160.

And one for children: Coke and ginger beer floats

Perhaps because ice cream and fizzy drinks were rationed in our family, nothing seemed quite as exciting as this, which combines them both. It makes a good midafternoon treat. Just fill one glass per person with either Coke or ginger beer and top with a scoop of ice cream.

Drinks for non-beer-drinkers to order in pubs and bars

4 Not being a great beer drinker, I often find myself stuck for a good drink in a pub. Neat spirits are all very well, but not at the beginning of the evening. I love cider, but all too often only Strongbow, which I don't love much at all, is on offer. Wine is too often too expensive and poor quality. Many drinks with mixers fall flat courtesy of the poor quality of on-tap tonic or because there is no ice and only a very thin, vinegary sliver of lemon. Here are some of the drinks I find work better.

Red vermouth and tonic

Red vermouth has a strong enough flavor to mask the taste of poor tonic. A pleasing and not too strong drink to have during the day if you're stopping off before a wedding or on a walk.

Gin gimlet

The consummate sitting-outside-on-a-patch-of-grass drink, if rather strong. This even tastes good out of a plastic cup. See p. 99.

Negroni

One of the best drinks in the world, and it can be made by pouring all three ingredients directly into the glass over a lot of ice. Failsafe. See p. 283.

Ginger wine

This is one everyone forgets, but it's lovely on a cold winter's day. See p. 240.

Whiskey and water

Definitely a one-for-the-road sort of order, but whiskey has such an intense flavor I find I drink a measure more slowly than others do a glass of wine. This is a good thing. See p. 243.

Cheap but still glamorous

5 The word *cocktail* has a disgracefully expensive ring to it, but provided the mixer is inexpensive, it can sometimes be cheaper, in pounds per alcoholic unit, to drink good spirits than it is to drink mediocre wine. None of the following will make you feel you are skimping, but they won't cost a fortune either.

Rum and soda, with Velma's stew chicken for dinner
Perfect for a family or larger party, the food and drink go together so well this always feels like a treat. See p. 147.

Mulled wine, in the days before the holidays
The mulling spices disguise a multitude of faults. You can get away with much cheaper wine in here than you might ordinarily drink. See p. 233.

Robbie's wassail cup, for chilly evenings
The bulk of the ingredients—the cider, the apples, the sherry—can be picked up at the lowest prices, but the recipe creates something that is more than the sum of its parts. Admittedly this works only if you are catering for larger numbers, because of the quantity of different ingredients that must be bought. See p. 234.

Prosecco with antipasti, for anytime
The light froth of prosecco gives a real lift and is much easier to drink than champagne. It's also relatively inexpensive—though if you are serving it with antipasti, these can ramp up the cost. If this is an issue, instead of cured meat, serve bruschetta. Just lightly toast a few slices of ciabatta or sourdough, rub with half a clove of garlic, and heap with

chopped tomato that you have previously marinated in salt, pepper, and olive oil. This could also be a first course, served at the table. I've put prosecco in the Spring chapter, but it is delicious year-round. See p. 110.

Vodkatini
The most glamorous drink of the lot, but also quite cheap. Just serve it nicely, with icy vodka and decent glasses, and it will feel very sleek indeed. See p. 282.

A lovely glass of chilled fino or manzanilla sherry
It never fails to astonish me that this bone-dry, salty, crisp drink costs so little when it feels so luxurious. If sherry were twice as expensive, I would still buy it. See p. 209.

Half a pint of cider and a ploughman's lunch
Simple, good food and drink to match. I'd rather have this than a stuffy Michelin-starred dinner any day. See p. 204.

ACKNOWLEDGMENTS

I would like to thank all those who have, generously and freely, given their time and expertise to help me write this book. Countless friends have assisted with the arduous task of drinking research. I will not name them all here, but they know who they are. Also Lizzy Kremer, for insisting I write this in the first place; Sally Bishop, for reading an early draft; Sara Holloway, for, among other things, her invaluable architectural input; and Daphne Tagg and Lesley Levene, for their careful eyes. And also Ted, who told me eleven years ago that I could write this book and never wavered in his belief that one day I would finally get around to it.

SELECT BIBLIOGRAPHY

This bibliography is intended to help readers find the books that are mentioned in the text.

Barham, Peter *The Science of Cooking* (Springer-Verlag, 2001)

Beauman, Fran *The Pineapple: King of Fruits* (Chatto & Windus, 2005)

Chandler, Raymond *The Long Goodbye* (Hamish Hamilton, 1953)

Craddock, Harry *The Savoy Cocktail Book* (Pavilion Books, 1999)

David, Elizabeth *Summer Cooking* (Penguin Books, 1965)

Davidson, Alan (ed.) *The Oxford Companion to Food* (OUP, 1999)

Edmunds, Lowell *Martini Straight Up: The Classic American Cocktail* (Johns Hopkins University Press, 1998)

Embury, David A. *The Fine Art of Mixing Drinks* (Faber, 1953)

Fleming, Ian *Casino Royale* (Jonathan Cape, 1953)

Greene, Graham *The Human Factor* (Bodley Head, 1978)

Hemingway, Ernest *Islands in the Stream* (Scribner, 1970)

Lawson, Nigella *How to Eat: The Pleasures and Principles of Good Food* (Chatto & Windus, 1998)

Parker, Dorothy *The Collected Dorothy Parker* (Viking, 1973)

Roden, Claudia *The Food of Italy: Region by Region* (Chatto & Windus, 1989)

Sherry Institute, The *The Perfect Marriage: The Art of Matching Food & Sherry Wines from Jerez* (Simon & Schuster, 2007)

INDEX

Acapulco, 141
Albariño, 266–7
alcohol-free drinks, 314–6
americanos, 284
apples, 200–4, 234
    apple brandy, 216
    apple juice, 76, 200,
      203, 264
aquavit, 264–5
Aristotle, 21
Armagnac, 12, 227, 243–5,
    311
Armstrong, Kevin, 17–8
Attila the Hun, 200

Baileys, 234, 311
Barham, Peter, 18, 20–1
Beauman, Fran, 160
beef, Thai, 250
beer, 205–6
    see also lager
Bellinis, 111–2
Between the sheets, 290, 317
Bibendum Oyster bar, 266
bitters, 6–7, 94, 98, 306
    angostura, 7, 225, 305
    Aperol, 7, 98
    Cynar, 7, 98
    Fernet-Branca, 7
    Peychaud's, 7
    see also Campari

blackberry liqueur, 193
Blake, Admiral, 150
blenders, 16, 74-80
bloodhounds, 131
Bloody Mary, 82–3, 315
Blumenthal, Heston, 207,
    211
Bollinger, Madame, 276
Bond, James, 99, 282
bourbon, 12, 101–2,
    305–9
    Buffalo Trace, 101,
      307, 309
    Woodford Reserve, 101,
      307, 309
Boyt, Mr., 29
brandy, 5, 11, 150, 173,
    243–5
    brandy Alexander, 238
    and eggnog, 237
    and ginger refresher, 231
    and sidecars, 289
    and wassail cup, 235
    see also Armagnac;
    cognac; fruit liqueurs
    and brandies
Brazil, 162–3
Brogdale Farm, 200–3
Buckingham Palace, 304
Burrough, James, 300

cachaça, 162–3
cafetières, 15, 63

caipirinhas, 162–3
Calvados, 11, 216
Campari, 7, 11–2, 15, 94-8,
    108–9
    and negronis, 283–4
Carter, Jimmy, 278
cava, 176
champagne, 175–6
    cocktails, 225–7
    demi-sec, 180–2
Chandler, Raymond, 99
Chase, Lorraine, 94
cheesy wafers, 229–30
cherries, 309
Chez Panisse, 308
chicken
    Thai chicken, 250
    Velma's stew chicken,
      148–9
China, 248
Churchill, Winston, 242,
    278, 281
cider, 204, 318–21
    pear, 175–6
    and wassail cup, 234–5,
      320
Cipriani, Giuseppe, 111
citron pressé, 117–8, 314
Clarence, Duke of, 197
Clark, Sam and Sam, 207
Club 55 restaurant, 171
Coca-Cola, 155, 170, 318
cocktail shakers, 15, 22